AF478124

Migration, Minorities and Citizenship

General Editors: **Zig Layton-Henry**, Professor of Politics, University of Warwick; and **Danièle Joly**, Professor, Director, Centre for Research in Ethnic Relations, University of Warwick

Titles include:

Rutvica Andrijasevic
MIGRATION, AGENCY AND CITZENSHIP IN SEX TRAFFICKING

Muhammad Anwar, Patrick Roach and Ranjit Sondhi (*editors*)
FROM LEGISLATION TO INTEGRATION?
Race Relations in Britain

James A. Beckford, Danièle Joly and Farhad Khosrokhavar
MUSLIMS IN PRISON
Challenge and Change in Britain and France

Gideon Calder, Phillip Cole, Jonathan Seglow
CITIZENSHIP ACQUISITION AND NATIONAL BELONGING
Migration, Membership and the Liberal Democratic State

Thomas Faist and Andreas Ette (*editors*)
THE EUROPEANIZATION OF NATIONAL POLICIES AND POLITICS OF IMMIGRATION
Between Autonomy and the European Union

Thomas Faist and Peter Kivisto (*editors*)
DUAL CITIZENSHIP IN GLOBAL PERSPECTIVE
From Unitary to Multiple Citizenship

Adrian Favell
PHILOSOPHIES OF INTEGRATION
Immigration and the Idea of Citizenship in France and Britain

Agata Górny and Paulo Ruspini (*editors*)
MIGRATION IN THE NEW EUROPE
East-West Revisited

James Hampshire
CITIZENSHIP AND BELONGING
Immigration and the Politics of Democratic Governance in Postwar Britain

John R. Hinnells (*editor*)
RELIGIOUS RECONSTRUCTION IN THE SOUTH ASIAN DIASPORAS
From One Generation to Another

Ayhan Kaya
ISLAM, MIGRATION AND INTEGRATION
The Age of Securitization

Zig Layton-Henry and Czarina Wilpert (*editors*)
CHALLENGING RACISM IN BRITAIN AND GERMANY

Georg Menz and Alexander Caviedes (*editors*)
LABOUR MIGRATION IN EUROPE

Jørgen S. Nielsen
TOWARDS A EUROPEAN ISLAM

Pontus Odmalm
MIGRATION POLICIES AND POLITICAL PARTICIPATION
Inclusion or Intrusion in Western Europe?

Prodromos Panayiotopoulos
ETHNICITY, MIGRATION AND ENTERPRISE

Aspasia Papadopoulou-Kourkoula
TRANSIT MIGRATION
The Missing Link Between Emigration and Settlement

Jan Rath (*editor*)
IMMIGRANT BUSINESSES
The Economic, Political and Social Environment

Carl-Ulrik Schierup (*editor*)
SCRAMBLE FOR THE BALKANS
Nationalism, Globalism and the Political Economy of Reconstruction

Vicki Squire
THE EXCLUSIONARY POLITICS OF ASYLUM

Maarten Vink
LIMITS OF EUROPEAN CITIZENSHIP
European Integration and Domestic Immigration Policies

Östen Wahlbeck
KURDISH DIASPORAS
A Comparative Study of Kurdish Refugee Communities

Lucy Williams
GLOBAL MARRIAGE
Cross-Border Marriage Migration in Global Context

Migration, Minorities and Citizenship
Series Standing Order ISBN 978–0–333–71047–0 (hardback) and
978–0–333–80338–7 (paperback)
(*outside North America only*)

You can receive future titles in this series as they are published by placing a standing order. Please contact your bookseller or, in case of difficulty, write to us at the address below with your name and address, the title of the series and the ISBN quoted above.

Customer Services Department, Macmillan Distribution Ltd, Houndmills, Basingstoke, Hampshire RG21 6XS, England

---

Labour Migration in Europe

Edited by

Georg Menz
Goldsmiths College, University of London, UK

Alexander Caviedes
State University of New York at Fredonia, USA

First published 2010 by
PALGRAVE MACMILLAN

Palgrave Macmillan in the UK is an imprint of Macmillan Publishers Limited,
registered in England, company number 785998, of Houndmills, Basingstoke,
Hampshire RG21 6XS.

Palgrave Macmillan in the US is a division of St Martin's Press LLC,
175 Fifth Avenue, New York, NY 10010.

Palgrave Macmillan is the global academic imprint of the above companies
and has companies and representatives throughout the world.

Palgrave® and Macmillan® are registered trademarks in the United States,
the United Kingdom, Europe and other countries.

ISBN 978–0–230–27482–2 hardback

This book is printed on paper suitable for recycling and made from fully
managed and sustained forest sources. Logging, pulping and manufacturing
processes are expected to conform to the environmental regulations of the
country of origin.

A catalogue record for this book is available from the British Library.

Library of Congress Cataloging-in-Publication Data
Labour migration in Europe / edited by Georg Menz.
      p.   cm. — (Migration, minorities and citizenship)
   Includes bibliographical references.
   ISBN 978–0–230–27482–2
   1. Foreign workers—Europe.   2. Foreign workers—Government
   policy—Europe.   I. Caviedes, Alexander.   II. Title.
   HD8376.5.L33 2010
   331.6′2094—dc22   2010027537

10   9   8   7   6   5   4   3   2   1
19   18   17   16   15   14   13   12   11   10

Printed and bound in Great Britain by
CPI Antony Rowe, Chippenham and Eastbourne

Contents

Section III: The Outsourcing of Migration Management

Section IV: Unauthorized Labour Migration

List of Tables and Figure

Tables

Figure

Notes on the Contributors

Alexander Caviedes is Assistant Professor in Political Science at the State University of New York at Fredonia. Among his publications, he includes articles published in the *Journal of European Public Policy* and the *EUSA Review*. During his previous career as an immigration attorney, his work appeared in the *Boston University International Law Journal*. In 2010, Lexington Books published: *Prying open Fortress Europe: The Turn to Sectoral Labor Migration*. That same year, his chapter on high-skilled migration will appear in *Migrants and Minorities* (Cambridge Scholars Publishing).

Vassilis Hatzopoulos is an associate professor at the Democritus University of Thrace (Greece), a visiting professor at the College of Europe, Bruges (Belgium), and a Special (Honorary) Lecturer at the University of Nottingham (UK). He has practised as a lawyer at the Athens Bar since 1995 in the fields of internal market (emphasis on services and free movement), network industries, and public procurement. He is the author of several books and over a hundred articles and case notes, in English, French, and Greek, on various topics of EU law. Recent work includes articles on the "Area of Freedom, Security and Justice" (*European Law Review* (33) 1/2008, 44–65), on the Services Directive (*Cahiers de Droit Européen* 3–4/2008, 299–358 and *Cambridge Yearbook of European Law* (2008) 215–261), and on the social dimension of the EU (in J. Baquero-Cruz and C. Closa (eds.) *European Integration from Rome to Berlin: 1957–2007*, Brussels: PIE Peter Lang, 2009, pp. 147–180).

Holger Kolb is Research Officer at the Scientific Council of German Foundations for Integration and Migration (*Sachverständigenrat deutscher Stiftungen für Integration und Migration*). He previously served as scientific assistant at the Institute for Migration Research and Intercultural Studies at the Universität Osnabrück, Germany.

Torben Krings is currently Postdoctoral Research Fellow at the Employment Research Centre at Trinity College in Dublin, Ireland. His recent publications include: "A Race to the bottom? Trade Unions, EU enlargement and the free movement of labour", *European Journal of Industrial Relations* 15 (1), 2009.

Willem Maas (PhD, Yale) is Jean Monnet Chair in European Integration and Associate Professor of Political Science and Public and International Affairs at York University in Toronto, Canada, where he directs the EU Centre of Excellence. His book *Creating European Citizens* explains the development of supranational rights culminating in EU citizenship. Professor Maas is currently researching the comparative politics of citizenship and nationality, the limits of tolerance and multiculturalism, and the intersection of migration and law.

Georg Menz is Reader in Political Economy at Goldsmiths College, University of London. His recent publications include *The Political Economy of Managed Migration: Nonstate Actors, Europeanization and the Politics of Designing Migration Policies* (Oxford: Oxford University Press, 2008), *Varieties of Capitalism and Europeanization: National Response Strategies to the Single European Market* (Oxford: Oxford University Press, 2005), *Internalizing Globalization: The Rise of Neoliberalism and the Decline of National Varieties of Capitalism* (co-edited with Susanne Soederberg and Phil Cerny, Basingstoke: Palgrave). His research has also led to publications in journals including the *Journal of European Public Policy, Journal of Common Market Studies, Debatte, German Politics*, and many more.

Ettore Recchi is a full professor of Political Sociology in the University of Chieti-Pescara, Italy. Among his recent publications are: E. Recchi and A. Favell (eds.), *Pioneers of European Integration: Citizenship and Mobility in the EU*, Elgar, Cheltenham, 2009; M. Braun and E. Recchi, *Free-Moving Western Europeans: An Empirically Based Portrait*, in H. Fassmann, M. Haller and D. Lane (eds.), *Migration and Mobility in Europe: Trends, Patterns and Control*, Elgar, Cheltenham, 2009, 85–101; E. Recchi, "Cross-State Mobility in the EU: Trends, Puzzles and Consequences", *European Societies* 10 (2), 2008, pp. 197–224.

Michael Samers (BA Clark University, MS, University of Wisconsin, D.Phil. Oxford University) is Associate Professor of Geography at the University of Kentucky, having previously taught at the Universities of Liverpool and Nottingham. He is the co-author of *Migration*, published by Routledge (2010) and co-author of *Spaces of Work* with Noel Castree, Neil Coe, and Kevin Ward (published by Sage in 2003). He is also currently working on issues of Islamic banking and finance, and serves as co-editor of Geoforum.

Anna Triandafyllidou is part-time Professor at the European University Institute (Robert Schuman Centre for Advanced Studies), Florence, Italy and Senior Research Fellow at the Hellenic Foundation for European and Foreign Policy in Athens, Greece. Since 2002, she has been Visiting Professor at the College of Europe in Bruges. Her main areas of expertise are migration, Nationalism, and European integration. Her most recent books include *Muslims in 21st Century Europe* (Routledge, 2010), *Irregular Migration in Europe: Myths and Realities* (Ashgate, 2010), *Migration in 21st Century Greece* (with T. Maroukis, Kritiki, 2010, in Greek).

1
Introduction: Patterns, Trends, and (Ir)Regularities in the Politics and Economics of Labour Migration in Europe

Georg Menz and Alexander Caviedes

Migration is an issue that commands ever greater attention, due to its transcending nature. It not only touches on the major issues in politics, sociology, economics, and geography in ways that connect such fields, but due to its capacity for bringing about change, it is a uniquely dynamic phenomenon. This holds true especially in the case of Europe, which is becoming acquainted with international integration to a degree that is novel to the continent in its temporal concentration, intensity and breadth. However, it is difficult to gain a complete and accurate understanding of post-war immigration in Europe without granting primary focus to labour migration. While a good deal of migration takes place outside of the economic context – and certainly states also make use of a variety of regimes for the management of the different forms of migration, whether they are dealing with asylum, refugees or family reunion – the impetus and development of migration in Europe traces its history to labour migration. For those who would break down the post-war European experience into different eras of migration, the initial period is always that characterized by the guest worker programmes that were initiated to address labour shortages during the rebuilding and expansion phases of western Europe's post-war economy (Appleyard, 2001; Messina, 1996). However, highlighting the roots of migration history should not obscure the fact that while economic concerns remain central in the motivations of would-be migrants, as well as the states that will host them, the exact nature of these concerns have shifted over time.

The macroeconomic changes of the last 30 years, typified by globalization, de-industrialization, rationalization of production, increasing sectoral differentiation, the shift away from Fordist-inspired mass production, and increasing regional integration have conspired to create a different labour market scenario than that which existed during the 1960s and 1970s in Europe. Not only has the broader composition of European economies undergone considerable change, but unfavourable demographic trends, skill shortages and purported recruitment difficulties, notwithstanding the backdrop of persistent mass unemployment, have led most European governments to reconsider the restrictive labour migration policies first instituted in the 1970s and to rediscover the benefits of "managed migration". However, given the pivotal role of the service sector and its notable bifurcation in terms of skill and pay levels, the profile of labour migrants courted by the newly emergent recruitment schemes differs from any precedent. The structural transformation of the European political economy – the twin phenomena of internationalization of economic production structure and (neo)liberalization of public policy regulation – has a profound impact on new strategies and designs of labour migration policy. In addition, the balance of power between trade unions and employer organizations has decisively shifted in favour of the latter, so that governments feel ever more compelled and capable of accommodating business demands for labour recruitment programmes. In (re-)discovering labour migration, Europe self-consciously enters a global competition for the "best minds", challenging more established recipient countries such as Canada, Australia and the US in the arena of human resources. Remittances from diasporas serve as important revenue sources, already dwarfing the size of western overseas developmental aid, yet the moral dilemmas of "brain drain" are considerable and not yet comprehensively addressed. Moreover, despite the intention to design carefully confined parameters of "managed migration" and close the doors firmly to those who do not fit said criteria, Europe has become a preferred target region of immigrants from economically and politically unstable and insecure regions, notably North and sub-Saharan Africa, Eastern Europe, Latin America, and Western and Southern Asia. While labour migration is certainly a phenomenon that is economic in nature, the sources of the changes described above cannot merely be read as economic, but also as political.

Economic migrants, itself a term previously often used as a slur in European political debates, have not only been re-discovered, but they are actively being courted by governments from Rome to Stockholm and from Dublin to Riga. Well trained and highly educated newcomers in particular are seen as making a potentially valuable contribution to economic growth and prosperity, a perception particularly common among employer associations and business groups, but to a large extent filtering into general public policy discourses. The re-conceptualization of migration policy as a national human resources strategy as opposed to a largely defensive security-driven domain more likely marks a long-term paradigmatic shift, notwithstanding the recession of the late 2000s and a largely sceptical public.

While attracting only limited scholarly attention between the 1970s and the early 1990s, the past 20 years have witnessed a virtual cotton industry of scholarly publications on European migration from a variety of disciplines (Angenendt, 1999; Brettel and Hollifield, 2007; Fassman and Münz, 1994; Geddes, 2003; Smeeding and Parsons, 2006; Soysal, 1994; Straubhaar, 2006; Uçarer and Puchala, 1997). In the political science literature, early efforts commonly were anchored in Stephen Castle's and Mark Miller's (1993) efforts to construct regulatory models, which over time led to a somewhat questionable tendency to favour the empirically rich description of allegedly idiosyncratic national case studies over comparative analytical efforts. Perhaps owing to the discipline's traditional core element, there is also a strong concentration on state activities and public policy, with sometimes insufficient attention being paid to non-state actors or individual institutions constituting the far from monolithic state apparatus. Only with the swelling ranks of immigration scholars have other actors received the attention they clearly warrant, including "organised interest groups, courts, ethnic groups, trade unions, law and order bureaucracies, police and security agencies, local actors and street-level bureaucrats and private actors" (Lahav and Guiraudon, 2006, p. 207). It is our contention that existing scholarship does not satisfactorily address the phenomenon of economic migration to Europe in all its depth and width. Few accounts systematically probe and analyse the most important elements shaping current labour migration flows and their regulation by governments and the role of private and non-governmental actors, highlighting the reasons for changes or in certain cases continuities in patterns, and, going forward examining continued trends. In fact, much labour migration proceeds through avenues either consciously or unconsciously abandoned by the regulatory control of the state (Guiraudon, 2001), for example, in the framework of the General Agreement on Trade and Services (GATS) liberalization of labour market access or through undocumented migration feeding into the underground segment of the economy. Much of the existing literature, especially in political science, assumes a fairly state-centric view and continues to treat migration policy as being the exclusive domain of governments. For political economy accounts of migration, one either has to travel back to the 1970s (Castles and Kosack, 1973; Piore, 1979) or rely on the few accounts published since (Cole and Dales, 1999; Freeman, 2006), including those by the editors (Caviedes, 2010; Menz, 2008). Worth noting is also Jim Hollifield's (1992) *Immigrants, Markets, and States: The Political Economy of Postwar Europe* which stresses the convergence of migration policies in light of labour market shortages, while linking it to developments in France, Germany, and the United States (US). However, this contribution seems to underestimate the differentiated impact (as argued by the literature cited above) that the distinct systems of political economy will have on policy output. It seemed apt to submit a joint fresh account, bringing together contributions from an international team of both junior and more established scholars.

Moreover, many of the existing contributions commit themselves exclusively to the subfield of migration studies and in doing so fail to take advantage of the developing theory in fields outside the narrower purview of migration, ignoring Bleich's (2008, p. 510) call for more "portable insights". As we contend, post-war immigration to Europe is rooted in economic migration, so it seems clear that a broad survey of economic migration trends should be embedded within the larger discourse on the changing political economy of Europe and the world. Of the most influential contemporary works in comparative political economy (Amable, 2004; Crouch and Streeck, 1997; Hall and Soskice, 2001; Scharpf and Schmidt, 2001; Yamamura and Streeck, 2003), none have yet been successfully linked with migration policy. Most of these works contain a central argument concerning the continued divergence between countries and sectors in the face of globalizing pressures, through case studies drawing from various policy areas from skills development to monetary to welfare policy. Despite the fact that many of these national policy responses address the very challenges for which labour migration often becomes a remedy, there has not yet been a systematic consideration of how these challenges have rendered European political economies more susceptible to certain types of migration policy solutions.

By providing a number of concrete case studies and exploring the impact of macroeconomic changes and micro-level corporate strategic change and their effects on labour recruitment, this book marries a comparative political economy and a migration perspective. To the extent that it highlights common aspects of national migration policies, the book challenges the literature's focus on national differences, yet it also aligns nicely with the conventional wisdom regarding increasing internal, sectoral, and labour force divergence. In this sense, our aim is to contribute to discussions in comparative and international political economy that examine the repercussions of globalization and national response and coping strategies, while examining an empirical issue area that, while central to the phenomenon of globalization, has often been overlooked in that body of literature.

This edited book endeavours to highlight *four* newly emerging themes in the politics of migration. In doing so, it is inspired by some of the insights generated by the rapidly unfolding literature on European migration in a number of disciplines, notably political science, yet examines issue-areas often neglected or even ignored.

Firstly, we argue that labour migration policies in Europe are increasingly driven by sector-specific considerations. The divergent institutional particularities of various models or varieties of capitalism can therefore help account for observed differences in the contours of new labour migration policies. The system of political economy prevalent in a given polity – be it national, regional, or sectoral – strongly shapes the types of labour migrants employers will be most interested in. It is likely that firms still face different institutional landscapes, depending upon which variety of capitalism is prevalent, leading to different policy demands and a resulting divergence in labour migration policies. Unlike the 1960s, when the demand for "guest workers" was more general, a simple transfer of excess labour from one sector to another has proven challenging. In response, countries have begun to incorporate large-scale labour recruitment policies, notably in sectors such as construction, agriculture and hospitality, but also extending to more highly skilled work in areas such as health care and information technology. In these areas, intra-company transfer practices have proven insufficient to satisfy the demands of the private sector and, together with the public sector, employers have been active agents in the creation of a highly developed system of high-skilled, yet often temporary migration.

Changes in political economy not only affect policies but also reconfigure power relationships within societies. In fact, the domestic politics of labour migration regulation have shifted considerably, showing great deference to employer preferences, due in no small part to the tendency of trade unions to adopt more pragmatic, and even fairly welcoming, stances. Unions embrace managed migration and legalization schemes as a preferential alternative to migration into the undocumented sector of the labour market and the consequent downward pressure on wages and working conditions (Haus, 2002; Watts, 2002). With the changes in the overall dynamics of international political economy, and due to the increased mobility of capital, the labour movement has been forced off the path of mere opposition onto one of adaptation. Not everywhere is labour acquiescence mere grudging accommodation to new and uncomfortable realities; in some cases unions share employer enthusiasm over economic growth potential unleashed by fresh immigration and an ideological commitment to international solidarity additionally arrests lingering discontent that may prevail at the grassroots level.

It is understood that the advocacy of labour migration is a politically delicate affair in an era of sceptical public opinion, concerns over political and religious extremism among the second and third generation, perhaps relatedly, poor records of scholastic achievement and labour market integration among some segments of these descendants, xenophobic far right parties and a dissipating public consensus on the virtues of multiculturalism in countries that used to embrace this approach to integration, such as the Netherlands and the United Kingdom (UK). However, these formidable obstacles notwithstanding, we posit that labour migration continues to be advocated by employers. One way of alleviating concerns – or, put somewhat more polemically, avoiding certain debates – is to separate immigration from integration discussions and focus on economic, but not humanitarian forms of migration. The public policy response in Europe seems to have combined more liberal provisions for labour migration with more restrictive attitudes towards humanitarian forms of migration, especially asylum. As liberal courts have curtailed governments' room for manoeuvre much more than the latter would care to admit, such restrictiveness takes the form of stricter enforcement of border controls, including the involvement of preventive detention by North African and Middle Eastern border police guards with more than chequered human rights records.

Secondly, labour migration policies are influenced by developments associated with globalization and Europeanization. European integration has always followed a market logic (Geddes, 2008), so it should come as no surprise that initiatives to further develop European Union (EU) migration law would implicate labour migration. However, not all attempts to create such new avenues for labour migration – both temporary and permanent – have been successful or indeed politically uncontested. The widening and deepening of European integration has meant that labour migration hails from substantially different sending regions than was the case a generation ago (Lavenex and Uçarer, 2002) and that some policies even benefit third country nationals. Demographic shortages notwithstanding, the anxieties over economic migrants from Central and Eastern Europe, spawning the debate over the ubiquitous "Polish plumber", have highlighted the very powerful possibility of a public opinion backlash against intra-EU labour migration. Intra-European migration is no longer the dog that does not bark and the old adage that "Europeans do not migrate" is an anachronism now.

The European Commission seeks to advance and coordinate pan-European immigration policy (Faist and Ette, 2007) but, facing member states reluctant or even openly hostile to the notion of Europeanized labour migration policy (Menz, 2008), it needs to proceed carefully, adopting a salami tactic of advancing in small steps focused on uncontroversial aspects of labour migration, concentrating, for example, on seasonal migrants, trainees interns, and researchers. The so-called European Blue Card (Council Directive 2009/50/EC) intends to create a pan-European temporary work and residency permit for highly skilled migrants, streamlining approval procedures and encouraging pan-European labour migration by the third-country beneficiaries. As the colloquial denomination already suggests, the proposal was meant as a direct challenge to the US Green Card and is inspired by the ultimately ill-fated Lisbon Agenda of increasing the EU's "competitiveness" by 2010. It also grew out of the 2005 Hague programme. Then Justice and Home Commissioner Franco Frattini explained: "Europe's ability to attract highly skilled migrants is a measure of its international strength. We want Europe to become at least as attractive as favourite migration destinations such as Australia, Canada, and the US. We have to make highly skilled workers change their perception of Europe's labour market governed as they are by inconsistent admission procedures. Failing this, Europe will continue to receive low-skilled and medium-skilled migrants only." The last sentence marks an odd non sequitur. Also, numerous national abrogations, most crucially the national right to set quotas, a reflection of sustained unease over communautarization in this area, water down its impact and the temporary nature itself constitutes a formidable difference to the US permanent residency permit. The conflicts in Brussels are largely related to the political desirability of communautarization, although some of the European Commission's initiatives might also be questioned and to some extent are by the member states. Demographic trends leading to a smaller and ageing work force need not be a problem if neoclassical growth postulates are relaxed (or abandoned altogether). Female labour market participation has often been merely rhetorically promoted and skilled migrant "import" in lieu of improved educational and vocational standards is a potentially highly problematic strategy. Whether a densely populated subcontinent can and should compete for immigrants with the world's most sparsely populated countries such as Australia and Canada, not least in light of pressing environmental considerations such as declining fossil fuel deposits, adverse climate change and serious concerns over the security of Europe's future energy supplies, is a somewhat different, nevertheless pertinent, question. Europe clearly wants immigrants, but whether it really needs them is an altogether different question. And time will tell whether skilled migrants will want Europe.

The vociferous debate over the EU directive on further liberalization of service provision – colloquially know as the Bolkestein Directive (2006/123/EC) – demonstrated the political limits to liberalization, as this sweeping project in its original incarnation would have permitted transnational service provision and posting of workers at home country standards, impeding efforts to effectively control adherence to standard wage levels. The posted workers controversy was particularly pronounced in the 1990s in countries with no statutory minimum wage such as Germany and Sweden (Menz, 2005), and Bolkestein reignited this problematique, but in the EU-27 which features wage gaps of a magnitude of 1:30, even greater controversy was guaranteed. Bolkestein came to be seen as synonymous with the Barroso presidency's infatuation with neoliberalism and contributed to the defeat of the Constitutional Treaty in referenda in France and the Netherlands. Whilst the pan-European liberalization of transnational service provision proved possible only after the principle of host-country wages as applicable minimum standards had been clarified (Menz, forthcoming), a regime on the free movement of services has been quietly constructed both within the EU and beyond. This is an often neglected area of labour migration over which states have deliberately ceded control, but it is one in which the European Union is already blazing a path that the WTO is also following, albeit at a slower pace. The GATS establishes an international labour migration regime for certain occupations within internal labour markets of multinational business that operate largely outside the discretion of the nation-state (Lavenex, 2006). Whether one is opposed to the pace of European integration in this area or not, it seems clear that this is the direction in which the global trade regime is moving as well.

Thirdly, there has been a considerable degree of privatization of migration control, and private actors and agencies play a more pronounced role in facilitating or detaining the flow of migrants. While the guest-worker programmes of the 1960s, with their foreign labour recruitment offices established in the sending countries and the bilateral labour treaties that served as legal foundation, reflected the attempts of governments to retain control over the official channels of migration, major employers often worked in tandem with governmental agencies, as in the case of French car manufacturers in North Africa and British Rail and British public transportation in the Caribbean. Today, labour recruitment is not exclusively state-centric, either: private recruitment agencies often operate either in lieu of or at the behest of national governments. Such actors have become primary conduits of information for both employers and would-be migrants, yet the absence of a scheme of regulation for such activities not only exacerbates the lack of official oversight within the process – which proves detrimental to governments seeking to maintain a degree of surveillance – it also renders it difficult to establish any system of coordination or self-regulation amongst those who provide these services. In many ways, this involvement of private sector agencies remains somewhat uncharted territory, even though agencies play obvious roles in facilitating, maintaining, and extending economic migration flows. The practical details of the migration process to Europe are quite often influenced by such actors, just as ethnic networks play a role in aiding in the transition and settlement process. Less than systematic evidence suggests that the liberalization of air transport and the emergence of budget airlines have supported the growth of East–West migration since the early 2000s as well as more temporary and even *pendel* forms of labour migration. Since the first round of EU enlargement in 2004, existing West European budget airlines have extended their network eastwards and have been challenged by new central and East European start-ups. The expansion of international air transport and real price decreases following market liberalization from the late 1970s onwards similarly facilitated immigration to Europe from outside regions, a development which European governments attempted to stem by integrating airlines into migration flow management and detention. European governments are therefore outsourcing certain control functions to private companies in the transportation sector (Lahav, 1998), with particular attention dedicated to perceived immigration "hotspots" in West Africa and South Asia, which has important implications for practical aspects of immigration. The limitation of air travel as a geographical access channel to Europe to passengers with travel documents and visas is meant to curb both undocumented migration, yet in practice also affects refugee and asylum seeker movements. Private sector involvement is also worth noting in the detention of migrants, though these tend not to be labour migrants.

Fourthly, moving beyond the regimes for documented labour migration, globalization also carries with it the understanding that advances in technology have shrunk geographic distances and fostered the transmission of information about work opportunities from host countries to sending communities around the globe. This has led to substantial flows of largely undocumented workers from Africa, Asia, Latin America and Eastern Europe into the less regulated sectors of (West) European economies. The presence of unauthorized workers within every EU member state points to the pervasiveness of work opportunities outside of the regulated labour markets that much of continental Europe is often associated with. Such labour flows are particularly pertinent for Southern European countries with sizable undocumented sectors of the economy, but also for Northwestern European countries with highly deregulated labour markets. These flows have resulted in a variety of government responses, ranging from legalization/amnesties, to attempts to tighten the physical control over borders, and to restrictions on other channels of entry that in the perception of European governments have come to attract "undesirable" economic migrants, notably asylum. The EU agency for border management Frontex coordinates the militarization of the physical borders of Europe, especially in the Mediterranean and Eastern Europe. Possibly of equal importance are bilateral treaties between European and North African governments that entail logistical, financial and know-how support for border enforcement in North Africa, a region that has emerged as a significant transit destination. Though the relationship between legal and clandestine flows of migration is uncertain – due in large part to the difficulties incumbent with producing accurate numbers of undocumented migrants and workers – there is clearly a synergy between the two that is particularly sanguine in certain economic sectors. As such, the presence and employment of undocumented workers is an issue that demands careful analysis and exploration, even if its exact dimensions and impact remain difficult to ascertain.

Managed migration in many – though not all – European countries has focused on skilled migrants; while there is considerably less appetite for unskilled migrants. These are often seen as unnecessary in the context of high unemployment, which tends to be negatively correlated with levels of formal education, and few job shortages. Relatively high levels of unemployment and comparatively poor levels of scholastic achievement amongst the second generation of European-born descendants of migrants further render low-skill migration akin to the post-war era very unattractive. The European Commission claims that opening up legal economic migration channels will both alleviate emigration pressure ("push factors") and reduce undocumented migration in general. But such argument ignores the approach of state apparatus tolerance – or possibly merely displaying malign neglect – towards widespread practices of undocumented forms of employment, which in certain sectors of Southern European economies have almost become structural and semi-permanent features. Attempts to regularize such undocumented migration channels and stock populations in Southern Europe have not truly succeeded in establishing state apparatus control, assuming this to be the original source of motivation. Notwithstanding often very hostile rhetoric employed by the media and the xenophobic parties of the far right, business often welcomes the manpower afforded by undocumented migrants, not least to fill unattractive and poorly remunerated positions in the agriculture and service sectors. However, such a stance is for obvious political reasons too controversial to spawn public pronouncements, not least because such employment commonly commands only substandard wages. Equally problematic and politically contested is "workfare", that is, the obligation for welfare payment recipients to perform often poorly remunerated jobs. Though hypothetically this constitutes a labour force that might replace migrant workers in this segment of the labour market, the political stigma attached to such proposals is considerable. The punitive ideological stance underpinning such proposals also remains unperturbed by employer complaints about lack of skills, motivation and often physical capability among such "forced labourers".

1. The transformation of European labour migration

The contributions in this book have several goals in mind. They seek to offer a wide array of perspectives on the factors that govern or at least influence labour migration in Europe. Whether the chapters are based on economic concerns, the impact of Europeanization, issues of management or the interaction between regular and irregular labour markets, a central concern of all contributors is to offer an assessment of the changes that appear in the European landscape in comparison to that one generation ago. Rather than to merely survey the changes and offer an empirical discussion of these issue areas, many of the authors have also sought explanations for these changes that draw from various theoretical disciplines. The aim is to offer an image of the changing nature of labour migration from a kaleidoscopic perspective, which nevertheless maintains a constant common thread that is based on this idea of change.

The first chapter explores the linkages between systems of political economy and labour migration policy. Georg Menz argues that different varieties of capitalism condition the types of migrants which employers will be interested in. Employers do not simply desire more migrants nor are they indifferent to their skills profile, but rather seek newcomers that can be easily accommodated and complement existing corporate strategies and skills requirements. However, they may also seek to "import" missing skills that domestic educational facilities do not generate. The profile of "desirable" economic migrants varies and is conditioned by production strategies and education and training schemes associated with different varieties of capitalism. Unions are considerably less influential for structural reasons. They generally passively accept regulated labour migration as the lesser evil compared to potentially substantial migration into the undocumented section of the labour market, which would jeopardize wages and working conditions throughout the economy. Employers cleverly influence public policy by rhetorically portraying the need for liberalized labour migration as a crucial component for continued international competitiveness and are fairly successful in doing so, as European governments have accepted central tenets of competition state ideology since the 1990s. Employers provide the data and arguments upon which West European governments base their economic migration policy design. They are represented in influential advisory councils and help co-manage migration flows considered of economic utility. Consequently, their influence is profound and seems to be underappreciated in most existing accounts of migration policy.

Also drawing upon the varieties of capitalism and how these provide different institutional landscapes that create varying employer preferences, Alexander Caviedes' contribution offers some caveats to the argument made by Menz in the previous chapter. The argument is that the workforce flexibility needs of employers drive them to seek labour migration policies, but that these flexibility concerns vary by economic sector. Compared with the rather general labour shortages that motivated guestworker programmes in the 1950s and 1960s, the transformation of the labour market since that time – in the direction of becoming service economies – has meant that in certain sectors such as information technology, hospitality and health care, flexibility has become a key concern. In a sense, this recognizes the presence of varieties of capitalism, however, it does not presume that these are exclusively national in character, but that they might be sectoral in nature so that similar needs and policies develop somewhat independently from national settings. Nevertheless, the analysis acknowledges that while employers' preferences may be converging across countries by sector, they still reside in national contexts that present varying domestic obstacles – in the form of industrial relations considerations and interest representation configurations – in the path towards further liberalization of labour migration. The identification of these differing logics opens up new questions as to what type of labour migration policies – if any – will be palatable in terms of further policy at the pan-European level as well.

Granting particular attention to one aspect of the sectoral nature of labour migration, Holger Kolb begins by asking the larger question about the logic behind states' immigration policy. Focusing on migration policies targeting the highly skilled, the chapter begins by providing a theoretical lens for understanding both the motivation behind and differentiation in policy instruments. Understanding the state as a form of club that provides a bundle of services to its members, Kolb explains that the state actively seeks to increase the membership of those who can contribute positively to this bundle. With the labour market for the highly skilled becoming more global in nature, the level of competition to attract the "best and brightest" from around the world while retaining one's own has also risen, pressuring states to draft policies that reflect both considerations. What results are migration policies that vary in terms of the degree of risk that states are willing to assume. While employer-driven policies offer the soundest assurance that migrants will be integrated into the labour market since they are guaranteed positions, policies for sectors with shortages are most concerned with preventing skills shortages in certain branches, while points-based systems appear to expose the state to the greatest risk in terms of relinquishing control over access to the labour market. Interestingly, rather than seeing one single type of policy emerge as the outcome of this imputed competition between states, states still differ in terms of their calculations and evaluations of what they see as the greatest vulnerabilities of their own particular bundle of collective goods.

A key area in which the landscape for policy formation has altered is in the role and stances of the labour movement. The chapter by Torben Krings points out that while trade unions were traditionally wary of labour migration, they have shown themselves to be pragmatic, especially during the growth years of the 1960s when they were quite complicit with employers in ensuring large flows of guestworkers into several European countries. While the 1970s witnessed a return to a more defensive stance, the last 15 years have generated greater adaptability on the part of unions. Recognizing the dedication of many governments to the labour market flexibility-enhancing properties of foreign workers, unions have altered their strategy. Large-scale labour migration has resumed and will continue, so rather than staunchly oppose the inevitable, unions – who have seen their stature within the policy-making process erode over the last 30 years – have sought to support those elements of policy that need not directly impinge on the prospects of their members, while criticizing only those elements that resemble the creation of an "industrial reserve army". Krings identifies the emergence of a consensus around government policy that is in the vein of "managed migration". Yet rather than unconditionally supporting such policies, unions differentiate between long-term policies, that they feel offer migrants stable and equitable perspectives, and short-term policies, in which migrants are denied the ability to bring family and where permanent perspectives are closed to them. Beyond the inequity of these programmes, unions recognize that it is the latter which constitute the most serious challenge to the employment perspectives of their constituency.

Ettore Recchi and Anna Triandafyllidou's discussion of East–West migration provides a clear image of the scale and nature of the dominant phenomenon that has characterized European immigration since the fall of the Iron Curtain. By looking beyond the numbers – which are certainly impressive in their own right – this examination makes several key points about the changing experience of those who migrate west from within Europe. The piece delineates the different stages in the status of those who come, tracing out the transition from having to "migrate" to eventually simply being able to exercise "movement". While the EU is celebrated as a facilitator of migration, whose very presence has certainly spurred much of these migration flows, Recchi and Triandafyllidou offer a sobering assessment of what *de facto* benefits "EU citizenship" has actually conferred upon workers from the accession states. They point out that changes in legal status have only gone so far towards opening opportunity in the West, where labour market segmentation still results in only certain types of jobs being available for Eastern Europeans, such that workers often find themselves assuming employment well below their qualifications. Beyond simply viewing this as an economic labour market issue, this chapter forces one to reflect on the impact of European integration in terms of both identity and political opportunity. When many new EU citizens still do not feel that they are treated as "full Europeans" what will this mean in terms of their embracing the political opportunities and obligations attendant to EU citizenship?

In a further consideration of the impression that European integration is making upon labour migration, the book is enhanced by Vassilis Hatzopoulos' consideration of the development of freedom of services from a legal perspective. While service providers are not often discussed in the same breath as migrants – due to employment activity that is often of more limited duration, as well as the fact that they are not usually subsumed under national immigration regimes – the former often serve as functional equivalents of the latter. Of particular impact has not only been the fact that EU rules on services open the door to workers from EU member states, but also that jurisprudence and legislation have increasingly extended the capacity of these rights even to third-country nationals under the employ of EU member state enterprises. While member states now accept that they must accord free movement to workers from fellow member states, they have always been able to rely on the fact that granting non-EU members access to EU labour markets has remained a national competence. In this regard, and perhaps somewhat surreptitiously, the expanding regime in services has certainly opened European labour markets further than some countries would have intended. As such, a legal framework that was in its infancy 30 years ago has changed the overall labour migration landscape in ways that were difficult to imagine then, and which are still difficult to fully appreciate and quantify now. As Hatzopoulos concludes, these rights not only have the potential to be further expanded, but as they do so, one should question to what degree they undermine the exclusive nature of the grant of citizenship rights attendant to the Treaty on European Union.

In a second contribution to this book, Georg Menz argues that the structural transformation of the European state and its embrace of neoliberal competition state priorities is often underestimated and underappreciated in current migration debates. Consequently, migration control efforts now involve private actors, especially transportation companies, but also private security companies. By devolving operational responsibility and imposing financial sanctions, airlines are forced to co-manage flows of "undesirable" migrants, such as refugees and asylum seekers. In addition, privatization has also occurred with regard to the detention of migrants, though usually limited to those deemed "undesirable", especially unsuccessful asylum applicants. The degree of reliance on such outsourcing seems to be directly correlated with the inroads that neoliberal inspired restructuration of the public sector and new public management ideas have made. Consequently, it is most pronounced in the UK and less so in the Netherlands and Germany, with fairly advanced degrees of outsourcing evident in Australia and the US. Ostensibly meant to reduce costs, such involvement of the private sector creates obvious principal-agent problems of accountability, oversight and transparency, and self-perpetuation, which do not seem to be particularly well addressed in any of the case studies. Activists also highlight recurring incidents of abusive treatment of inmates, which are not helped by often substandard working conditions and inadequate training for the security staff. The chapter importantly highlights new forms of migration management, especially the somewhat less easily palatable mechanisms of curbing migration flows outside of the newly created access channels for "desirable" economic migrants.

Undocumented migration is by its nature difficult to chart and assess empirically, and it is an even more taxing exercise to theorize its role and function in the European political economy. Michael Samers' contribution highlights the structural embeddedness of undocumented or "black" labour markets in certain European economies and the somewhat uneven responses by employer associations and governments to dealing with such segments. The response by the state apparatus is often contradictory because it recognizes the preferences of employers to rely on undocumented labour for certain activities and in certain tiers of the labour market, yet it also seeks to re-establish political and economic control over such segments (often unsuccessfully) in order to generate tax revenues. In Italy and France, the state apparatus also responds somewhat eclectically because on one level political parties and politicians of the right desire to be seen as taking "tough" action on deportation, border security and re-establishment of state regulatory control, yet on another level, the capitalist state can ill afford to alienate business interests and politically well-connected members of the bourgeoisie. Neo-Marxist migration analyses have long drawn on the Marxist concept of the "reserve army" to argue that capital and the state conspire to maintain access to cheap labour. Drawing on empirical material from these two Mediterranean countries, Samers argues that undocumented migration is often subject to "malign neglect" by the state apparatus.

According to Willem Maas, the state apparatus is not necessarily unwilling to take strong action against undocumented migration, but rather, at least in Spain, is structurally and organizationally incapable of doing so. Maas examines the regularly deployed instrument of "regularizations" of undocumented migrants in Spain, a tool previously used elsewhere in Southern Europe, including in France and Italy. The rapid economic expansion of Spain over the past 20 years and the attendant construction and real estate boom have led to an exponential growth in immigration, much of which has taken the form of visa overstayers from Latin America. Maas seeks to establish the rationale underpinning regularization in the Spanish context. Clearly, assuming it to have been part of a "carrots and sticks" policy, it has failed to act as a deterrent. Yet, part of the explanation might simply be the structural lack of capacity, manpower and organizational structure to police the labour market adequately, coupled with the welcome contribution that migrants have made towards economic growth. It remains a valid question whether such a permissive attitude will be retained in the face of the economic downturn that has affected the Spanish economy, and especially the real estate sector, with particular vehemence. First attempts to entice migrants to return by offering return premiums (also experimented with by France in the 1990s) seem to generate little interest, so the question remains open as to what further policy responses remain available.

2. New dynamics and new actors in migration policy-making

In sum, this book has three principal objectives. Firstly, it explores and analyses the politics of economic migration, which, though a quantitatively smaller phenomenon than the substantial inflow of beneficiaries of family reunion and asylum, are important precisely because the European state still commands significant margins of manoeuvre in this area. This is also fairly uncharted territory. The re-discovery of economic migration is a novel phenomenon, yet labour migration to Europe itself is obviously not unprecedented. However, we argue that a qualitative difference exists between the patterns of labour recruitment of the 1950s–1970s (and indeed those during the rapid onset of industrialization in Britain during the early nineteenth century and in France and Germany during the latter part of it), reflecting the structural transformation of the European economy since. We analyse new patterns, new trends and new actors. Intra-European migration has re-emerged, albeit with an East–West rather than a South–North focus. Traditional countries of emigration such as Greece and Spain have attracted significant numbers of immigrants, either from economically challenged Eastern European countries, the linguistically and culturally related countries of Latin America, or simply geographically proximate and economically and politically unstable Africa. The old paradigm of zero immigration seems to have been well and truly abandoned. Governments embrace migrants deemed valuable for economic purposes. Employer associations and business groups have re-discovered an appetite for labour migration and have abandoned much more sceptical positions that used to prevail, including in France and Germany. Unions now support and endorse managed migration. New actors such as airlines, trucking companies, and private security companies are co-opted into the administration and detention of migrant movements.

Secondly, we seek to overcome the state-centric bias of much of the political science literature on migration by explicitly considering the role and activities of non-state actors, notably trade unions and employers. In a way, these would appear to be interest groups with an obvious stake in the issue, even more so in traditionally neocorporatist continental Europe, but their role remains underspecified in existing scholarly accounts. Public policy is designed in a much broader arena than political science scholars sometimes acknowledge, notwithstanding efforts to curtail limits to this venue, control the number and nature of participants, or simply shift and create new venues. It is also possible to shape and colour the cognitive framework and nature of public discourse, which is an effective way of agenda setting. The re-discovery of labour migration has been difficult to market politically because high structural unemployment, hostile public opinion and clearly apparent social and political problems emanating from past migration waves and often only modestly successful attempts at their integration do not make for amenable conditions. The state apparatus is also often aware of substantial flows of undocumented migration, yet is either incapable of or unwilling to impose its regulatory power in certain segments of the labour market. Adherence to standard wages and working conditions in Spanish vineyards, in London restaurants and hotels, in Sicilian fields and in the nurseries of the children of Milan's *haute bourgeoisie*, or on the building sites of Berlin would substantially alter the economic logic of these enterprises. Businesses welcome governmental "malign neglect" both because it keeps personnel costs in check and because the autochthones are often neither inclined or indeed truly capable of tolerating poor working conditions and substandard pay levels.

Thirdly, we examine and sketch the impact of major macroeconomic global and European changes on strategies of economic recruitment, corporate restructuring and firm-level strategies. European economies today have diverged considerably, yet have obviously all undergone the shift towards the tertiary sector, with the decline of manufacturing now slowly affecting Southern and Eastern Europe as well. There is little interest in sheer manpower; instead there is highly differentiated appetite for skilled migrants to slot into select sectors of the economy, where deficiencies in domestic training institutions, rapidly and newly emerging sectors, and employer preferences for flexibility imply shortages. Europe openly challenges existing traditional countries of immigration and enters the competition for the best brains. Labour markets are also opened in less than conspicuous ways, for example, through the temporary posting of highly skilled employees of multinational corporations or under the auspices of service provision. An evolution and transformation of economic structures, corporate strategies and, very importantly, an ideological preference for neoliberal growth strategies and the resultant attempt to optimize investment conditions and accumulation have conspired to transform European migration policies. However, the backlash against forms of migration that threaten to jeopardize wage levels and social standards demonstrates the political limits to the liberalization of migration regulation. At the same time, Europe's poor record regarding the integration of existing ethnic minorities into the labour market highlights shortcomings of educational opportunities afforded and raises important questions for public policy designers devising new schemes of managed migration. More pragmatic labour migration also seems to coincide with more restrictive policy regarding other forms of migration, deemed "undesirable", notably refugees and asylum seekers. As in the 1960s, there was a call for human resources, but human beings arrived, as Swiss author Max Frisch sardonically commented. But different human resources are being solicited and presumably different human beings will consequently arrive.

The patterns and trends we identify here point to a systematic and fundamental transformation of migration policy design that is unlikely to be affected by the worst economic recession since the early 1930s that surfaced in Europe in the autumn of 2008. While legal channels for low-skilled migrants, existing in small numbers in the UK, might be closed and the quantitative scope of highly skilled migration might be temporarily limited throughout much of Europe, it seems unlikely that this recession will play a similar functional role to the OPEC crisis of 1973. By 2011, existing restrictions on intra-European migration originating in the 2004 accession countries will have to be ended; by 2014, full labour mobility will encompass even the 2007 newcomers. By then, Croatian and Icelandic membership may have become reality. There is thus a sizable labour pool for pan-European labour mobility, even in the absence of full membership for Turkey. The newly discovered paradigm of managed migration seems unlikely to succumb to economic recession and its implications. In fact, initial but less than systematic evidence suggests that return migration to either Eastern European or third countries is limited. A more radical rethinking of migration policy design might be precipitated by serious effects of climate change, energy shortages and spiralling fossil fuel prices. This might also engender the abandonment of neoclassical postulates of unfettered economic growth, which has long underpinned the academic training of EU and national administrative and political elites. However, at present, such paradigmatic change still appears to be at least one decade away.

Labour migration is a complex, multi-layered and multi-tiered phenomenon. Its fairly recent renaissance in Europe might account for the ultimately limited scholarly interest this particular form of migration has attracted recently. Within a mere decade, migration studies have moved from a somewhat exotic *Orchideenfach* to being a highly topical and current focal point of enormous scholarly productivity. In public policy discourses and public debate, migration has become an issue that simply refuses to go away. With this study of the recent transformation of European labour migration policy design, we endeavour to contribute to both of these debates and generate fresh and hopefully progressive arguments about conundrums and denouements.

This book has had a fairly long gestation process. The editors discovered their joint interest in European labour migration policy via Martin Rhodes, at the time professor of public policy at the EUI in Florence, whilst Alex was a visiting scholar there en route to carrying out his doctoral research on new avenues for labour migration to Europe in the early 2000s. His doctoral thesis, submitted to the University of Wisconsin, has now been published as *Prying Open Fortress Europe: The Turn to Sectoral Labor Migration* (2010).

Georg had come to the subject of labour migration through an interest in the politics of service provision liberalization and later spent time at the EUI as a Jean Monnet Fellow, drafting the manuscript of what was to become *The Political Economy of Managed Migration* (2008). A pint in South London's rough and ready New Cross in 2003, while watching the coaches go by outside the pub windows that ferried Polish and Czech would-be migrants to central London, preceded chats over espresso in the arguably marginally more appealing environs of the *Badia* in 2006. More extended talks on the fringes of the Council for European Studies and EUSA conferences in Chicago and Montreal eventually spawned this edited collection.

Georg would like to express his gratitude to the National Europe Centre at Australian National University, a perfect Antipodean hideaway from the quotidian reality of South London, where his two chapters were drafted during a sabbatical in late 2008. The British Academy Small Grant Scheme and Goldsmiths College helped fund research trips to Germany, the Netherlands, Italy, Ireland, Poland, and the US and conference presentations in the US and Canada.

Alex would like to thank SUNY Fredonia for funding further research in Germany, the UK, and the Netherlands in 2008, to supplement the original studies that were undertaken while finishing the dissertation at the University of Wisconsin. Further, he has benefited from travel grants to attend conferences where he could present his own work and, perhaps more importantly, continue to be exposed to the research of others that confirms the dynamic and continuing transformation of labour migration in Europe.

Bibliography

Amable, B. (2004) *The Diversity of Modern Capitalism* (Oxford: Oxford University Press).

Angenendt, S. (ed.) (1999) *Asylum and Migration Policies in the European Union* (Berlin: Europa Union Verlag).

Appleyard, R. (2001) "International Migration Policies 1950–2000", *International Migration* 39(6): 7–18.

Bleich, E. (2008) "Immigration and Integration Studies in Western Europe and the United States: The Road Less Traveled and a Path Ahead", *World Politics* 60(3): 509–538.

Brettel, C. and Hollifield, J. (eds.) (2007) *Migration Theory: Talking Across Disciplines* (London: Routledge).

Castles, S. and Kosack, G. (1973) *Immigrant Workers and Class Structure in Western Europe* (Oxford: Oxford University Press).

Castles, S. and Miller, M. (1993) *The Age of Migration: International Population Movements in the Modern World* (London: Guildford Press).

Caviedes, A. (2010) *Prying Open Fortress Europe: The Turn to Sectoral Labor Migration* (Lanham, MD: Lexington Books).

Cole, M. and Dales, G. (eds.) (1999) *The European Union and Migrant Labour* (New York: Berg).

Crouch, C. and Streeck, W. (eds.) (1997) *Political Economy of Modern Capitalism: Mapping Convergence and Diversity* (Thousand Oaks, CA: Sage).

Faist, T. and Ette, A. (eds.) (2007) *Europeanization of National Policies and Politics of Immigration* (Basingstoke: Palgrave Macmillan).

Fassmann, H. and Münz, R. (eds.) (1994) *European Migration in the Late Twentieth Century* (Aldershot: Edward Elgar).

Freeman, G. (2006) "National Models, Policy Types, and the Politics of Immigration in Liberal Democracies", *West European Politics* 29(2): 227–247.

Geddes, A. (2003) *The Politics of Migration and Immigration in Europe* (London: Sage).

Geddes, A. (2008) *Immigration and European Integration: Beyond Fortress Europe*, 2nd edn (Machester: Manchester University Press).

Guiraudon, V. (2001) "De-nationalizing Control: Analyzing State Responses to Constraints on Migration Control", in V. Guiraudon and C. Joppke (eds.) *Controlling a New Migration World* (New York: Routledge), pp. 29–64.

Hall, P. and Soskice, D. (eds.) (2001) *Varieties of Capitalism: The Institutional Foundations of Comparative Advantage* (Oxford: Oxford University Press).

Haus, L. (2002) *Unions, Immigration and Internationalization: New Challenges and Changing Coalition in the United States and France* (New York: Palgrave).

Hollifield, James (1992) *Immigrants, Markets, and States: The Political Economy of Postwar Europe* (Cambridge, MA: Harvard University Press).

Lahav, G. (1998) "Immigration and the State: The Devolution and Privatisation of Immigration Control in the EU", *Journal of Ethnic and Migration Studies* 24(4): 675–694.

Lahav, G. and V. Guiraudon (2006) "Actors and Venues in Immigration Control: Closing the Gap Between Political Demands and Policy Outcomes", *West European Politics* 29(2): 201–223.

Lavenex, S. (2006) "The Competition State and the Multilateral Liberalization of Skilled Migration", in A. Favell (ed.) *The Human Face of Global Mobility, International Highly Skilled Migration in Europe, North America and the Asia-Pacific* (New Brunswick, NJ: Transaction Publishers), pp. 29–54.

Lavenex, S. and Uçarer, E. (eds.) (2002) *Migration and the Externalities of European Integration* (Lanham, MD: Lexington Books).

Menz, G. (2005) *Varieties of Capitalism and Europeanization: National Response Strategies to the Single European Market* (Oxford: Oxford University Press).

Menz, G. (2008) *The Political Economy of Managed Migration* (Oxford: Oxford University Press).

Menz, G. (2010) "Are You Being Served? Europeanizing and Re-Regulating the Single Market", *Journal of European Public Policy*.

Messina, A. (1996) "The not so Silent Revolution: Postwar Migration to Western Europe", *World Politics* 49(1): 130–154.

Piore, M. (1979) *Birds of Passage* (Cambridge: Cambridge University Press).

Scharpf, F. and Schmidt, V. (eds.) (2001) *Welfare and Work in the Open Economy: Volume I: From Vulnerability to Competitiveness* (New York: Oxford University Press).

Schmidt, V. (2002) *The Futures of European Capitalism* (Oxford: Oxford University Press).

Smeeding, T. and Parsons, C. (eds.) (2006) *Immigration and the Transformation of Europe* (Cambridge: Cambridge University Press).

Soysal, Y. (1994) *Limits of Citizenship: Migrants and Postnational Citizenship in Europe* (Cambridge: Cambridge University Press).

Straubhaar, T. (2006) "Labour Market Relevant Migration Policy", *Zeitschrift für Arbeitsmarktforschung* 39(1): 3–172.

Watts, J. (2002) *Immigration Policy and the Challenge of Globalization: Unions and Employers in Unlikely Alliance* (Ithaca, NY: Cornell University Press).

Yamamuro, K. and Streeck, W. (2003) *The End of Diversity? Prospects for German and Japanese Capitalism* (Ithaca, NY: Cornell University Press).

Uçarer, E. and Puchala, D. (eds.) (1997) *Immigration into Western Societies* (London: Cassell).

Section I

Labour Migration and European Capitalisms

2
Employers, Trade Unions, Varieties of Capitalism, and Labour Migration Policies

Georg Menz

1. Introduction

Over the past 15 years, European governments have re-discovered labour migration. The restrictive approaches that dominated the period between the mid-1970s and the mid-1990s have given way to more liberal policy design regarding "desirable" labour migrants, though not other migration categories, such as humanitarian ones. Current debates in political science migration studies explore a number of agents active in migration policy-making, including "organised interest groups, courts, ethnic groups, trade unions, law and order bureaucracies, police and security agencies, local actors and street-level bureaucrats and private actors" (Lahav and Guiraudon, 2006, p. 207).

This chapter contributes to this literature by exploring the political activities of employer associations, actors which have remained curiously bereft of scholarly attention. Adopting a perspective that is both influenced by the comparative capitalisms approach in comparative political economy and previous work on the role of organized interest groups in migration studies (Freeman, 1995, 2002, 2006), it is argued that the interest and advocacy positions of employer associations are shaped by the particularities of the national production systems they are embedded in. This is operationalized in terms of Hall and Soskice's (2001) ideal-types of varieties of capitalism, as amended by Hancké et al. (2007). In methodological terms, the chapter adopts the case study method, by focusing on the four European case studies best representing these ideal types, Germany, France, Poland, and the United Kingdom (UK). Empirically, it focuses on the analysis of labour migration policy between 1995 and the present. Thus, employer preferences for labour migrants will be conditioned by considerations of complementarity with existing production strategies, easily adding to, but in the case of liberal market economies (LMEs) also "importing" skills to existing portfolios. The rest of this chapter is organized as follows.

In the second section, the theoretical contribution is outlined, drawing on both the migration and comparative political economy literature. The main propositions are presented in more detail. Employers will want migrants to complement and not complicate existing production strategies and expect them to easily fit with skills and training strategies.

In the third section, the influence of employers in shaping public policy is explored in empirical detail. Fourthly, a conclusion succinctly summarizes the insights derived from the analysis of previously neglected actors in migration policy-making and advocates application of tenets of comparative political economy to studying migration.

2. Models of capitalism, employer associations, and labour migration policies

European migration policies are rapidly changing. A formerly restrictive approach, assumed after the end of the post-war boom in the early 1970s, has been slowly abandoned in favour of more pragmatic and liberal labour migration policy. Notwithstanding the impediments to resuming labour recruitment (Messina, 1990) and the obvious shortcomings of the guestworker concept of the post-war decades, European governments from Ireland to Italy, from France to the Czech Republic have commenced recruiting economic migrants again. Thus, between 1999 and 2006 the annual net flow of foreign workers into the UK rose from 42,000 to 62,700; in Germany it rose from 304,900 in 1999 to 380,300 in 2004 (OECD, 2008: Table A.2.1.). This general trend holds true across European OECD (Organisation for Economic Co-operation and Development) members.

But who drives these changes? A "gap" between restrictionist rhetoric and slightly more permissive practice (Hansen, 2002) exists. It has previously been partially accounted for by the activities of liberal courts (Hollifield, 1992; Joppke, 1998), though these pertain predominantly to humanitarian forms of migration, especially family reunion, but also asylum seekers and refugees. Other relevant actors recently addressed in the migration literature include political parties (Bale, 2008), the media (Demo, 2004), and trade unions (Haus, 2002; Watts, 2002). Nevertheless, "prevailing scholarship...has been inconclusive with regard to the role and nature of domestic actors on national immigration policy-making" (Lahav and Guiraudon, 2006, p. 207).

Obviously, not all of these actors have a stake in labour migration policy. Little scholarly attention has been paid to the role of employer associations in migration studies (exceptions are Cerna, 2009 and Caviedes in this book), though organized business played a pivotal role in earlier Marxist-inspired analytical contributions (Cole and Dale, 1999; earlier: Castells, 1975; Castles and Kosack, 1973; Piore, 1979). This is surprising, for it would seem *prima facie* fruitful to explore the role of these actors in understanding how and why national-level labour migration policy has come to be liberalized across Europe since the mid-1990s onwards. While the "gap" puzzle is still unresolved, it is worth noting that with respect to labour migrants, official discourse is strikingly less restrictive than regarding "undesirable" migrant groups. The framework proposed addresses the interest positions assumed by employers since the mid-1990s.

This chapter bridges the gap between the migration literature and the rapidly evolving scholarship on comparative political economy, "mainstreaming" migration by marrying it with fresh insights from a different subfield. In doing so, the weakness of the political science literature on European migration to treat the field as a *sui generis* subfield is addressed. Freeman (2006) refers to this as a tendency to construct idiosyncratic national models. Similarly, the commonly state-centric bias is addressed by focusing on somewhat under-researched non-state actors, namely employer associations.

Recent advances in comparative political economy have stressed the resilience of national models or varieties of capitalism (VoC) (Coates, 2000; Hall and Soskice, 2001; Hancké et al., 2007). This highly influential though also criticized (Coates, 2005) approach highlights the persistence of multiple equilibria in the institutional configuration of systems of political-economic governance, encompassing systems of industrial relations and labour market regulation, vocational training and education, corporate governance and finance, and intra-firm relationships. For all its strengths, it is a very theoretical body of literature and can be strengthened by further empirical applications, especially in a field such as labour migration which is logically linked to many of the core components of these varieties. However, this link has not been exhaustively explored in the literature (an exception is Menz, 2008).

One of the most valuable endeavours towards exploring the role of interest groups and explaining the puzzle of expansionary policies behind a backdrop of restrictive public sentiment is Freeman's pioneering work (1995, 2002, 2006). Inspired by Wilson (1980), it has emphasized the importance of client politics in liberal democracies, though principally the United States (US), where well-organized business groups and ethnic advocacy coalitions combine efforts to press for liberal policies from which they benefit and whose costs are diffused. For labour-oriented non-permanent migration both costs and benefits are concentrated (2006, p. 230), leading to "interest group politics", while for permanent migration channels the benefits are concentrated and the costs are often diffuse, which leads to a low-conflict mode of client politics. With costs diffuse in the latter case, opponents to immigration may find it difficult to organize and rally effectively. In the former case, we would expect organized labour to be a natural opponent to immigration (cf. Freeman, 2006, pp. 233–234), yet research on recent European trade union positions suggests that carefully managed labour immigration is preferred to a restrictive approach and substantial unregulated migration (Haus, 2002; Watts, 2002). Though compelling in its empirical application and rightfully applauded for its introduction of a political economy angle, Freeman's work has been criticized for not being applicable to the European context, where ethnic advocacy groups thus far play a limited role and hence "client politics" play out quite differently (Joppke, 1999; but see Freeman, 2006, pp. 234–235). Immigration is also framed and perceived differently by actors (Statham and Geddes, 2006) in countries which for decades have described themselves as not open to immigrants (Hansen, 2002).

Modifying Freeman's analysis somewhat, it is maintained that in the European context employers will not simply lobby for "more liberal" policy, but rather for migrants with certain skill profiles which correspond to the predominant production strategy. Employers do not univocally advocate the recruitment of identical profiles of economic migrants. Their interest will be conditioned by the model of capitalism (and thus the production strategy) they are embedded in, ensuring complementarity. Skill sets of migrants differ along two dimensions, the level (low versus highly skilled) and the specificity (sector-specific versus generalist). Following Salt (1997, p. 5), highly skilled is defined as "tertiary level education or its equivalent in experience". Aside from skills, labour shortages will also influence employer positions, but will be filtered by considerations of results produced by present educational and vocational systems. It is true that "countries' policies cannot thus be deducted from a simple division into...VoC groups" (Cerna, 2009, p. 146). However, the advocacy position of employers is indeed shaped by the production system and the respective model of capitalism. Employers may also use labour migration to escape confines imposed by training systems. LME employers may encounter skill

Table 2.1 Interest positions of employers in liberal and coordinated market economies

Skill Level ▶	Unskilled/Low Skilled	Highly Skilled
Skill Specificity ▼		
	LME employer interest (synergy)	LME employer interest (supplementarity)
Sector-Specific	No CME employer interest	CME employer interest (synergy)
Generalist	LME employer interest (synergy)	LME employer interest (synergy)
	No CME employer interest	CME employer interest (supplementarity)

shortages among the domestic labour pool due to the traditional weakness of LME education systems to generate vocational training schemes (Table 2.1). Coordinated market economies (CME) employers face a different challenge: in certain sectors, especially those rapidly evolving due to technological change, CME education and training systems may perform inadequately, because they are geared towards gradual not radical product innovation. "Importing labour" to overcome or "circumvent institutional constraints" is recognized as an explicit business strategy in recent VoC literature (Herrmann, 2009). Employers will thus seek to secure employees with skills that are complementary in the first instance, creating obvious *synergy* effects, but they will also turn to labour migration as a source of *supplementarity* to overcome limitations of domestic training systems.

In LMEs, as a rule there is more generalist, employer-specific, and on-the-job training provided (Thelen, 2004) as opposed to sector-specific skills education, hence migrants with a variety of past training and skill levels can be accommodated. "Individuals and employers are free to determine levels and types of skill investment and acquisition" (Keep and Mayhew, 1997, p. 372). Thus, employers in LMEs will welcome migrants with general skill profiles and those who are highly skilled. There is a substantial service sector in the UK, accounting for 75 per cent of total employment in 2003, according to the OECD (Hall, 2007, p. 67), some of which is based on "a lower-cost, lower-price strategy, underpinning service-sector expansion" (Hancké et al., 2007, pp. 32–33). Here, high staff fluctuation and quickly shifting labour demand are important factors in influencing employer demands, not least because low-skill low-wage jobs are inherently difficult to recruit for due to low wages, poor morale and prestige, and unappealing working conditions, as Piore's dual labour market thesis (1979, p. 17) highlighted.

Employers in CMEs will lobby for skilled migrants that either complement existing production modes directly or provide valuable synergies if they permit the "import" of skills that are not, or not sufficiently, generated domestically, thus permitting radical product innovation. Highly skilled foreigners may have skills equivalent to CME-style vocational training or tertiary education; they may thus either possess generalist or specific skills. However, there is no interest in unskilled migrants. The absence of a sizable low-skill low-wage service sector renders low-skilled or unskilled individuals difficult to employ. Employers have no institutional incentive to upset the "high skill equilibrium" (Culpepper, 1999; Culpepper and Finegold, 2001), which is a crucial component of the CME model, but face potentially very costly consequences for doing so.

Despite their heterogeneity and hybrid status (Molina and Rhodes, 2007, pp. 224–229), mixed market economies (MMEs) such as France have often sizable high-skill high-wage clusters in the secondary sector. EMEs (Emerging Market Economies) such as Poland, where CME-style coordination is very weak and underdeveloped (Mykhnenko, 2005), would appear to be slowly constructing these, but, setting themselves apart from Southern and Northwestern Europe, also still possess sizable primary sectors.

Therefore, the embedded environments of LMEs and CMEs shape the preferences of actors and create demands for different sets of labour migrants. Different national production strategies influence employer advocacy coalitions. Recent trends towards economic liberalization notwithstanding, the differences in production strategies are more pivotal in the present than they were during the post-war phase of labour recruitment. Furthermore, post-war labour migration was not exclusively driven by economic factors such as skill profiles and labour shortages and often more influenced by (post-)colonial ties (Castles with Miller, 2003).

However, migration advocacy does not unfold in a depoliticized environment. Addressing Statham and Geddes' (2006) concern regarding framing, it is argued that employer associations endeavour to define "competitiveness" as a central concern for national policy-makers and attempt to demonstrate how immigration can help provide the required human resources necessary to ensure economic competitiveness. This competition-state agenda is defined by Cerny (1995) as the provision of a relatively favourable investment climate for transnational capital, including a circumscribed range of goods that retain a national-scale public character human capital, infrastructure, and general maintenance of a public policy environment favourable to investment and profit making. Thus, discourse, "used to construct and legitimate... the necessity and appropriateness of reform... can exert a causal influence" (Schmidt, 2002, p. 169). While analysts influenced by the Copenhagen School have alerted us to immigration often being conflated with threats to national security (Buzan et al., 1993; Huysmans, 2006; but: Boswell, 2007) and indeed the dynamics of the rhetorical construction of this very term, economic competitiveness can also be framed as an issue of national security, in line with Rudolph's (2003) suggestion.

> H1 (VoC hypothesis): Employer preferences are shaped by the variety of capitalism they are embedded in.

LME employers will make demands for migrants with both generalist and sector-specific skills, and both for highly skilled and low skilled. Such labour migrants can be easily accommodated into flexibility-oriented production strategies and complement existing training schemes or provide a useful synergy by "importing" skilled labour. CME employers will be interested in migrants with high skills, either of a generalist nature or sector-specific. There will be no interest in the unskilled. Similar considerations will influence MME and EME employers, thus they will advocate both highly skilled generalists and sector-specific highly skilled in the MMEs and the EMEs. The "importation" of skills is of interest, as high-value-added high-skill "islands" emulate CME strategies.

But employer associations face considerable hurdles in influencing public policy and need to establish new channels to ministries of interior affairs. Influence is defined as a substantial similarity between non-state actors' publicly stated interests, assessed in interviews and the review of primary sources, and the actual regulatory outcome. *Employer preferences translate into successful influence on policy only if employers are internally united on this issue and successfully influence public policy through skillful rhetoric invoking competitiveness.* Employers therefore need to be very explicit about emphasizing the economic utility of migration.

> H2 (coherence hypothesis): Internal consensus on migration policy among employers will lead to tangible impact on public policy.

> H3 (competition rhetoric hypothesis): Influence on policy will be superior if employers successfully portray economic migration as a core component of securing or maintaining economic competitiveness.

In the following section, the three hypotheses will be juxtaposed with empirical developments in four European countries.

3. The politics of advocating liberalized labour migration policy

3.1. France

Analysts have struggled to categorize the *French* political economy given its mix of statist structures and policies, liberalized elements, and subtle power shifts between actors over the years (Clift, 2007; Culpepper, 2006; Woll, 2006). In the VoC literature, it is characterized as a mixed market economy (Hall and Gingerich, 2004), combining "market regulation with some elements of coordinated regulation as well as state-compensating coordination" (Hancké et al., 2007, pp. 13–14).

For many years, French employers' interest in labour migration was limited (Watts, 2002).[1] French policy-makers began exploring active labour migrant recruitment in the late-1990s. In 1998, an internal administrative circular had advised provincial governments to consider "fast-tracking" (or at least treat with leniency) residency permit application from information technology experts, spawning a 2001 governmental initiative to grant working and residency permits to a total of 4000 information technology specialists.[2] Despite the restrictive Pasqua Laws being only a few years old, there were signs that the paradigm of zero (illegal) immigration was slowly being abandoned[3] among the political Right.[4] The 1998 Chèvenement Law permits the fast-track processing of residency and work permit applications by "desirable" labour migrants. The number of permanent work permits issued fluctuated between 6403 in 2000 and 8920 in 2005 (Régnard, 2006).

Until the early 2000s, however, there was no firm consensus within the French business camp on strategies for labour recruitment (interview FR-BUS-1). The major internationally active players were not opposed to recruiting highly skilled migrants, but relied largely on home-grown talent. Some sectoral employers, for example, in the construction sector, even assumed a somewhat protectionist position, preferring recruitment of established "migrant" communities to active soliciting. Critical analysts (Terray, 1999) argue that employers do rely on undocumented migrants already present. He highlights successful employer lobbying activity against the March 1997 Barrot Law that would have shifted the burden of proof on the employer in cases of infractions against employment laws. The status quo permitted the necessary flexibility.

De facto, a secondary labour market already exists and many, though not all, of these "three D" jobs (dirty, dull, dangerous) are filled by foreigners. This is particularly true in sectors of the economy such as gastronomy, construction, seasonal agricultural work, and textile (Samers, 2003). Remarkably, the most common infraction found by French labour inspectors (Ministère de la Justice, 1999) is *not* the employment of individuals not entitled to work on French territory, but rather illicit forms of employment that contravene existing labour laws, for example, regarding working hours, remuneration, or health and safety. Given the ready availability of a domestic low-skill labour pool, employable at substandard conditions, there was little incentive for additional lobbying for many years.

This somewhat divided and reticent stance changed in the early 2000s. Employer association *Mouvement des entreprises en France* (MEDEF) itself remained reluctant to endorse active labour recruitment in public (correspondence with the author, March 2006). But the business-friendly think tank Institut Montaigne, founded in 2000 by outspoken Claude Bébéar, senior manager of insurance giant AXA, began advocating the introduction of migration quotas and the active recruitment of highly skilled migrants in particular (*Le Point*, 7 May 2002; *Le Figaro*, 15 February 2006). While it does not maintain direct links with MEDEF, its list of financial supporters reads like a who's who of major French blue chip corporations, including, among others, Total, LVMH, Bouygues, BNP Paribas, Carrefour, Capgemini, Sodexho, Vivendi, and Suez. Its publications make the link between competitiveness and selective immigration very explicit, criticizing that human right considerations have taken precedence over economic concerns in past French migration policy, while suggesting that an immediate doubling of migration flows, based on a "sélection des candidates" (Institut Montaigne, 2003, p. 192) would immediately address worrying labour shortages. The notion that the "doors for immigration" need to be opened to raise competitiveness and meet the challenges of globalization surfaces throughout its publications (Institut Montaigne, 2006, p. 19).

While the very notion of quotas and actively managed and selected immigration remains highly controversial among the political Left,[5] former minister of the interior and current president Nicholas Sarkozy[6] warmed up quickly to the notion of embracing "actively managed, not encountered immigration policy", based on the principles of "growth perspectives, labor market needs, and accommodation capacity" (*Le Monde*, 8 February 2006; interview FR-GOV 1).[7] The new National Agency for the Reception of Foreigners and Migrants (*Agence Nationale de l'Accueil des Etrangers et des Migrations* = ANAEM) are responsible for administering the new "reception and integration contracts" rolled out first as pilot projects in 2003 and nationwide since 2005 (enshrined in Law 2005–32 of 18 January 2005), which oblige new migrants to partake in cultural and linguistic training programmes and to accept the legal and cultural "republican" national values.While remarkable, this represents further movement into this direction, solidifying the institutional framework for future policy. Sarkozy's assessment of alleged past failures emphasizes the economic contribution migrants ought to make: "France is the only developed country which robs itself of the possibility to invite on its territory migrants that it needs to contribute to growth and prosperity" (*Le Monde*, 15 April 2006). A 2006 report commissioned by the Ministry of Finance explicitly calls for active labour market recruitment of skilled migrants (MinFin, 2006). At the 2006 MEDEF summer school Sarkozy repeatedly emphasized the benefits of "chosen immigration" for "those for whom we have work" rather than the "tolerated" flows arriving through family reunion (MEDEF, 2006), the latter of which accounting for 70 per cent of all permanent immigration in 2005 (Régnard, 2006). This stance has spawned the 24 July 2006 so-called Sarkozy II Law, "regarding immigration and integration" (*loi relatif à l'immigration et à l'intégration; loi 2006–911, Journal Officiel 170*) (interviews FR-GOV-1; FR-GOV-2, *Le Monde*, 15 April 2006, 18 June 2006). This law combines a more restrictive approach towards family reunion in particular, motivated by concerns over rising numbers in this category as well as asylum seekers (interview FR-GOV-2), with new work permits aimed at highly qualified migrants. The government is now obliged to draw up a list of economic sectors experiencing labour shortages and to facilitate economic migrant access. The law also aims to smoothen the transition for foreign graduates of French universities into the labour market. Informed by the rhetoric of "chosen" (*choisie*) rather than "imposed" (*subie*) migration, President Sarkozy also created a separate Ministry for Immigration and National Identity in 2007 (*Libération*, 2 April 2007). Most innovative, however, is the introduction of the *carte compétences et talents* for skilled migrants, motivated by the desire to raise the skill profile of labour migrants and to abandon the previous principle of a general labour market review as one condition for approving new work permits. The law found approval in both houses of parliament, though some of the provisions regarding family reunion were modified somewhat (*Le Monde*, 18 June 2006). MEDEF, which was informally consulted throughout the drafting process, enthusiastically supported the new chosen direction in labour migration. The internationally active companies were particularly vocal in supporting facilitated access to the best brains (interview FR-GOV-2).

The recent, but fairly comprehensive, embrace of skilled migration recruitment thus coincided with MEDEF's awakening interest in adding to the skills profile already present in the MME. The employer-friendly think tank served as an important conduit for voicing preferences for public policy reform that has been enacted under President Sarkozy.

3.2. Germany

Recent transformations notwithstanding (Streeck and Höpner, 2003), the *German* political economy is regarded as the paradigmatic CME in the VoC literature. Employers, organized in the BDA (Confederation of German Employers' Associations) and for larger internationally oriented companies also the interest group BDI (Federation of German Industries), are interested in maintaining and enhancing institutions that provide public goods, notably education.

In the late 1990s German employers re-discovered the attractions of labour migration. This changed stance originated within the BDI and can be traced to its outspoken late-1990s president Hans-Olaf Henkel. Henkel called for more avenues for legal labour migration in a general quest to render Germany's economy more dynamic and competitive.[8] Henkel himself was part of two government expert commissions on immigration and harshly criticized the Christian Democrats' rejection of labour migration quotas (*Manager Magazin*, 16 October 2000). His successor in office rejected any quantitative limits to quotas, or at least setting them at 300,000 annually, a tenfold increase over the quota proposed by the 2001 commission (*Süddeutsche Zeitung*, 11 June 2001). The BDA enthusiastically welcomed the "new paradigmatic change" inherent in the hotly contested 2002 draft bill that contained a liberalization of labour migration, even claiming to have demanded such change "for a long time" (BDA, 2002). Convinced of the necessity to "compete for the best brains" and "internationally mobile high flyers" to address "labour market shortages" and to ensure the continued "competitiveness of Germany as place to do business", regulation concerning economic migration is seen as needing to be liberalized, permitting both temporary and long-term migration flows, with minimal discretion for local and regional administrative interventions, "while more stringent procedures and increased deportations should render asylum less attractive" (BDA, 2002); with the latter presumably rendering the former more palatable to the electorate.

This newly discovered interest in labour migration was strongly supported by the metalworking employer association *Gesamtmetall*. Its president Martin Kannegiesser claimed in 2004 that there were shortages of skilled employees that were not sufficiently addressed by the vocational system of training. That same year, the employers remarkably published a joint position paper with the unions in which the desirability of long-term permanent migration, accompanied by greatly enhanced integration measures, including language classes, was strongly emphasized (DGB and BDA, 2004).

The employers also launched a vociferous and financially well-endowed public relations vehicle to popularize their demands for neoliberal restructuring. Founded in 2000 by *Gesamtmetall*, the New Social Market Economy Initiative (*Initiative Neue Soziale Marktwirtschaft*) aims to influence public opinion and media reports (Leif, 2004), drawing on an annual budget of ten million euros. Immigration of "highly qualified foreigners" is one of its many proposals based on the "know how" and "contribution to economic growth" and "the future" that skilled migrants make (Initiative Neue Soziale Marktwirtschaft, 2002, p. 8; 2004, 2006).

The Red-Green government launched a temporary labour recruitment programme in 2000 for 20,000 highly skilled migrants, particularly in IT (the so-called "green card" initiative). The next summer, the Minister for the Interior Schily commissioned a report from an expert commission composed of academics, legal experts, the social partners, and politicians from all parties, headed by moderate Christian Democrat Süssmuth. However, in light of sustained opposition from the Christian Democrats, Schily was unwilling to heed the call for annual migration quotas despite the fervent support of the representative of the employers in the commission. The law was finally accepted by the Bundestag on 1 July and by the Bundesrat on 9 July 2004, bearing the revealing title "Law on the management and limitation of inward migration and the regulation of the residence and integration of EU citizens and foreigners" (*Gesetz zur Steuerung und Begrenzung der Zuwanderung und zur Regelung des Aufenthalts und der Integration von Unionsbürgern und Ausländern*), and came into effect as of 1 January 2005 (BGBl Part I No. 41 1950 of 5 August 2004).[9] Art. 18 specifies that in processing an application for a work permit (henceforth linked to a residency permit), consideration should be given to the labour market situation, the fight against unemployment, and the exigencies of securing national competitiveness. The employer association had been consulted throughout the drafting of the bill (interviews DE-BUS-1, DE-GOV-1). Both BDA representatives within the commission strongly lobbied in favour of more "demand oriented managed migration" and less bureaucratic lee-way for regional labour market administrations in the context of more "competition for the best brains", coupled with faster asylum decisions and more rigorously enforced deportations to "avoid any signal that could be understood in countries of origin that immigration for non-labor market related reasons will be expanded" (BDA, 2002). Employers were particularly interested in highly skilled migrants, not least due to the positive experiences with the IT sector programme, and contributed to the demand for an annual migration quota, based on a points sys-tem (interview DE-BUS-1). Consistent lobbying led to the creation of migration channels for highly skilled high-wage professionals in the new immigration bill, namely entrepreneurs investing at least one mil-lion euros and creating at least ten new jobs and carefully delineated categories of highly skilled migrants were permitted access, including teachers, scientists, and skilled managers earning in excess of 100,000 euros (all defined in Art. 19). In addition, foreign graduates of German universities were permitted to remain in the country for one additional year to search for employment.

Following a meeting of ministers in Merseburg in August 2007, fur-ther business-friendly concessions were made effective as of November 2007, including facilitated access for Central and East European engi-neers, three-year work permits for foreign graduates of German univer-sities, and the creation of a working group within the Ministry of Labour and Education charged with developing "a labor market-oriented man-agement of migration", including the examination of a points-based system measuring qualification levels, age, and language skills (*Berliner Zeitung*, 6 and 25 August 2007). Vice-chancellor and Minister of Labour Müntefering announced that there was no need for low-skill labour migration. The employers enthusiastically welcomed the liberalization of access, emphasizing labour shortages not only in engineering, but also in banking and business services (BDA, 2007a), and continued their advocacy of the "long overdue introduction" of such points-based sys-tem (BDA, 2007b), pointing to Britain as a possible model (BDA, 2007c, 2007d).

The Ministry of Labour drafted a bill on the "management of the migration of the highly qualified" during the summer of 2008. The key changes entailed were further reducing the annual income required for highly qualified migrants eligible for "fast-tracking" from 86,400 euros to 63,600 euros, permitting labour market access for university graduates from the EU-8 accession countries, and creating a permanent council advising and evaluating labour market needs for skilled employees, which would include a representative of the employers. It also facilitated labour market access for already resident temporarily "tolerated" refugees if they could demonstrate successful completion of a three-year tertiary training programme. The bill was accepted by the *Bundestag* on 17 November and by the *Bundesrat* on 19 December 2008. Complaints over minor details notwithstanding, the project was warmly welcomed by the employers (BDA, 2008).

BDA began to warm up to the idea of liberalized labour migration following the impetus from BDI, but very quickly became an outspoken advocate in its own right. In doing so, it was aided by *Gesamtmetall* which was concerned over shortages among highly skilled engineers (interviews DE-BUS-1, DE-BUS-2), presumably key to high-value-added CME production. There was no serious internal disagreement regarding the new liberal stance. In fact, even a sectoral employer association of which one might have intuitively expected advocacy for low-skilled migration, the association for gastronomy did not pursue such action (interview DE-BUS-3). Its main point of criticism of the 2008 legislation is thus not the exclusive focus on highly skilled migrants, but rather the focus on academic degrees as a measure of such skills, which in the hotel sector in particular is often somewhat inadequate (DEHOGA, 2008).

Thus, internal dissent was non-existent, though certain sectoral associations, notably *Gesamtmetall*, were more enthusiastic than others, creating internal consensus and a common external front among the German employers (interviews DE-BUS-1, DE-BUS-2).

3.3. The United Kingdom

The *UK* system of political economy has commonly been subsumed under the category of liberal market economy (Hall and Soskice, 2001, p. 8). The decline of apprenticeship and common training schemes further encourages labour "poaching", which in turn can appear preferable to costly in-house training. Such incentive structure has important implications for human resource strategies, including a willingness to rely on "imported" skilled labour.

Employers in the UK assume an active stance in advocating immigrants considered of economic utility (interview UK-BUS-1). Employers are ideationally unified and present a common position. They very strongly support the persistence of largely deregulated labour markets and the use of economic migrants, both skilled and unskilled (interview UK-BUS-1).

The flexibility, additional skill base, often superior training and educational standards, and soft skills such as higher motivation associated with economic migrants are factors leading UK employers to embrace managed migration and strongly lobby in its favour. A CBI (Confederation of British Industry) representative asserted in an interview with classic British understatement that the association had "no aversion" to economic migration (interview UK-BUS-1). In mid-2005 CBI president Digby Jones stressed the advantage the UK enjoyed thanks to its flexible labour markets and pragmatic labour migration schemes, having earlier proclaimed that "capital can't afford to be racist for lots of reasons" (CRE, 2003).[10] His public intervention was made in response to the Conservative Party's plan to introduce tightly capped migration quotas. This position has been warmly received by the government; during an April 2004 speech at the CBI then prime minister Tony Blair argued that "recognition of the benefits that controlled migration brings not just to the economy but to delivering the public and private services on which we rely" was needed (Geddes, 2005).

UK employers assume an active stance in advocating immigrants considered of economic utility, both in very highly skilled service sector jobs, especially in finance, law, health, natural science research, and in low-skill jobs in food processing, agriculture, gastronomy, and construction and both regarding generalist and sector-specific skills (interviews UK-BUS-1, UK-BUS-2). An official publication (CBI, 2005: 2) highlights that immigration "is no alternative to raising the skills levels of the home-grown workforce – nor should immigration be seen as negating the need for effective active labour market policies to tackle the problem of economic inactivity." However, the same position paper highlights that "20% of the UK workforce lack appropriate levels of functional numeracy and literacy – raising the skill levels of this group would help to ease recruitment difficulties faced by employers." In an interview, a CBI representative confirmed sectoral and firm concerns over poor "employability" of domestic workers in some sectors and highlighted the advantages of hiring "better trained" graduates of "continental vocational training schemes" and universities, despite their marginally higher average age (interview CBI). By contrast, there is no real interest in asylum matters (interview UK-BUS-1). The CBI conducted a detailed survey among its members to produce a detailed response to the White Paper "Secure Borders, Safe Haven" in 2002. Along with the union and certain NGOs, its representatives are invited to the bi-annual "user panel" planning sessions of the Immigration and Nationality Directorate in the Home Office. The CBI is also part of the employer taskforce group, which is responsible for providing policy suggestions to the Home Office's Border and Immigration Agency. Recommendations from this group have fed into the establishment of an Australian-style high-skill migration programme in February 2008 and the illegal working stakeholder group (interview UK-BUS-1). Within this taskforce group, along with a trade union delegate, major internationally oriented businesses such as Shell, Ernst & Young, Tesco, Citigroup, and Goldman Sachs are represented as well as sectoral employer associations in engineering, hospitality, and employment services, alongside NASSCOM, the Indian IT sector chamber of commerce. Both formal responses to government initiatives and informal avenues to the Home Office are fairly well received (interview UK-GOV-1) and the CBI has positioned itself well to influence governmental deliberations. An added strength of the CBI is its internal ideational consensus on the desirability in principle of economic migration and its vast benefits, shared by all members, including small and medium sized enterprises (interview UK-BUS-1). Internal cohesion is strong and the degree of centralization is high given the successful monopolization of business representation the CBI enjoys despite comparatively low representation among its core clientele, encompassing only about 13 per cent of all companies in the private sector.

UK labour migration regulation has undergone considerable changes in recent years. After repeated legislative measures had limited the legal access to the labour market considerably, three key entry avenues remained for non-EU citizens, all of them tightly regulated: the Working Holidaymaker programme, principally geared at short-term working experiences for Commonwealth citizens, an annual quota of 10,000 temporary work placements principally in agriculture, prior to 2004 for CEE (Central and Eastern Europe) citizens and later for Romanians and Bulgarians, and case-by-case work permits granted to highly skilled individuals whose employers filed applications for them in select economic sectors experiencing labour shortfalls. The 2002 Act itself changed little, as it was principally geared at limiting territorial access by asylum seekers and undocumented migrants – thus rendering UK migration policy indeed "firmer", though not necessarily "fairer and faster" as the 1999 Green Book had promised. However, since then, there has been considerable activism in this domain. The main thrust of the reforms is to re-structure and ultimately limit the schemes pertaining to low-skill migration, based on the strategy that CEE citizens would fill these jobs from 2004 onwards, while streamlining procedures for high-skill migrants into a points-based system, reflecting qualifications and labour market needs. Thus, the agricultural working scheme has been reduced in size in 2004. The working holidaymaker scheme was first broadened in scope in 2003 to make greater allowances for New Commonwealth countries for foreign policy reasons, only to be quantitatively limited again in February 2005. Meanwhile, an explicit quota scheme was introduced for low-skill short-term labour migration in select sectors (sectors-based scheme, Immigration Rules HC 395, paras. 135I-135K, Ensor and Shah, 2005), especially gastronomy and food processing. The 2001 Highly Skilled Migrants Programme (HSMP) first introduced an explicit point system, taking into consideration formal level of education, work experience, salary level, overall qualification, and qualification of the spouse. Additional points were added for applicants in sectors with shortages – especially medicine – and, unlike the previous procedure, applicants themselves filed the application rather than their employer. Such a point system is also used to evaluate application by "entrepreneurs" who plan to establish businesses. The HSMP was replaced in 2008 by a new points based system with two tiers for "highly skilled" and "skilled" migrants, respectively, also taking into account available funds and past UK residence or educational experience (*The Guardian*, 30 October 2007).

This marks somewhat of a change from the original policy proposal, but its logic remains similar to that apparent in the proposal's subtitle "Making Migration Work for Britain", namely based on a "flexible, employer-led" logic (Home Office, 2005, p. 9).[11] Indeed, the document reiterates on 12 occasions that employers will be consulted or that the scheme is employer-led. Some independent advisory body on skills will also be consulted. The UK points-based scheme is a paradigmatic example of business-driven labour recruitment schemes. It is also very clearly emblematic of its competition-state logic and rhetoric, as in pronouncements emphasizing that: "Managed migration is not just good for our country. It is essential for our continued prosperity" (Home Office, 2005, p. 7). In sum, UK employers welcome both skilled and unskilled labour migrants who are offering either additions to the national skills portfolio or feed into a largely unregulated low-skill sector where manpower rather than skills are important.

3.4. Poland

Central and Eastern European political economies defy easy categorization and confound much taxonomy. The implementation of privatization, privileging insiders with party and state apparatus connections, led one observer to describe the process in Poland as "not a result of the expansion of the traditional private sector, but...a peculiar linkage of political power and capital" (Staniszkis, 1991, p. 128). However, encompassing privatization programmes of the 1990s have created a private sector accounting for 70 per cent of the GDP in Poland and up to 80 per cent elsewhere in CEE. Given the predominance of small companies in the economy, government steering and intervention in the economy, including protectionist barriers to investment, the decentralized industrial relations, feeble employee protection, a low degree of unionization, an underdeveloped stock market, but a relatively small private banking sector as well, a weak "Latin-style" welfare state, and underdeveloped secondary educational institutions, one analyst of the Polish political economy (Mykhnenko, 2005) finds it to constitute an odd blend, confounding Hall and Soskice's (2001) typologies, uniquely combining elements that seem to constitute oddities, rather than complementarities. The Polish political economy may be best conceived as a hybrid, containing elements from various types or as an "emerging market economy" (Hancké et al., 2007).

The employer camp is organizationally divided and lacks organizational coherence, but shares an ideational lacklustre attitude towards new instruments in labour migration (interview PL-BUS-1). It enthusiastically welcomed the legislative measures brought underway in 2004,[12] creating a new and simplified labour permit scheme. The legislative status quo meets all current labour needs, permitting labour immigration in highly skilled service sector positions and, given the absence of visa requirements for Ukrainians, paths to flexible if undocumented economic migration in the agricultural, construction, and personal care sectors. Though work permit applications imply a bureaucratic process and significant employer initiative, including proof that no Polish (or, where applicable, EU) citizen is available for the position, and while the job seeker him or herself needs to apply from abroad, this is still an improvement over the legislative status quo ante. Ministry of Economic Affairs and Labour data indicate that 46 per cent of all migrants are employed as managers or consultants, mostly from EU countries, Oceania, and North America (Korys and Weinar, 2005, p. 8). Most self-employed business owners, making up another 26 per cent of the total, come from Asian countries, including prominently Vietnam and Turkey. Russia and other former Soviet republics are highly represented among both legal and, according to less reliable evidence, illegal migrants as well. In 2004, 7845 of the total 18,841 permanent residency holders in Poland stemmed from the EU-15, 2750 from Ukraine, another 2181 from successor republic to the USSR, and 3563 from Asia. Though organizationally perhaps not best positioned to affect governmental policy, labour migration regulation meets employer interests and, though restrictive, permits the recruitment of high-skill service sector employees.

Previous legislation in the field of labour migration was more burdensome for employers. The 29 December 1989 Act on Employment (Journal of Laws of 1989, No. 75, item 446) introduced the obligation to obtain agreement from the regional (*voivod*) labour office before work permits to foreigners could be issued, which was required to consider regional labour market trends before doing so. The 14 December 1994 Act on employment and combating unemployment (Journal of Laws of 1995, No. 1, item 1) reiterated this requirement, limited the initial duration of such work permit to 1 year, and fixed the cost at the equivalent of one average monthly salary, thereby *de facto* reducing its scope to high wage positions. The number of work permits issued annually throughout the early 1990s hovered around 11,000 according to the Ministry of Interior, but this met employer needs at the time (interview PL-BUS-1). From the late 1990s onwards, larger companies and Polish branches of MNCs began to attract more Western high-skill migrants and communicated this development to the employer associations (interview PL-BUS-1). Partially in response, the 9 September 1997 Decree of the Ministry for Labour and Social Affairs specified exceptions to the work permit requirement for foreign employees and fine-tuned work permit procedures. In light of emerging short-term labour market shortages, the government looked favourably upon applications from its eastern neighbours, especially Ukraine, Russia, and Belarus. Partially as a result of the flexibilization, the number of work permits issued rose to 15,307 in 1997 and reached 21,487 in 2004; 74 per cent of which applied to key staff in multinational corporations and only 339 to unskilled workers (Kicinger, 2005, p. 20). Local discontent notwithstanding (interview PL-UNI-2), the relevant 1997 Act on Aliens which rendered deportation of illegally employed foreigners possible was not applied rigorously, with labour inspections in 2003 unearthing only 2700 cases of illegal employment of foreigners (Kicinger, 2005), despite estimates of up to 500,000 undocumented employees. This undocumented pool of immigrants constitutes a flexible buffer that renders advocacy of regularized low-skill migration less pertinent, while relatively bureaucratic and costly procedures deter employers from work permit applications in such instances. The 13 June 2003 Act on Aliens (Journal of Laws 2003, No. 128, item 1175) increased the duration of legal residency required for applicants for permanent residency to 5 years, stipulated the conditions to be met for temporary residency, containing the interesting stipulation that individuals engaged in "an economic activity... beneficial to the national economy and in particular, contributes to the development of investments, transfer of technology, innovations or job creation"(Art. 53 1.2) were to receive preferred treatment. This can be read as indication that Poland was starting to attract highly skilled migrants and invoked competition rhetoric, without, however, much pressure from the employers in this instance.

It has been argued that Polish (and much of CEE) migration policy "has arisen almost entirely as a result of the requirements of EU accession and that EU policy models and ideas about borders, security and insecurity have been exported to CEE countries" (Geddes, 2003, p. 173) and indeed this observation is largely accurate for asylum and refugee policy (Lavenex, 2001), but may obstruct the view on domestic initiative regarding economic migration. Beyond the legislative acts presented, the Polish government does not yet see the need for specific labour recruitment programmes (interview PL-GOV-1, GOV-2). Undocumented labour in low-skill sectors, especially agriculture, informal language tutoring, baby-sitting, care for the elderly, and gastronomy continues. It is not always clear whether the relatively lax enforcement at the local level is politically motivated or simply a function of administrative incapacity. The Polish economy does encounter skill shortages, but the government is extremely reluctant to implement a full-scale labour migration policy or even revive and remodel a briefly functional bilateral labour agreement with Ukraine. In skilled professions, emigration and brain drain remain problems. In a revealing reaction to the EU Green Paper on Labour Migration, the Polish government very clearly highlighted the problem of high structural unemployment and expressed scepticism towards the prospect of European policy in this field, demonstrating its willingness, however, to contemplate sector-specific flexible labour recruitment (Korys and Weinar, 2005, p. 27) in line with the *de facto* policy today.

As an EME, Poland's approach to labour migration is expectedly mixed. On one level, there are some skill shortages in islands of highly skilled high-value-added production islands that resemble CMEs, but increasingly there are also pure manpower shortages in low-skill jobs that are filled largely through undocumented migration. The employers are thus far unwilling to acknowledge the need for LME-style unskilled labour migration and prefer to focus on the quantitatively more limited and politically more palatable area of advocating highly skilled migration.

4. Conclusion

Employer associations have re-discovered an appetite for labour migrants. The need for liberalized labour migration is portrayed rhetorically as being pivotal in securing and maintaining "competitiveness" and thus crucial to national security. But employers are selective in terms of the migrant profile they seek to attract; their preferences are conditioned by the systems of political economy they are embedded in. In the view of organized business, ideal migrants should fit easily into existing production systems and complement corporate strategies. Ideational unity and skilful public relations aid in lobbying for new channels, especially as the migration domain remains highly politicized and sensitive, while detractors are quick to point to generally high levels of unemployment and poor records of economic and societal integration among second and third generation descendants of migrants.

Employers have been very active lobbyists, especially in the UK and Germany. The first hypothesis stating that different varieties of capitalism condition employer preference is largely borne out by the empirical evidence.

Thus, UK employers have become actively concerned with labour migration policy. Labour recruitment focuses on the service sector and seeks to compensate for deficiencies in domestic training institutions. Concerns over such shortages, especially in engineering, IT, and finance, have spawned advocacy of liberalized immigration channels. By contrast, French employers have only recently discovered the benefits of labour migration, given that skills shortages were not strongly apparent. Lack of unity and, for a while, interest impeded effective lobbying. Recent French government activities suggest an embrace of actively managed labour migration policy aimed at highly skilled migrants, complementing existing high-skill sectors. German employers, especially those in the manufacturing sector, notably metal processing association *Gesamtmetall*, have been strongly supportive of highly skilled migration, complementing a high-skill high-value-added production strategy. Polish employers have only very recently become active in interacting with government authorities with a view to liberalizing labour migration. Much simplified procedures for highly skilled migrants now facilitate economic migration and largely meet current employer demands.

Internal unity – pertaining to the second hypothesis – does promote more efficient and effective lobbying efforts. In France, it was not strongly present at first, while later the influential internationally oriented larger companies affected ideational change. In Germany, a common consensus similarly emerged relatively late. While the federation of larger industry BDI was very enthusiastic from early on, not all sectoral employers shared this sense of urgency. However, by the time major reforms of immigration legislation were underway, the BDA had embraced the new impetus. In Poland, ideational interest among employers developed only in the early 2000s. Finally, in the UK such general consensus was reached relatively early and was widely shared.

The third hypothesis entails the claim that clothed in the rhetorical terms of the purported need to compete for the best brains appeals by business to government to ensure national competitiveness in their design of labour migration policy have been much more successful. This is equally borne out by evidence from three of the four countries, where the rhetorical invoking of concepts of national competitiveness and the purported need for flexible liberalized economic migration channels was conducted successfully, either in the form of employer-led public relation campaigns as in France and Germany or directly through the pronouncements of employers. Where employers did not employ such tactics, as in Poland, their influence was also somewhat more limited.

Future research should establish to what extent the framework proposed here could be applied to other European countries. From Tallinn to Rome governments are designing schemes that will facilitate the inflow of the "best brains", yet employers insists that these brains (or muscles) fit into existing systems of political economy. Their political activities have been highly successful in influencing regulatory outcomes.

Interviews

FR-GOV-1 interview with senior official at French Ministry of Interior Affairs, Paris.

FR-GOV-2 interview with senior official at French Ministry of Interior Affairs, Paris.

DE-GOV-1 interview with senior official at German Ministry of Interior Affairs, Berlin.

DE-BUS-1 interview with official at employer association BDA, Berlin.

DE-BUS-2 interview with official sectoral employer association Gesamtmetall, Berlin.

DE-BUS-3 interview with official at sectoral gastronomy employer association DEHOGA, Berlin.

UK-BUS-1 interview with official at employer association CBI, London.

UK-BUS-2 interview with official at sectoral gastronomy employer association BHA, London.

UK-GOV-1 interview with official at UK Home Office [Ministry of Interior Affairs], Croydon/London.

PL-BUS-1 phone interview with official at employer association PKPP, Warsaw.

PL-GOV-1 interview with senior official at Polish Ministry of Interior Affairs, Warsaw.

PL-GOV-2 interview with senior official at Polish Office for Repatriation and Aliens, Warsaw.

PL-UNI-1 interview with senior trade union official at All-Polish Alliance of Trade Unions OPZZ, Warsaw.

Notes

1. Historically, French business, especially primary sector companies in the first part of the twentieth century and major manufacturing companies in fields such as construction, automobile assembly, metallurgy, and iron and steel during the post-war boom, were, of course, highly interested in labour recruitment, even assisting, and arguably surpassing the efforts and indeed the importance of the governmental labour recruitment office ONI and earlier its pre-World War I predecessor SGI (Weil, 1991). While the ONI – and before it the SGI and the bilateral treaties it helped administer – focused exclusively on European migrants, its slow and inefficient operations and its *de facto* inappropriate brief given not only the importance of non-European countries of origin, but also the fact that migration from the Iberian peninsula had to be clandestinely in nature on account of the authoritarian nature of the Franco and Salazar regimes, meant that the employers almost designed and operated labour migration themselves, or at least heavily influenced both the broad contours. They were actively involved in facilitating administration at the microlevel. Renault representatives recruiting workers in Algerian villages or local authorities legalizing *post-hoc* the new arrivals provided they could prove stable employment point to the pre-eminent role played by business in labour recruitment in France historically. By 1968, such post-hoc *régularisations* represented more than 80 per cent of all entries. In this sense, the 1974 recruitment stop also meant a restatement of statist authority. However, seasonal labour migration continued even after 1974 and entailed up to 100,000 work permits annually, especially in agriculture (Hollifield, 2000, 121). But by the mid-1990s, the number of slots had dwindled to approximately 10,000 annually, largely due to increasing mechanization in harvesting. These permits are granted to citizens of countries with which bilateral agreements had been signed, especially Morocco (treaty signed on 1 June 1963), Tunisia (1 August 1963), and Poland (20 May 1992).
2. Circulaire DPM/dm2-3/98/767 du 28 décembre 1998, see also Morice (2000).

3. This was stated explicitly in the joint Franco-British-German proposal tabled at the Council of Ministers meeting in Luxembourg on 4 October 1999, in preparation of the Tampere summit. Note, however, that this call for a CAMP carried also strong language about the danger of illegal migration and crime, often confounding the two (Joint Note by France and Germany concerning asylum/migration for the European Council in Tampere, 15/16 October 1999, dated 17 September 1999 and UK, France, Germany Note, 4 October 1999).

4. In a much noted 3 August 2000 article in the influential centre-right daily *Le Figaro*, the authors argued that "the call for foreign labor does not only target 'brains', [...] but also low-skill or unskilled workers, seasonal and not". As early as 1999, Alain Juppé surprised some of his party friends by arguing that in light of changing mentalities and demographics, "Europe will need the inflow of foreign labor" in a 1 October 1999 *Le Monde Diplomatique* article (Morice, 2000).

5. See, for example, the arguments presented in an interview with historian Patrick Weil who had overseen the influential Weil Report, informing the immigration policy of the Socialist Jospin government in *Libération* (6 November 2005).

6. In a press conference in 2004, Sarkozy argued: "We are now in a situation where immigration is uncontrollable because we refuse to demand an immigration we choose and for which we are responsible. Our integration system has broken down" (cited in Kretzschmar 2005, p. 15).

7. In the course of this press conference, the minister also stated: "The question of quotas, in other words, 'immigration by choice' as opposed to 'immigration by submission', must be the subject of true debate without taboos or exclusions. [We must] not be content with the failure which, after ten years of illegal immigration, leads all governments to debate wide-ranging integration" (cited in Kretzschmar 2005, p. 15). Sarkozy also makes passing reference to a "quantitative objective" in his book "Libre" (Sarkozy, 2003, also *Le Monde* 15 April 2006, interview GOV-FR-2).

8. See, for example, his articles in *Frankfurter Rundschau* (10 May 2000) and *Allgemeines Deutsches Sonntagsblatt* (17 and 24 March 2000).

9. It contained the following main provisions: The previous bewildering array of five categories of residency permit (Morris, 2002, esp. 47ff.) were being reduced to two (unlimited and limited), a new coordinating agency for migration and refugees, reporting to the ministry of interior and assuming the duties of the central unit for asylum claims, creating labour migration channels for entrepreneurs investing at least one million euros and creating at least ten new jobs and carefully delineated categories of highly skilled migrants, including teachers, scientists, and skilled managers earning in excess of 100,000 euros (all defined in Art. 19), permitting foreign graduates of German universities to remain in the country for one additional year to search for employment, a minor improvement for the "tolerated" refugees who are granted residency permits if no deportation can be implemented within 18 months, and eligibility for language and civic culture courses for newcomers, with this right becoming an obligation for specified resident migrants. Language skills are now a mandatory requirement for both ethnic Germans and Jewish migrants from the successor states to the Soviet Union.

10. In a 5 January 2006 policy statement (CBI, 2006), the CBI re-affirmed this position, announcing that: "The CBI believes that migration is beneficial to the UK. Migrants have made an important contribution to the UK economy – bringing valuable and scarce skills that have benefited UK business and helped contribute to economic growth. Migrant workers are an integral part of the UK workforce and the CBI shares the Government's belief that a carefully managed migration policy can bring further benefits to the UK. [...] The CBI supports the Government's plans, outlined in a five year strategy, to introduce a points test for skilled migration and rely on EU migration for lower-skilled workers, with a reduced role for schemes such as the SBS and SAWS. It is important that the Government maintains a range of routes into the country in order to react to labour market needs. The CBI has written to the Home Office opposing the imposition of employer bonds for migrant workers and the use of on-the-spot fines for illegal working."

11. The original plan would have replaced all of these schemes with a single, points-based labour migration system, comprising four tiers, the first one reserved for highly skilled professionals in fields such as IT, finance, medicine, and engineering, as well as "entrepreneurs". Applicants in these groups would have received permission to enter the UK to assist them in their job search. The second category is geared towards applicants in sectors experiencing shortages that cannot be filled domestically or within the EU, especially in nursing and teaching. The third tier would have consisted of short-term, tightly quantitatively limited quota schemes that can be opened – and presumably closed – on short notice, replacing the agricultural and sector-based schemes. Finally, the fourth tier would have encompassed the working holiday schemes and short-term schemes for students. Both of these bottom two tiers will only be open to nationals of countries which have concluded repatriation agreements with the UK.

12. (Dziennik Ustaw, No. 27 – item 236–239 of 11 March 2004 and the 20 April Act on the Promotion of Employment and Labour Market Institutions, Dzienne Ustaw 2004, No. 99, item 1001.)

Bibliography

Bale, Tim (2008) "Turning Round the Telescope: Centre-Right Parties and Immigration and Integration Policies in Europe", *Journal of European Public Policy* 15 (3): 315–330.

BDA (2002) "Stellungnahme zum Zuwanderungsgesetz", 16 January 2002, Berlin: BDA.

BDA (2007a) "Newsletter: Diskussion um Fachkräftemangel gewinnt an Dynamik", Berlin: BDA.

BDA (2007b) "Arbeitgeberpräsident Dr. Dieter Hundt: Einführung des Punktesystems ist ein längst überfälliger Schritt", Press Release 46/2007, Berlin: BDA.

BDA (2007c) "Arbeitgeber begrüßen Beschluss des Bundeskabinetts zu kurzfristigen Maßnahmen gegen Fachkräftemangel", Press Release 67/2007, Berlin: BDA.

BDA (2007d) "Arbeitgeberpräsident Dr. Dieter Hundt: Gezielte Zuwanderung ja, undurchdachte europäische Gesetzgebung nein!", Press Release 105/2007, Berlin: BDA.

Bleich, E. (2008) "Review Article: Immigration and Integration Studies in Western Europe and the United States", *World Politics* 60: 509–538.

Boswell, C. (2007) "Migration Control in Europe After 9/11: Explaining the Absence of Securitization", *Journal of Common Market Studies* 45 (3): 589–610.

Buzan, B., O. Waever, M. Kelstrup, and P. Lemaitre (eds.) (1993) *Identity, Migration, and the New Security Agenda in Europe* (London: Pinter).

Castells, Manuel (1975) "Immigrant Workers and Class Structure in Western Europe", *Politics and Society* 5 (1): 33–66.

Castles, S. and Gundula Kosack (1973) *Immigrant Workers and Class* (Oxford: Oxford University Press).

Castles, Stephen with Miller, Mark J. (2003) *The Age of Migration: International Population Movements in the Modern World (Third Edition).* Basingstoke: Palgrave-Macmillan.

CBI – Confederation of British Industry (2006) "Business Summaries: Immigration and Illegal Working", London: CBI.

Cerna, Lucie (2009) "The Varieties of High-Skilled Immigration Policies: Coalitions and Policy Outputs in Advanced Industrial Countries", *Journal of European Public Policy* 16 (1): 144–161.

Cerny, P. (1995) "Globalization and the Changing Logic of Collective Action", *International Organization* 49 (4): 595–625.

Clift, B. (2007) "French Corporate Governance in the New Global Economy: Mechanisms of Change and Hybridization within Models of Capitalism", *Political Studies* 55 (3): 546–567.

Coates, D. (2000) *Models of Capitalism: Growth and Stagnation in the Modern Era* (Cambridge: Polity Press).

Coates, D. (ed.) (2005) *Varieties of Capitalism, Varieties of Approaches* (Basingstoke: Palgrave Macmillan).

Cole, Mike and Gareth Dale (eds.) (1999) *The European Union and Migrant Labour* (Oxford/New York: Berg).

CRE (2003) – Commission for Racial Equality, "Capital can't afford racism", *Catalyst Magazine*, Winter 2003/2004.

Culpepper, Pepper (1999) "The Future of the High Skill Equilibrium in Germany", *Oxford Review of Economic Policy* 15: 43–59.

Culpepper, Pepper and Finegold, David (eds.) (2001) *The German Skills Machine: Sustaining Comparative Advantage in a Global Economy*, New York: Berghahn Books.

Culpepper, P. (2006) "Capitalism, Coordination and Economic Change: The French Political Economy since 1985", in P. Culpepper, P. Hall, and B. Palier (eds.) *The Politics that Markets Make* (Basingstoke: Palgrave Macmillan): pp. 29–49.

Demo, A. (2004) "Policy and Media in Immigration Studies", *Rhetoric and Public Affairs* 7 (2): 215–229.

DGB and BDA (2004) "Gemeinsame Erklärung von...DGB und...BDA: Miteinander statt Nebeneinander: Integration durch Fördern und Fordern", DGB/BDA: Berlin.

Ensor, J. and A. Shah (2005) "United Kingdom", in J. Niessen, Y. Schibel, and C. Thompson (eds.) *Current Immigration Debates in Europe: A Publication of the European Migration Dialogue* (Brussels: MPG).

Freeman, G. (1995) "Modes of Immigration Politics in Liberal Democratic States", *International Migration Review* 19 (4): 881–908.

Freeman, G. (2002) "Winners and Losers: Politics and the Costs and Benefits of Migration", in A. Messina (ed.) *West European Immigration and Immigrant Policy in the New Century* (Westport, CT: Praeger): pp. 77–96.

Freeman, G. (2006) "National models, policy types and the politics of immigration in liberal democracies", *West European Politics* 29 (2): 227–247.

Geddes, A. (2003) *The Politics of Migration and Immigration in Europe* (London/Thousand Oaks, CA: SAGE).

Geddes, A. (2005) "United Kingdom", in J. Niessen and Y. Schibel (eds.) *Immigration as a Labour Market Strategy – European and North American Perspectives* (Brussels: MPG).

Hall, Peter (2007) "The Evolution of Varieties of Capitalism in Europe" in Hancké, Bob, Martin Rhodes, and Mark Thatcher (eds.) *Beyond Varieties of Capitalism* (Oxford: Oxford University Press): pp. 39–88.

Hall, P. and D. Soskice (eds.) (2001) *Varieties of Capitalism: The Institutional Foundations of Comparative Advantage* (Oxford: Oxford University Press).

Hall, P. and D. Gingerich (2004) "Varieties of Capitalism and Institutional Complimentarities in the Macroeconomy: An Empirical Analysis", Discussion Paper 04/5, Cologne: Max-Planck-Institut für Gesellschaftsforschung.

Hancké, B., M. Rhodes, and M. Thatcher (eds.) (2007) *Beyond Varieties of Capitalism* (Oxford: Oxford University Press).

Hansen, R. (2002) "Globalization, Embedded Realism, and Path Dependence: The Other Immigrants to Europe", *Comparative Political Studies* 35 (3), April: 259–283.

Haus, L. (2002) *Unions, Immigration, and Internationalization: New Challenges and Changing Coalitions in the United States and France* (New York: Palgrave Macmillan).

Herrmann, A. (2009) *One Political Economy, One Political Strategy? Comparing Pharmaceutical Firms in Germany, Italy, and the UK* (Oxford: Oxford University Press).

Hollifield, J. (1992) *Immigrants, Markets and States: The Political Economy of Postwar Europe* (Cambridge, MA: Harvard University Press).

Hollifield, J. (2000) "Immigration and the Politics of Rights: The French Case in Comparative Perspective", in M. Bommes and A. Geddes (eds.) Immigration and Welfare: Challenging the borders of the welfare state (London: Routledge): pp. 109–139.

Home Office (2005) *Controlling our Borders: Making Migration Work for Britain – Five Year Strategy for Asylum and Immigration*, February 2005, London: Home Office.

Huysmans, J. (2006) *The Politics of Insecurity: Fear, Migration and Asylum in the EU* (London: Routledge).

Initiative Neue Soziale Marktwirtschaft (2002) *Deutschland im Reformstau: Muster-Koalitionsvertrag*, No. 72 (Berlin: Initiative Neue Soziale Marktwirtschaft).

Initiative Neue Soziale Marktwirtschaft (27 February 2004) "Deutschland braucht qualifizierte Zuwanderer" (Berlin: Initiative Neue Soziale Marktwirtschaft).

Initiative Neue Soziale Marktwirtschaft (3 July 2006) "Deutschland muss die Zuwanderung aus eigenem Interesse steuern" (Berlin: Initiative Neue Soziale Marktwirtschaft).

Institut Montaigne (2003) "Compétitivité et vieillissement" (Paris: Institut Montaigne).

Institut Montaigne (2006) "Mondalisation: Réconcilier la France avec la compétitivité" (Paris: Institut Montaigne).

Joppke, C. (1998) "Why Liberal State Accept Unwanted Migration" *World Politics* 50 (2): 266–293.

Joppke, C. (1999) *Immigration and the Nation-State: The United States, Germany and Great Britain* (Oxford/New York: Oxford University Press).

Keep, Ewart and Mayhew, Ken (1997) (2nd ed) "Vocational Training and Education and Economic Performance", in Tony Buxton, Paul Chapman, Paul G. Chapman, Paul Temple (eds.) *Britain's Economic Performance*: pp. 367–398.

Kelly, R., G. Morrell and D. Sriskandarajah (2005) *Migration and Health in the UK: An IPPR Factfile* (London: IPPR).

Kicinger, A. (2005) "Between Polish Interests and the EU Influence – Polish Migration Policy Development 1989–2004", CEFMR Working paper 9/2005, Warsaw: Central European Forum for Migration Research.

Korys, P. and A. Weinar (2005) "Poland", in J. Noesse and Y. Schiebel (eds.) *Immigration as a Labour Market Strategy – European and North American Perspectives* (Brussels: MPG).

Kretzschmar, C. (2005) "Immigration as a Labour Market Strategy: France", in J. Niessen and Y. Schibel (eds.) *Immigration as a Labour Market System – European and North American Perspectives* (Brussels: Migration Policy Group).

Lahav, G. and V. Guiraudon (2006) "Actors and Venues in Immigration Control: Closing the Gap between Political Demands and Policy", *West European Politics* 29 (2): 210–223.

Lavenex, S. (2001) "The Europeanization of Refugee Policies: Normative Challenges and Institutional Legacies", *Journal of Common Market Studies* 39 (5): 851–874.

Leif, T. (2004) Die politischen Strategien der *Initiative Neue Soziale Marktwirtschaft* (Düsseldorf: Hans-Böckler-Stiftung).

MEDEF (2006) "Intervention de Nicolas Sarkozy", Speech at the MEDEF Summer School, 31 August (Paris: Medef).

Menz, G. (2008) *The Political Economy of Managed Migration* (Oxford: Oxford University Press).

Messina, Anthony (1990) "Political Impediments to the Resumption of Labor Migration to Western Europe", *West European Politics* 13 (1): 31–46.

MinFin (14 January 2006) "Immigration sélective et besoins de l'économie française", available at: www.minefi.gouv.fr, internet accessed on 9 March 2010.

Ministère de la Justice (1999) "Le travail illégal et sa répression", Infostat Justice, No. 54, Paris: Ministry of Justice.

Molina, O. and M. Rhodes (2007) "The Political Economy of Adjustment in Mixed Market Economies: A Study of Spain and Italy", in B. Hancké, M. Rhodes and M. Thatcher (eds.) *Beyond Varieties of Capitalism* (Oxford: Oxford University Press): pp. 223–252.

Morice, Alain (November 2000) "De l'immigration zero aux quotas", *Le monde diplomatique*, 6–7.

Morris, Lynda (2002) *Managing Migration: Civic Stratification and Migrants' Rights* (London: Routledge).

Mykhnenko, V. (2005) "What type of Capitalism in Eastern Europe? Institutional Structures, Revealed Comparative Advantages, and Performance of Poland and Ukraine" CPPR Discussion Paper Series, No. 6 (September).

OECD (2008) *International Migration Outlook*, Paris: OECD.

Piore, Michael (1979) *Birds of Passage: Migrant Labor and Industrial Societies* (Cambridge: Cambridge University Press).

Régnard, C. (2006) "Immigration et presence étrangère en France 2005: Rapport annuel de la direction de la population et des migrations" (Paris: Ministère de l'emploi, de la cohesion sociale et du logement).

Rudolph, C. (2003) "Security and the Political Economy of International Migration", *American Political Science Review* 97 (4): 603–620.

Salt, J. (1997) "International Movement of the Highly Skilled", *OECD Occasional Paper 3*, London: International Migration Unit, 3.

Samers, M. (2003) "Invisible Capitalism: Political Economy and the Regulation of Undocumented Immigration in France", *Economy and Society* 32 (4): 555–583.

Sarkozy, Nicholas (2003) *Libre*. Paris: Edition Pocket.

Schmidt, V. (2002) "Does Discourse Matter in the Politics of Welfare State Adjustment?", *Comparative Political Studies* 35 (2): 168–193.

Staniszkis, J. (1991) *The Dynamics of Breakthrough* (Berkeley: University of California Press).

Statham, Paul and Geddes, Andrew (2006) "Elites and the 'Organised Public': Who Drives British Immigration Politics and in Which Direction?", *West European Politics* 29 (2): 248–269.

Streeck, W. and M. Höpner (eds.) (2003) *Alle Macht dem Markt? Fallstudien zur Abwicklung der Deutschland AG* (Frankfurt: Campus).

Terray, E. (1999) "Le travail des étrangers en situation irrégulière ou la delocalisation sur place", in E. Balibar, M. Chemilllier-Gendreau, J. Costa-Lascoux, and E. Terray (eds.) *Sans-Papiers: L'archaïsme fatal* (Paris: La Découverte).

Thelen, K. (2004) *How Institutions Evolve: The Political Economy of Skills in Germany, Britain, the United States and Japan* (Cambridge: Cambridge University Press).

Unabhängige Kommission (2001) *Zuwanderung gestalten, Integration fördern* (Berlin: Unabhängige Kommission Zuwanderung).

Watts, J. R. (2002) *Immigration Policy and the Challenge of Globalization: Unions and Employers in Unlikely Alliance* (Ithaca, N.Y.: Cornell University Press).

Weil, P. (1991) *La France et ses étrangers: L'aventure d'une politique de l'immigration.* (Paris: Calmann-Lévy).

Wilson, James (1980) *The Politics of Regulation* (New York: Basic).

Woll, C. (2006) "National Business Associations under Stress: Lessons from the French Case", *West European Politics* 29 (3): 489–512.

3
The Sectoral Turn in Labour Migration Policy

Alexander Caviedes

Labour migration and the recruitment of foreign workers have seen a fluctuation in intensity as well as a transformation in kind. For those countries that have actively pursued foreign labour, the 1960s and early 1970s witnessed the zenith of guest worker programmes, followed by a roughly 20-year period during which recruitment was largely terminated. Since the 1990s, labour migration from non-EU countries[1] once again features prominently in many countries, but its return has been characterized by a rise in sector-specific programmes in response to the worker flexibility needs of particular economic sectors. In addition to programmes designed to attract seasonal labour for agriculture there has been a proliferation of programmes to facilitate the entry of workers into branches such as information technology, health care, and hospitality. This expansion of sectoral policy is not simply a reflection of altered demand, but has often been reliant on parallel shifts in industrial relations – namely greater decentralization of bargaining authority within employers' associations and increased differentiation among unions – that are not merely country – but even sector-specific. Globalization and de-industrialization exerts common pressures, but European labour migration policy responses have been less broad in scope, with liberalization largely limited to policy in certain specific economic sectors.

To explain similar labour migration patterns in terms of peak periods and termination of programmes, even in countries with less reliance on labour recruitment, this chapter begins by reviewing labour migration theory, and then develops an argument about the centrality of employer flexibility concerns. This argument is then illustrated through an analysis of labour migration schemes in information technology (IT) and hospitality in the UK, Germany, the Netherlands, and Austria. The cases span countries which were heavily involved in recruiting foreign labour as well as the UK, which was not, and countries in which a more corporatist style of government might be expected to strengthen the power of unions to the point that one would not expect a liberalization of labour migration. Integrating media reports, annual organizational reports, press statements, and individual interviews with representatives of government, trade unions, and employers' and trade associations this chapter demonstrates how employers have been affected by changes in the overall structure of the labour market that generate preferences which differ by industry. Where employers have been able to couch their policy demands in economic terms, avoiding larger societal debates over immigration, they have been successful in achieving labour migration liberalization, provided that peak level employers extended their support in the case of opposition from the labour movement.

1. Who drives labour migration policy?

While courts can play an important role in expanding the rights of immigrants (Joppke, 1999), political parties are most identified with playing an important role in the development of general immigration policy. In the last decade, populist and Right-wing parties have successfully courted voters by brandishing xenophobic rhetoric, and, together with the media, have pressured established parties to address this issue. However, the profile of parties remains subdued in the area of labour migration policy. In the past, both business-friendly conservative and union-allied social democratic parties sponsored restrictive policy, while the broadest recent expansions in labour migration occurred under Germany's Social Democrats (SPD) and the UK's Labour Party. Germany's Christian Democrats (CDU) and SPD, as well as Labour and the Tories in the UK, generally kept the issue de-politicized and essentially under administrative purview (Hansen, 2000, p. 128; Joppke, 1999, p. 65; Katzenstein, 1987, p. 221).[2] The accession to power of anti-immigration parties such as Austria's Freedom Party and the Netherlands' List Pim Fortuyn produced a focus on integration measures, but did not lead to any curtailing of labour migration (Caviedes, 2010). While government institutions and its party composition can constrain or facilitate the labour migration policy designs of employers, this analysis does not postulate them as the determinative agenda-setters in the policy-making process.

The key factor to analyzing labour migration policy is the involvement (or lack of involvement) of the social partners, whose influence over policy and its implementation is shielded from public scrutiny (Freeman, 1979). Predominantly, studies have centred on the role of trade unions, who should oppose labour immigration because of its potential for lowering wages within regulated labour markets and providing alternative labour in times of conflict (Castles and Kosack, 1973; Haus, 2002; Zolberg, 1989). Despite this, unions in countries such as Germany, Austria, Switzerland, Sweden, and the Netherlands displayed pragmatic behaviour during the period of rapid economic growth in the 1960s, which was fuelled in large part by access to foreign labour (Joppke, 1999; Katzenstein, 1987; Kindleberger, 1967). After the 1973 oil crisis and the demise of full employment in Western Europe, the preferences of unions were seen to have once again solidified in favour of restriction (Castles, 2006; Münz, 2001; Wrench, 2000), though a recently developing body of research documents that the labour movement has actually become more open to immigration (Cachón and Valles, 2003; Haus, 2002; Watts, 2002). Business is seen as uniformly supporting immigration due to the propensity of migrant workers to lower wages, hamper labour market regulation, and divide the labour movement (Castles and Kosack, 1973). Too little consideration has been given to the changing nature of the labour force such that employers might also have a heightened interest in retaining their skilled workers, as opening up certain labour markets to foreign labour could destabilize the regulated conditions under which employers currently refrain from poaching each other's workers (Wood, 2001). The conditions that make foreign labour an attractive alternative to the domestic work force do not prevail throughout every sector.

Employers' associations constitute optimal units of analysis for focusing on the development of labour migration. First, while the state drafts and executes the relevant laws and regulations, in an open, democratic setting it seldom unilaterally seizes the initiative in identifying the area and magnitude of policy needs (Traxler, 1999); and instead it relies on private organizations that possess the relational knowledge necessary to target policies towards the most likely participants (Culpepper, 2003, p. 53). Second, compared to individual firms that suffer a great deal of uncertainty as to the effects of any change and the costs of advocacy, a private association has the overview to assess the ramifications of a given policy and to facilitate cooperation in the execution of that policy. Third, in an area such as labour market policy where benefits are concentrated within certain producer groups yet costs remain diffuse, employers are unlikely to encounter much resistance beyond that represented by organized labour (Freeman, 1979). However, in contrast to trade unions whose interest in this area lies in preserving the status quo, employers actively identify labour needs and forward policy proposals (Schneiberg and Bartley, 2001). Though trade union stances are relevant, since they can constitute the major obstacle stemming labour migration, the role of employers – as the primary force conveying preferences to the government for implementation – remains central to this study.

2. Business preferences on labour migration

When addressing preferences for international labour migration, broader societal immigration debates generally assume secondary importance and mainly serve to delineate the outer boundaries for acceptable policy. Preferences for labour migration develop in the business community within firms and their associations,[3] so to generate the framework for analysis we build upon two established approaches that provide hypotheses about employer preferences.

Theory informed by the Marxist concept of the secondary labour force views employers as sharing a pro-immigration bias (Castles and Kosack, 1973; Piore, 1979). Employers and trade unions alike derive benefits from the perpetuation of a secondary labour force that remains highly exposed to market forces and managerial discretion, while at the same time shielding a primary work force comprised of domestic workers who enjoy extensive rights and exhibit organizational strength. Immigrant labour props up secondary-type pools of labour in some less-regulated economic sectors such as agriculture, care provision, and hotels and restaurants (Piore, 1979), suggesting that employer preferences vary by specific economic branch. For example, in the construction industry unions and employers united to demand greater labour market regulation within the EU, and subsequently demanded extended waiting periods before granting free movement to workers from the Eastern European accession countries (Faist et al., 1999; Menz, 2005). Employers in some sectors expect essentially the entire workforce to expose itself to considerable vulnerability, so greater emphasis should be placed on employers' flexibility concerns than simply on the tension between foreign and domestic workers. This point has not been granted sufficient consideration, even by the more recent work that acknowledges growing union support for liberalizing labour migration (Haus, 2002; Watts, 2002).

The other theoretical direction offering insight into employer preferences is the varieties of capitalism approach (Hall and Soskice, 2001; Menz, 2005). Viewing labour migration as tantamount to labour market deregulation, it would suggest that firms in liberal market economies like the UK should exhibit greater support for labour migration while firms in coordinated market economies such as Austria and Germany would likely be concerned that a deregulating influence upon the labour market could also diminish the comparative advantages that employers draw from established industrial relations and vocational training institutions. The "varieties" approach is often criticized for focusing on national economies as its unit of analysis (Howell, 2003; Watson, 2003) and would be enriched by theory and empirical work identifying which types of sectors best exemplify a particular national variety of capitalism and which sectors align less comfortably with other national institutions (Herrmann, 2009).[4]

Areas of policy convergence between countries that practise different strands of capitalism, as well as divergences within countries, suggest that certain sectors are differently embedded within their imputed national variety of capitalism. Marginson and Sisson argue that "the homogeneity of institutions, practices and customs that gives national systems their distinctive character is being fractured as new forms of 'isomorphism' reach across borders and within sectors and MNCs [multinational corporations]" (2002, p. 680). General economic policies may reflect the preferences of the most powerful sectors within a national economic pluralist system (Bearce, 2003; Rogowski, 1987), but the accretion of sectoral labour migration policies signals both an absence of consensus amongst employers and the insufficient influence of any single sector or group of sectors to secure the passage of policies extending beyond its own sector. Firms are the drivers of institutional change, and in the cases observed they are responding to institutional incentives that are inextricably integrated within the industrial structure at the sector level (Marginson and Sisson, 2002). Building on the varieties of capitalism's understanding of varying employer preferences, and the secondary labour market theory's recognition of employers' fixation on flexibility, the following section explains which sectors' labour force flexibility needs cannot be solved within the firm or national labour market.

2.1. Employer's sectoral flexibility concerns

The primary determinant of firm preferences on immigration has been the shift in overall characteristics of the labour market. The growth of the service economy and the decline in manufacturing has been gradual, yet pronounced when comparing the size of the principal economic sectors in the 1970s to that of today (Howell, 2002; Vogel, 2001).

From 1975 to 2000, manufacturing jobs in the EU decreased by over one-quarter from 31.2 to 21.8 per cent, while service jobs expanded by one-third from 50.8 to 67.8 per cent (Eurostat, 1976–2002). The shift is further reflected in the type of labour initially recruited by countries such as Germany or the Netherlands in the 1960s, when predominantly unskilled foreign labour entered the labour market in both the service and manufacturing sectors (Kindleberger, 1967; Münz and Ulrich, 1997). In contrast to this common demand for unskilled labour spanning most industries, new foreign labour now mostly enters into select service sector branches (Biffl, 2003; Office for National Statistics, 1998, 2003; SOPEMI, 1999; Zimmermann, 1993).

The analysis of employer preferences proceeds in two stages: the first relates to identifying flexibility needs, while the second addresses societal factors that impact on employer strategies. The first stage acknowledges that shifts in the labour market due to technological advances and changes in production methods have led to more particularized labour market needs than a generation ago. With the exception of firms in the IT sector, most of these employers operate in sectors where local workers should meet their needs because no extensive skills set is being sought. Nevertheless, some employers still court foreign labour, despite the costs of finding foreign workers and the potential challenges of integrating them into their workforce, suggesting a perceived qualitative difference between foreign and domestic workers.

The term "flexibility" connotes the quality employers seek, which contemplates a more fluid labour market that allows for greater differentiation in pay and qualification schemes, so that changes in demand can be dealt with quickly. Among the various types of flexibility, employers are especially interested in using labour migration as a means for improving the numerical, temporal, and wage flexibility of their workforce. Numerical flexibility is the ability to hire-and-fire rapidly in step with demand fluctuations, while temporal flexibility allows employers to adjust the amount of labour utilized according to cyclical or seasonal demand shifts. Finally, wage flexibility requires independence from collective bargaining or statutory pay scales (Regini, 2000).

Labour migration presents employers with workers more transient than their own domestic labour force. Following Piore's logic, this increases when the foreign workers are only entitled to limited stays, so employers in sectors that experience rapid demand fluctuations prefer that foreign workers are entitled to only a limited stay. Thus, temporal flexibility is supported through seasonal and short-term labour permits that nevertheless allow for sizeable influxes of foreign labour during periods for which shortages are foreseeable. Finally, employers have an interest in carving out a degree of wage flexibility in those sectors where the jobs offered are unattractive to local workers. Such jobs, common in agriculture and hospitality, are seldom sufficiently productive to generate profits unless wages remain depressed. Therefore, employers want to assure that policies governing foreign workers place these workers in a different status from domestic workers whose greater security and access to benefits render them less willing to accept such conditions. The IT, agriculture, and hospitality branches all strive for at least one variant of flexibility, driving employers to pursue non-permanent, limited duration visa schemes for foreign workers. Table 3.1 illustrates the flexibility profiles of IT and hospitality, but also includes metalworking, a branch once heavily reliant on international labour migration, to illustrate the impact of changing flexibility profiles.

In industries with labour shortages, numerical and temporal flexibility are key concerns, while temporal flexibility is most salient in sectors that are unable to adjust to consumer demand fluctuations through hiring and firing but, rather, seek workers who accept shift work. However, the urgency of such needs alone does not automatically produce policy: employers must first navigate certain domestic institutions that can influence how employer interests are transmitted to the government, and whether they eventually are reflected through policy change.

Table 3.1 Flexibility needs in Information Technology and Hospitality

Flexibility Type	Sector		
	Information Technology	**Hospitality**	**Metal work**
Numerical	Yes – Limited stay allows for managerial discretion.	Yes – Unskilled foreign workers can be quickly integrated.	No – Slow growth means few rapid demand fluctuations.
Temporal	Yes – Foreign specialists prepared to work longer hours.	Yes – Foreigners work seasonally and for longer hours.	Yes – However, this can be dealt with through shift work.
Wage	Yes – Foreign workers accept lower wages.	Yes – Foreigners accept low wages despite poor conditions.	No – Internationally competitive branches must keep wages low – unions comply.

While these changes in the labour market have taken place to similar degrees across industrialized nations, the labour migration preferences of firms in industrialized Western Europe cannot be understood in isolation from their respective national labour market institutions (Vogel, 2001), which include training programmes, collective bargaining arrangements, and the configuration of industrial relations. First, drawing on the varieties of capitalism (Crouch and Streeck, 1997; Hall and Soskice, 2001), it is important to realize that, especially in continental Europe, firms' preferences are shaped by and aggregated through their membership in various associations. Often, the initial preferences at the individual firm or sectoral association level are subordinated to the broader interests of a larger confederation whose constituency spans the entire economy (Thelen, 2001). With respect to labour migration, this means employers must weigh the costs of seeking a policy that is not in accord with their confederation's position.

A second aspect rooted in industrial relations is that, before bringing their demands to the government, employers often take into account the position of the trade unions. Unions do not constitute a monolithic anti-immigration bloc or organize pro-actively as policy entrepreneurs on labour migration issues, but their presence is a further key element refracting the employers' demands. Employers must factor in the organizational strength of unions and their influence over the government to assess whether union opposition must be addressed and compensated for. Where unions are well organized and able to point out feasible flexibility alternatives that privilege their domestic members, employers must negotiate in advance with their union counterparts before bringing policy proposals to the government. These two domestic institutional configurations testify to the validity of varieties of capitalism thinking, as they highlight the different sets of obligations and opportunities that can exist for firms depending on whether they are situated in a coordinated or liberal market economy.

The third factor impacting the preference formation and expression process is the degree to which labour migration is debated, not in economic terms but under the broader topic of immigration. In Austria and the Netherlands the rise of populist parties espousing anti-immigrant sentiment (and the murders of a couple of its most vocal Dutch proponents) have led to demands that immigration be curbed or that greater effort be invested towards the integration of foreigners. However, when the List Pim Fortuyn in the Netherlands and the Freedom Party in Austria came into government, no new restrictions were placed upon labour migration. Although Germany and the UK are not untouched by this issue, especially in the aftermath of 9/11 and the 2005 London bombings, policy restrictions in the past decade has been limited to more stringent asylum law provisions or deportation procedures. A debate over labour migration policy reform argued purely in terms of economic costs and benefits (or, better yet for employers, not argued at all) stands a better chance of being resolved in favour of liberalization.

To summarize, the path from preference formation to policy change begins within the context of macroeconomic changes that are manifested by labour shortages in certain service sector industries. These cause firms to identify particular flexibility needs that cannot be adequately met by the local workforce, leading them to make labour migration policy demands for short-term workers in particular sectors. Whether these demands blossom into policy depends on whether domestic institutions – in the form of employers' association support, union opposition, or the larger immigration context – serve to buttress employer claims or make them politically uncomfortable for the government to implement.

3. Labour migration in the information technology and hospitality sectors

Factories have traditionally been home to a large proportion of foreign workers. During the economic boom of the 1960s, manufacturers were among the most vocal advocates and biggest beneficiaries of foreign worker recruitment (BDA, 1962; Joppke, 1999; Kindleberger, 1967). However, manufacturing is no longer the destination for foreign workers. A surge of economic growth throughout Europe in the latter 1990s accelerated the economic shifts that lead employers, in certain service sectors first, to experience a heightened need for work force flexibility. Closer examination of two of these sectors, IT, which employs highly skilled workers, and hospitality, which employs mostly the unskilled, highlights how employers made and government responded to calls to liberalize labour migration. While both sectors experienced labour shortages, policy has not simply reflected employer needs due to the variable influence and mentality of domestic unions and employers' associations.

3.1. Information technology

Information Technology skills shortages have been a common impetus for expanding and recasting the entire debate over labour migration in

Europe. At the 2000 Lisbon Summit, national leaders of the European Union member states set the goal for the EU to become the most competitive knowledge-based society in the world by 2010 (European Commission, 2002). Although IT jobs constitute a fraction of the total service sector, the sector has experienced enormous growth in the last 10 years, with a 40 per cent rise in computer workers as a percentage of total employees in the EU from 1995 to 1999 (OECD, 2002; SOPEMI, 2002). Most IT occupations are high skill, yet, due to the industry's infancy most countries' systems for training workers proved unable to meet the intense rate of increased demand. Rapid sector growth inhibited the development of an extensive regulation, and businesses have been anxious to avoid regulations setting firm wage rates or job descriptions in a field where the workers themselves prefer flexible pay arrangements and working hours (BITKOM, personal communication, 21 August 2003; Intellect, personal communication, 29 September 2003). These conditions led employers throughout Europe to view foreign labour as an ideal short-term means to achieving numerical flexibility.

On 23 February 2000, at Germany's annual convention for information and communication technology, the CeBIT, Chancellor Schröder announced that the administration was planning to introduce a short-term work permit for IT specialists. The announcement came in response to an ongoing dialogue between government representatives and large businesses in a steering group of Initiative D21, a pro-technology initiative composed of several of Germany's largest companies (Initiative D21, personal communication, 15 December 2003). Initial protests by Labour Minister Walter Riester and the German Trade Union Federation (DGB) that domestic unemployment problems had to be solved first were undermined when Education Minister Buhlman admitted that training programmes could not cover the immediate existing shortage (Sharma, 2000). To allay labour's fears of foreign specialists permanently substituting domestic workers, the government allocated an additional 100 million euros for vocational training in IT to the Department of Labour. Significantly, the Federal Union of German Employers' Associations (BDA) pledged to double the IT apprenticeships offered by its member firms to 60,000, taking a measure of responsibility for the shortage of qualified workers (Greifenstein, 2001).

On 11 July 2000, the *Bundesrat* passed the "Green Card" regulation, admitting up to 10,000 IT specialists annually on limited 5-year work permits passing through an expedited Labour Ministry review in about one week.[5] Despite a downturn in the industry and lukewarm response to the programme – not all of the allotted 20,000 permits were issued – the Green Card provision was renewed on 16 July 2003[6] before it was superseded in 2005 by the new immigration without special IT worker provisions. Business leaders insist that regardless of the current labour market situation, foreign workers are a necessary component. IT specialists are and remain qualitatively different from other foreign workers because they also bring with them contacts to foreign markets and business partners (BITKOM, personal communication, 21 August 2003; VDI, personal communication, 4 September 2003; "Mixed reaction", 2007), and this is an argument that even the labour movement is prepared to accept (DGB, personal communication, 14 August 2003; ver.di, personal communication, 8 September 2003; Ministry of Interior, personal communication, 11 June 2008), especially since the 2005 law provides no special conditions for the highly skilled; applicants for visas are now admitted based primarily on surpassing a somewhat hefty (64,000 euro) minimum salary requirement.

Similarly, in February 2000, British Home Office Minister Barbara Roche announced that as many as 100,000 foreign workers annually were needed to satisfy the UK's labour market needs. One month later, after little public debate, the Home Office unveiled rules changes to the work permit structure placing several ITCE (Information Technology, Communications and Electronics) occupations on the shortage occupation list (Work Permits UK, personal communication, 9 December 2003). This designation allowed permits to be issued to such specialists without requiring UK firms to advertise these positions and further eliminated the requirement for a two-year postgraduate degree for ITCE managers.

While trades associations such as Intellect, representing the IT sector, and the peak business association, the Confederation of British Industry (CBI), had been major supporters of liberalizing the work permit process (CBI, 2002; Intellect, personal communication, 29 September 2003), with the bursting of the dot-com bubble and general downturn in the IT industry, business reversed its stance on labour migration. Intellect and the Professional Contractors Group (PCG), representing freelancers, claimed that after more than 50,000 ITCE work permits had been issued in the first 2 years (PCG, 2002), as of 2002, home-grown IT skills were no longer in short supply. Amicus, representing engineers and other science-related professionals, had warned of the danger of flooding the job market, but without the requisite conviction or supporting data (PCG, personal communication, 10 December 2003; Intellect, personal communication, 29 September 2003; Amicus, personal communication, 11 December 2003). Citing an unemployment rate of 26 per cent within the branch, the PCG convinced the IT Sector Panel to remove ITCE occupations from the shortage list in August of 2002. Given the downturn in the industry, the CBI did not object at the time (CBI, 2002). The UK's current solution to employers' sectorally-varying needs was to introduce a points-based system in 2007 (see Kolb, this book), under which foreign labour permit applicants are graded on criteria including education and previous work experience. Applicants earn further points if they are in a "shortage occupation", thus the power to periodically designate these occupations is tantamount to a sector-specific permit scheme that can be reconfigured to serve several different sectors – quite a boon to employers concerned with numerical flexibility in times of heightened demand.

The growth of jobs in the Netherlands' computer services/ICT from 1995 to 2000 was explosive, more than doubling from 47,500 to 115,900 (Kolb et al., 2004, p. 152). From 1996 to 2000, work permits issued to foreigners in IT rose by over 400 per cent from 414 to 2209, comprising nearly 10 per cent of all permits issued (Dobson and Salt, 2004, p. 135). Even this amount did not satisfy the needs of industry during a time when the industry's growth was at its zenith; especially since Dutch firms have difficulty retaining foreign workers in these branches as wages are modest and many treat the Netherlands as a proving ground before passing on to more lucrative employment in other countries (OECD, 2005). Since Dutch provisions for international intra-company transfers do not extend to workers with technical skills, even large firms are relatively more reliant on standard work permits than is the case in Germany or the UK (personal communication with VNO-NCW, 2003).

In 2000, a coalition of the peak employers' association, VNO-NCW, the Federation of Dutch IT Firms (FENIT), and a few large firms including Germany's Siemens and the Netherland's own Phillips, lobbied the government for relief. Citing the EU's Lisbon Agenda and the German Green Card initiative, they hoped for a quota system for foreign IT workers and recruitment assistance for businesses through some manner of centralized coordination (personal communication with VNO-NCW, 2003). The government's response was almost immediate. As of 1 May 2000, Article 13 of the Aliens law (*Vreemdelingenwet*) was altered to eliminate the existing requirement that employers first engage in a domestic job search for IT workers. A further regulation (the *AD-regeling*) that went into effect on 22 February 2001, exempted employers from the duty to advertise their vacancies for ICT jobs at the higher vocational education level. Like the previous cases, this victory for employers was somewhat short-lived, since the ensuing economic downturn in IT led the government to terminate the programme as of 1 January 2003.

Nevertheless, the unique situation of the IT sector was re-affirmed on 1 October of the following year, when Immigration Minister Verdonk introduced the knowledge worker regulation (*kennismigrantenregeling*), an accelerated procedure for issuing permits to highly skilled workers. Foreign "knowledge workers" earning more than 45,000 euros need merely qualify for residence. A half-year into the programme, only about 400 foreigners had taken advantage of the procedure ("Netherlands faces", 2005) suggesting no dearth of high-skilled workers at top-wage levels. Rather than abandoning the idea, in recognition of employers' numerical flexibility needs, changes were made in the 2006 immigration law that went into effect in 2008. Under a points-based system that allows other criteria to compensate in the case of lower wages, the adjudication of work and temporary stay permits is now merged, speeding up the process.

Policy change to attract IT specialists has been the most publicized and radical among the industries being compared. The rapid growth of the industry and the inability to predict the duration of labour shortages has led employers throughout the industrialized world to voice their numerical flexibility needs and call for liberalization of migration. The relatively unadulterated transmission of preferences to actual policy has been the result of strong employers' confederation support, little union opposition, and ineffective training systems. The more pluralistic system of interest representation in the IT sector has meant that the employers' greater resources have been parlayed into new policies under which business was afforded access to potentially large numbers of foreign IT specialists. The domestic constraints often in place in the form of established patterns of industrial relations are less relevant here.

3.2. Hospitality

A leading contributor to the service sector's expansion has been the growth of the hospitality industry, comprised of restaurants, hotels, and other tourist-related business. While the percentage of EU employees in services grew by 7.1 per cent from 1990 to 2000, the percentage in hospitality grew by 19 per cent during the same time span.[7] These employers often lament their ability to attract sufficient staff, especially during peak seasons. Trade unions counter that the low wages and unappealing and physically demanding working conditions of occupations within the industry are the culprits for the endemic labour shortages. Unlike in the IT industry, where unions initially conceded that labour shortages could not be covered by domestic workers, unions in the hospitality branches have been more vocal in blaming employers for failing to train their own workers or provide attractive working conditions.

One UK method for responding to employer flexibility needs was the Working Holidaymaker programme allowing young people (aged 17–27) from the Commonwealth countries to work in the UK without a work permit. However, this programme proved insufficient to cover the labour shortages in the branch, and, in response to CBI pleas (CBI, 2002) and after consultation with several associations including the British Hospitality Association, the government introduced a sectors-based scheme for hotels and catering in the summer of 2003 (Work Permits UK, personal communication, 9 December 2003). Similar to the IT programme, sectors-based schemes allow employers to receive short-term work permits for up to 20,000 applicants in unskilled professions designated as shortage occupations, without showing individual employer need. Since the determination resulted through sector panels comprised of employers and unions, the absence of objections from the unions on the panel – TGWU and GMB – signalled to the government a consensus that the shortages claimed by employers were genuine and immediate. Only following the EU accession of the Eastern European countries in 2004, did the vast number of low-skilled workers entering the UK labour market lead to the program's initial reduction in 2004 and cessation in 2005.

In Germany, where the branch relies heavily on foreign labour (Vogler-Ludwig, 1999) the situation has been more contentious. The German Restaurant and Hotel Federation, DEHOGA, has supported labour migration schemes since the termination of recruitment in 1973 (Edye, 1987). After the fall of the Wall, Germany introduced programmes in 1991 targeting foreign workers from former East-bloc countries. The guest worker programme brings in a small, symbolic quota of young labourers with the stated aim of transmitting experience and know-how. Though over 50 per cent of the participants work in hospitality, in 2000 this amounted to less than 4000 workers (Zentralstelle für Arbeitvermittlung, 2001). The seasonal workers programme that also recruits labourers from Eastern Europe for economic branches that experience seasonal fluctuations has led to larger influxes of foreign workers, but only 15,000 of the 260,000 seasonal workers recruited in 2000 worked in hospitality rather than agriculture (Beauftragte, 2001; Zentralstelle, 2001). These numbers are hardly sufficient to meet shortages estimated at 80,000 by DEHOGA in 2001 (DEHOGA, 2001a). The claims were dismissed as exaggerations by the Union for Food, Consumption and Restaurants (NGG), which challenges the wisdom of recruiting foreigners when unemployment levels still rise within the industry (NGG, telephone communication, 25 November 2003). Beyond facing union scepticism, DEHOGA feels inadequately represented by the BDA and the industry confederation, BDI, which lent greater support to the IT industry while only tepidly supporting changes in labour migration provisions for unskilled workers (DEHOGA, personal communication, 29 August 2003). In a response paper solicited by the independent commission on the 2002 immigration law, DEHOGA questioned why the government has not met its demands for a Green Card-type programme akin to that of the IT industry (DEHOGA, 2001b). DEHOGA has had to be satisfied with minor changes to the seasonal worker system, such as the extension of the duration of permits from three to 4 months in 2003, and 6 months in 2008. The lack of response on the part of the government, and its continued denial of free movement rights to Eastern Europe accession country workers, has left the industry feeling hard done by.

Hospitality is also a growth industry in Austria, where only 3.4 per cent of the workforce was employed in the branch in 1969, but where nearly 6 per cent worked at the millennium's end (Hauptverband der österreichischen Sozialvericherungsträger, 1969–2002). The share of foreigners working in hospitality has risen from 2 per cent in 1964 to 28 per cent in 2002 (Österreichisches Institut für Wirtschaftsforschung, 1962–2002). Though employers in the sector use standard work permits for long-term skilled labour such as specialty cooks, most foreign workers in hospitality enter through the seasonal *Saisonier* programme. *Saisoniers* receive a six-month, once-renewable, employer-specific permit, but thereafter the worker must exit Austria for at least 2 months before reapplying. The system is subject to a quota of 8000 workers on average, meaning that in peak months this number can be exceeded. These visas are also available to workers in agriculture, so to prevent counterproductive competition between the two branches, there is a separate 7000 permit allotment that is only valid for a few weeks during the harvest time.

The Tourism and Leisure Industry Section of the Austrian Business Chamber represents employers, while the Union for Hotels, Restaurants and Personal Services (HGPD) is its vocal counterpart. Employers and the regional HGPD offices cooperate closely in the process of granting individual work permits, but the issue of seasonal work is thornier. At the root are tremendous fluctuations in employment, with only three-quarters as much staff employed in the off-season when unemployment rises almost 200 per cent (Biehl and AMS, 2003, p. 57). These fluctuations render temporal flexibility considerations uniquely salient for employers who feel further hemmed in by Austria's rigid working hour regulations (Brauchen neue, 1996), but they also fuel union opposition.

In response to such union arguments, the Austrian Hotel Federation (*Hotelvereinigung*) asks aloud why even in the high season when hotels struggle to find sufficient help 20,000 workers can remain unemployed (Mehr Saisonniers, 2001).

In response, unions have emphasized that despite the quota of 8000 workers, in actuality, the number of foreign workers that enter each year is far higher. The pro-labour think tank, the *Arbeiterkammer*, pointed out that in 2001, on average 9299 seasonal workers were employed (25.211 oder, 2002). Despite this largesse, in 2002 employers were once again bemoaning shortages, and the WKÖ and Hotel Federation implored the government to introduce greater flexibility into the scheme or risk having hotels turn away vacationers (Zu Saisonstart, 2002). Cautious to avoid overtly raising the quota, the government's response the following year was to create a weighting system under which seasonal workers who stay less than six weeks do not count against the quota. Aided by the creative redefinition of statistics, the number of foreigners in the industry continues to rise. However, it is interesting that despite domestic constraints in the form of vocal union opposition and significant levels of public debate over the efficacy of the programme, Austrian employers at both the sectoral and peak level have successfully convinced the government that their temporal and wage flexibility needs are both genuine and largely beyond resolution through recourse to the national labour market.

While the pressures upon the labour market and the ensuing claims by employers in hospitality are similar in each country, German and Austrian employers face additional obstacles. The absence of strong support from the central business and employers' confederations and the labour movement's ability to effectively contest the necessity for labour migration has led to German government caution in meeting employer demands. Austria's highly institutionalized procedure for negotiating the entry of seasonal workers plays in favour of unions and the status quo, but, in recognition of the sector's pressing need, the government has resorted to a creative solution that suggests a desire to favour business despite the ire that this policy created among unions. In the UK the absence of powerful unions and need for sectors to receive CBI approval creates a more direct path from employer preference to final policy that spawned sectoral solutions.

4. Conclusion

While it is not surprising that business preferences on migration depend on labour market conditions, today's pressures are qualitatively different from those in the more immediate post-war era. The prevailing employer preferences and attitudes towards labour migration of that time often no longer reflect current labour market conditions. However, businesses are not necessarily free to pursue sectoral interests that may only just have become apparent through the economic growth spurt that characterized the latter 1990s. Instead, certain national or sectoral institutions may alternately strengthen or challenge employers' demands for the liberalization of labour migration.

The absence of extensive regulation in IT makes it fertile ground for liberal labour migration. The novelty of the sector also renders factors such as union opposition and existing training systems less salient, resulting in new programmes to recruit IT specialists in all four countries. The hospitality industry features similarly low levels of regulation, but the presence of established unions and the reserved support from the employers' confederation for employers in this sector have prevented it from realizing its demands in Germany, and have forced policy to be ad hoc and even surreptitious in Austria. In the UK, where these factors did not weaken the case advanced by employers, employers' demands were addressed through a sectoral programme before the advent of the free flow of labour from the newly acceded Eastern European countries.

The salience of sectoral concerns becomes even more evident when one considers that with regard to opening their labour markets to workers from fellow EU countries from the East, rather than following the UK or Swedish example of allowing in all workers, countries such as Germany, Belgium, the Netherlands, and France have only opened to workers in particular occupations, such as engineering, care-giving, or food processing. Furthermore, the Blue Card, the initiative to create a common EU-wide work permit, covers only highly skilled workers in technology or management fields. While the gates of Fortress Europe – both collectively and among individual countries – have swung open once again after several decades of low volumes of migration, these gates open much more selectively than in the past, reflecting the ever-greater specialization of production and labour markets that has resulted from the structural transformation of industrialized economies over the last 30 years.

Notes

1. Though the free movement of workers is mandated within the European Union, non-EU foreigners constituted roughly two-thirds of all foreign workers in Germany (6 out of 9 per cent) and the UK (2.5 to 3 per cent

out of 4 to 4.5 per cent) from 1985–2003 (*Eurostat, Labour Force Sample Survey*, 1985–2004).
2. Immigration featured prominently in the UK Conservatives' 2005 campaign, but this strategy proved far from successful.
3. While the terms "firms" and "employers" are used interchangeably, "firms" refers to individual companies, in line with the varieties of capitalism approach based on the logic of the firm. Use of the term "employers" is meant to encapsulate both firms and the larger associational entities in which firms are organized.
4. Garrett and Way (1995) and Shafer (1994) respectively employ the term "sector" to mean either public versus private or traded or non-traded sectors. Without definitive criteria for delineating sectors, I follow Hiscox (2001), who roughly equates the term with industry branch.
5. Bundesgesetzblatt I, p. 1146.
6. Bundesgesetzblatt I, p. 1471.
7. While the hospitality sector in the UK grew apace with services overall during the last 10 years (10 per cent compared to 8 per cent), in Germany growth was significantly higher (31 per cent compared to 11 per cent).

Bibliography

"25.211 oder 52.000: Wie viele Saisoniers arbeiteten 2001?" (2002) *Der Kurier*, June 8.

Abramovsky, L., Griffith, R., and Sako, M. (2004) *Offshoring of Business Services and its Impact on the UK Economy* (Oxford: Advanced Institute of Management Research).

Bearce, D. H. (2003) "Societal Preferences, Partisan Agents, and Monetary Policy Outcomes", *International Organization* 57(2): 373–410.

Beauftragte der Bundesregierung für Ausländerfragen (2001) *Migrationsbericht der Ausländerbeauftragten im Auftrag der Bundeseregierung* (Berlin).

Biehl, Kei and AMS (2003) "Beschäftigung und Arbeitslosigkeit", in S. Leodolter and R. Kaske (eds.) *Tourismus in Österreich: Zukunftsbranche oder Einstieg in die Arbeitslosigkeit?* Verkehr und Infrastruktur, No. 18 (Vienna: AK Wien), pp. 35–73.

Biffl, G. (2003) "Mobilitäts- und Verdrängungsprozesse auf dem österreichischen Arbeitsmarkt: Die Situation der unselbständig beschäftigten AusländerInnen", in H. Fassmann and I. Stacher (eds.) *Österreichischer Migrations- und Integrationsbericht: Demographische Entwicklungen – sozioökonomische Strukturen – rechtliche Rahmenbedingungen* (Vienna: Verlag Drava Klagenfurt/Celovac), pp. 62–86.

"Brauchen neue Ausländerpolitik" (1996) *Wirtschafts Blatt*, 11 June, p. A3.

Bundesvereinigung der Deutschen Arbeitgeberverbände (BDA) (1962) *Jahresbericht der Bundesvereinigung der Deutschen Arbeitgeberverbände, 1961* (Düsseldorf: BDA).

Cachón, L. and Valles, M. S. (2003) "Trade Unionism and Immigration: Reinterpreting Old and New Dilemmas", *Transfer. European Review of Labour and Research* 3 (3): 469–482.

Castles, S. and Kosack, G. (1973) *Immigrant workers and Class Structure in Western Europe* (London: Oxford University Press).

Castles, S. (2006) "Guestworkers in Europe: A Resurrection?" *International Migration Review* 40(4): 741–766.

Caviedes, A. (2004) "The Open Method of Coordination in Immigration Policy: A Tool for prying open Fortress Europe?" *Journal of European Public Policy* 11(2): 289–310.

Caviedes, A. (2010) *Prying Open Fortress Europe: The Turn to Sectoral Labor Migration Policy* (Lanham, MD: Lexington Books).

Confederation of British Industry (CBI) (2002) *CBI Response to the Government's White Paper on Immigration, Asylum and Nationality* (London: CBI).

Crouch, C. and Streeck, W. (eds.) (1997) *Political Economy of Modern Capitalism: Mapping Convergence and Diversity* (London: Sage).

Culpepper, P. D. (2003) *Creating Cooperation: How States Develop Human Capital in Europe* (Ithaca, NY: Cornell University Press).

DGB (1985/1989/1993) *Geschäftsbericht des Bundesvorstandes des Deutschen Gewerkschaftsbundes* (Düsseldorf: Deutscher Gewerkschaftsbund).

DEHOGA (2001a) "Hotellerie und Gastronomie Befürworten 'Green Card' Vorstoß des Bundeskanzlers", Press Release, 2 February.

DEHOGA (2001b) "Stellungnahme des Deutschen Hotel- und Gaststättenverbandes e.V. gegenüber der unabhängigen Kommission 'Zuwanderung' ", Press Release, 1 March.

Dobson, J. and Salt, J. (2004) "Review of Migration Statistics", in M. Bommes, K. Hoesch, U. Hunger and H. Kolb (eds.) *Organisational Recruitment and Patterns of Migration: Interdependencies in an Integrating Europe*, IMIS Beiträge 25 (Osnabrück, Germany: Institut für Migrationsforschung und Interkulterelle Studien), pp. 99–140.

Edye, D. (1987) *Immigrant Labour and Government Policy: The Cases of the Federal Republic of Germany and France* (Brookfield, VT: Gower).

European Commission (2002) *Towards a Knowledge-Based Europe: The European Union and the Information Society* (Brussels: Directorate General for Press and Communication).

Eurostat (1976–2002) *Labour Force Sample Survey* (Luxemburg: Statistical Office of the European Communities).

Faist, T., Sieveking, K., Reim, U., and Sandbrink, S. (1999) *Ausland in Inland: Die Beschäftigung von Werksvertagsarbeitnehmern in der Bundesrepublick Deutschland* (Baden-Baden: Nomos).

Freeman, G. P. (1979) *Immigrant Labor and Racial Conflict in Industrial Societies: The French and British Experience 1945–75* (Princeton, NJ: Princeton University Press).

Garrett, G. and Way, C. (1995) "The Sectoral Composition of Trade Unions, Corporatism, and Economic Performance", in B. Eichengreen, J. Frieden, and J. Von Hagen (eds.) *Monetary and Fiscal Policy in an Integrated Europe* (Heidelberg: Springer Verlag), pp. 38–61.

Greifenstein, R. (2001) *Die Green Card: Ambitionen, Fakten und Zukunftsaussichten des deutschen Modelversuchs* (Bonn: Friedrich Ebert Stiftung).

Hall, P. and Soskice, D. (eds.) (2001) *Varieties of Capitalism: The Institutional Foundations of Comparative Advantage* (New York: Oxford University Press).

Hansen, R. (2000) *Citizenship and Immigration in Post-war Britain* (New York: Oxford University Press).

Haus, L. (2002) *Unions, Immigration, and Internationalization: New Challenges and Changing Coalitions in the United States and France* (New York: Palgrave Macmillan).

Heckley, G. (2005) "Offshoring and the Labour Market: The IT and Call Center Occupations Considered", *Labour Market Trends* (September): 373–385.

Herrmann, A. (2009) *One Political Economy, One Competitive Strategy? Comparing Pharmaceutical Firms in Germany, Italy and the UK* (New York: Oxford University Press).

Hiscox, M. J. (2001) "Class versus Industry Cleavages: Inter-Industry Factor Mobility and the Politics of Trade", *International Organization* 55(1): 1–46.

Howell, C. (2003) "Varieties of Capitalism: And Then There Was One?" *Comparative Politics* 36(1): 103–124.

Howell, D. R. (2002) "Increasing Earning Inequality and Unemployment in Developed Countries: Markets, Institutions and the 'Unified Theory' ", *Politics & Society* 30(2): 193–243.

IG Metall (1961–2002) *Geschäftsbericht des Vorstandes der IG Metall für die Bundesrepublik Deutschland* (Frankfurt a.M.: Industriegewerkschaft Metall).

Joppke, C. (1999) *Immigration and the Nation-State: The United States, Germany, and Great Britain* (Oxford: Oxford University Press).

Katzenstein, P. J. (1987) *Policy and Politics in West Germany: A Semi-Sovereign State* (Philadelphia, PA: Temple University Press).

Kindleberger, C. P. (1967) *Europe's Postwar Growth: The Role of Labor Supply* (Cambridge, MA: Harvard University Press).

Kolb, H., Murteira, S., Peixoto, J., and Sabino, C. (2004) "Recruitment and Migration in the ICT Sector", in M. Bommes, K. Hoesch, U. Hunger, and H. Kolb (eds.) *Organisational Recruitment and Patterns of Migration: Interdependencies in an Integrating Europe*, IMIS Beiträge 25 (Osnabrück, Germany: Institut für Migrationsforschung und Interkulterelle Studien), pp. 147–178.

Marginson, P. and Sisson, K. (2002) "European Industrial Relations: A Case of Convergence *and* Divergence?" *Journal of Common Market Studies* 40(4): 671–692.

"Mehr Saisonniers, weniger Schwarzarbeit" (2001) *Die Presse*, 21 January.

Menz, G. (2005) *Varieties of Capitalism and Europeanization: National Response Strategies to the Single European Market* (New York: Oxford University Press).

Münz, R. (2001) "Geregelte Zuwanderung: Eine Zukunftsfrage für Deutschland", *Aus Politik und Zeitgeschichte*, B 43/2001: 3–6.

Münz, R. and Ulrich, R. (1997) "Changing Patterns of Immigration to Germany, 1945–1995: Ethnic Origins, Demographic Structure, Future Prospects", in K. Bade and M. Weiner (eds.) *Migration Past, Migration Future: Germany and the United States* (Providence, RI: Berghahn Books), pp. 65–119.

"Netherlands faces mass shortage of top expats" (2005) *Expatica News*, 4 May. Available at http:/www.expatica.com/source/site_article.asp?subchannel_id=1&story_id=19772 (accessed 02 November 2006).

NGG (1962–1998) *Geschäftsbericht. Gewerkschaft Nahrung-Genuß-Gaststätten* (Hamburg: Gewerkschaft Nahrung-Genuß-Gaststätten).

OECD (2002) *International Mobility of the Highly Skilled* (Paris: OECD).

OECD (2005) *Science, Technology and Industry Scoreboard* (Paris: OECD).

Office for National Statistics (1998) "Flows and Stocks of Foreign Labour in the United Kingdom", *Labour Market Trends* (July): 371–380.

Office for National Statistics (2003) "Work Permits and Foreign Labour in the UK: A Statistical Review", *Labour Market Trends* (November): 563–574.

Piore, M. (1979) *Birds of Passage: Migrant Labor and Industrial Societies* (New York: Cambridge University Press).

Professional Contractors Group (2002) *PCG Position Paper,* 19 November 2002.

Regini, M. (2000) "The Dilemmas of Labor Market Regulation", in G. Esping-Andersen and M. Regini (eds.) *Why Deregulate Labour Markets?* (Oxford: Oxford University Press), pp. 11–29.

Rogowski, R. (1987) "Political Cleavages and Changing Exposure to International Trade", *American Political Science Review* 81(4): 1121–1138.

Schneiberg, M. and Bartley, T. (2001) "Regulating American Industries, Markets, Politics, and the Institutional Determinants of Fire Insurance Regulation", *American Journal of Sociology,* 107(1): 101–146.

Seifert, W. (1995) *Die Mobilität der Migranten: Die berufliche, ökonomische und soziale Stellung ausländischer Arbeitnehmer in der Bundesrepublik* (Berlin: Edition Sigma).

Shafer, M. D. (1994) *Winners and Losers: How Sectors Shape the Developmental Prospects of States* (Ithaca: Cornell University Press).

Sharma, Y. (2000) "Germany Accepts that it Needs Foreign Labor", *Inter Press Service,* 25 February.

SOPEMI (1999) "Report on the Temporary Employment of Foreigners in Several OECD Countries", in SOPEMI, *Trends in International Migration: Continuous Reporting System on Migration* (Paris: OECD), pp. 185–198.

SOPEMI (2002) "Labour Shortages and the need for Immigrants: A review of Recent Studies", in SOPEMI, *Trends in International Migration: Continuous Reporting System on Migration* (Paris: OECD), pp. 103–118.

Thelen, K. (2001) "Varieties of Labor Politics in the Developed Democracies", in P. Hall and D. Soskice (eds.) *Varieties of Capitalism: The Institutional Foundations of Comparative Advantage* (Oxford: Oxford University Press), pp. 71–103.

Traxler, F. (1999) "The State in Industrial Relations: A Cross-National Analysis of Developments and Socioeconomic Effects", *European Journal of Political Research* 36(1): 55–85.

Vogel, S. K. (2001) "The Crisis of German and Japanese Capitalism: Stalled on the Road to the Liberal Market Model?" *Comparative Political Studies* 34(10): 1103–1133.

Vogler-Ludwig, K. (1999) "Deutschland", *Beschäftigungsobservatorium SYSDEM Trends* 32: 20–24.

Watson, M. (2003) "Ricardian Political Economy and the 'Varieties of Capitalism' Approach: Specialization, Trade and Comparative Institutional Advantage", *Comparative European Politics* 1(2): 227–240.

Watts, J. (2002) *Immigration Policy and the Challenge of Globalization: Unions and Employers in Unlikely Alliance* (Ithaca, NY: Cornell University Press).

Wood, S. (2001) "Business, Government and Patterns of Labor market Policy in Britain and the Federal Republic of Germany", in P. Hall and D. Soskice (eds.) *Varieties of Capitalism: The Institutional Foundations of Comparative Advantage* (New York: Oxford University Press), pp. 247–274.

Wrench, J. (2000) "British Unions and Racism: Organisational Dilemmas in an Unsympathetic Climate", in R. Penninx and J. Roosblad (eds.) *Trade Unions, Immigration and Immigrants in Europe, 1960–1993* (New York: Berghahn Books), pp. 133–156.

"Zentralstelle für Arbeitvermittlung" (2001) *ZAV-Info*, May.

Zimmermann, K. (1993) "Industrial Restructuring, Unemployment and Migration", in L. Bekemans and L. Tsoukalis (eds.) *Europe and Global Interdependence* (Bruges: European Interuniversity Press), pp. 25–52.

Zolberg, A. R. (1989) "The Next Waves: Migration Theory for a Changing World", *Interational Migration Review* 23(3): 403–430.

"Zu Saisonstart fehlt Personal" (2002) *Salzburger Nachrichten*, 13 November.

4
Emigration, Immigration, and the Quality of Membership: On the Political Economy of Highly Skilled Immigration Politics

Holger Kolb

1. The end of easy solutions: The changing face of immigration policies in the OECD world

Immigration has been one of the most heavily disputed political topics in many OECD (Organisation for Economic Co-operation and Development) states for a long time. Being a topic that still serves as a popular tool to mobilize alleged political supporters before elections, immigration politics in many OECD-states nevertheless have been exposed to a fundamental change. Recent debates about migration are no longer centred on the basic question of whether immigration should be allowed or not. The core of the current immigration discussion instead revolves around what kind of migration should be allowed, who should become a new member, and how the admission process should be organized. At present there is no industrialized country that still pursues a policy of general open borders.[1] The era of minimum state intervention into immigration processes – the "liberal moment in the history of international migration" (Zolberg, 1992, p. 322) – ended in the nineteenth century (Moch, 1992, p. 107). States neither accept nor reject immigrants as a rule and even countries such as Germany, which have been described as "undeclared" (Thränhardt, 1992) or "reluctant" (Martin, 1992) countries of immigration, now openly confirm their new status as immigration countries. In light of this, the central thrust of current debates on immigration in most OECD countries is not the question as to whether or not there should be any immigration. Instead, debates focus on technical questions such as the kind of migration that should be allowed, the characteristics of potential members that are considered desirable, or the management of the admissions process. A common denominator of immigration politics in the OECD world over the last decades would be that access for medium- or low-skilled workers has been restricted while the level of competition for highly skilled migrants has been increasing. As a general trend this implies the "end of the easy solutions" in the way that neither pursuing a policy of open borders nor the other extreme, the categorical denial of entrance to outsiders, seem to be realistic options for Western liberal democracies.

The reasons for the end of the "easy solutions" deserve further attention. Particularly immigration advocates sometimes wonder why immigration is such a hotly debated issue and argue that, in the long run, labour mobility benefits everyone (Simon, 1989; see for this critique Freeman, 1995; Hillman, 1994). From an economic perspective, migration is understood as a function of mobility costs and welfare differentials (Pies, 1995, p. 151) and thus a phenomenon of arbitrage that contributes to the correction of market imperfections. From this view, migration should be generally approved of by states because it contributes to increased economic efficiency (Straubhaar, 2002, pp. 52–53). This general statement, however, loses its validity when welfare state arrangements are introduced. As the modern nation-state primarily is a welfare state (Bommes and Halfmann, 1998, p. 87), unregulated immigration may undermine the welfare state's capacity to provide services to its populations. In particular, tax-financed benefits, where they are paid independently of previous contributions, may operate as a magnet for certain immigrant groups (Borjas, 1999) who thus contribute less to the state than they receive. It is therefore in the self-interest of a state to restrict immigration for those groups (Straubhaar, 2002, p. 84), or, in other words, welfare states must maintain an external "threshold of inequality" (Stichweh, 1998, pp. 49–61).[2] A second, less economic reason why industrialized nation-states have abandoned a laissez-faire immigration policy is related to the reduced value attributed to the population size of a state. The move from the prohibition of emigration to the restriction of immigration mirrors the rejection of a mercantilist population policy that was primarily aimed at increasing the population size. Indeed, a growing population is no longer automatically associated with an increase in power or competitiveness (Stichweh, 1991). Most states allow emigration (exit) because population quantity is neither a central determinant of military power (which in any case may be less important than in the past), nor is it a precondition for economic competitiveness (Tietzel, 1995, p. 128). As a consequence, the main rationale for increasing the population size has become less important.

This indicates that the option of unrestricted migration as a means of inducing or accelerating population growth can be excluded as a realistic state option.

If unrestricted immigration is not a realistic option, then one might expect states to aim for simple exclusion by totally prohibiting immigration. This approach, however, has not been followed in state policies. Even leaving aside states' commitments to certain channels of humanitarian migration, attempts to completely prohibit immigration would result in tremendous costs and are therefore not pursued. This is the "liberal paradox" (Hollifield, 1992) that confronts many states. Despite the existence of domestic political forces, such as the electorate that prefer rather restrictive immigration policies[3] and that push states towards increasing closure, international economic forces have the opposite effect and push states towards greater openness.[4] North Korea may well be the only nation-state that refuses any form of integration into the globalized economy. Open societies are indeed able to manage economic structural changes much more smoothly by allowing factor mobility and by enhancing their potential for growth by attracting immigrants who complement indigenous production factors. Neither a policy of open borders nor the total prohibition of migration can be serious policy options given the current and expected future international economic context. As a consequence of the end of easy and categorical solutions, highly skilled migrants, as one specific group of migrants, have gained increasing importance. The impact of this quantitatively small group on economic competitiveness is far greater than the relatively small numbers of migrants suggest (Salt, 1992). The emergence of highly skilled migrants as one particularly important migration group and the evolution of specific attraction policies targeted at highly skilled persons living outside the respective country is the main focus of this chapter. For a better explanation of the mentioned attraction policies, the first step will be to provide a theoretical framework that is meant to sketch out the relevant political and economic contexts that created the preconditions for these policies.

2. Albert O. Hirschman's model of state membership and cross-border migration

In his book *Exit, Voice, and Loyalty: Responses to Decline in Firms, Organizations, and States*, which nowadays is appreciated as a milestone of interdisciplinary social science research, Albert O. Hirschman (1970) discussed two central modes of articulating protest against quality deterioration within organizations. Whereas "exit" is discussed as the relevant strategy of an unsatisfied consumer to react to the declined quality of a certain commodity and thus is assumed to be a major topic for economists,[5] "voice" was understood as a key element of the political process and thus seemed to be reserved as a bread-and-butter issue of political science (Dowding et al., 2000, p. 470). Hirschman overcomes this dichotomy and aims for an integrated discussion of both strategies by generalizing "from the market to the polity" and by "introducing the mechanisms of politics into the economy" (Rokkan, 1974, p. 27). In general he is interested in feasible "Responses to Decline in Firms, Organizations, and States" (the book's subtitle). Most emphasis, however, is placed on "firms and organisations" (Pfister, 2006, p. 43), while "states" are only discussed to a very limited degree.[6] As a consequence, migration, as a specific form of exit, was barely touched in the analysis. This gap triggered authors like Jonathan Moses to refer the Hirschman model explicitly to state action and to cross-border mobility. Moses (2005) argues that shrinking mobility costs, the resulting increasing numbers of migrants, and – related to this – the amplification of the exit strategy as a way to articulate discontent against deterioration of state "citizenship bundles" (Moses, 2005, p. 70) will induce new cleavages in the form of mobile against immobile members. According to this, governments increasingly will be responsive to the wishes, preferences, and claims of those groups of the population who are mobile and might use their exit options as a threat. What has been left out by Moses and others is the utilization and further development of these considerations for the understanding of immigration politics and specifically the recent changes in the patterns of attraction schemes for highly skilled migrants.

Instructive for the theoretical foundation of the emergence of highly-skilled immigration politics are the remarks of Hirschman in the paragraph on loyalty (chapter 7). Hirschman argues that membership in a state is a precious resource because it allows for the utilization of a specific bundle of state-provided goods (see also Stichweh, 2005, p. 152). A more detailed description of the goods can be found elsewhere (Kolb and Fellmer, 2008), but the core of this bundle without doubt constitutes the state-provided social security benefits against the basic risks of life such as old age, unemployment, disability, illness, and need of care. Additionally, however, these goods feature certain particularities, since contrary to normal goods and services they are produced and consumed by the members at the same time: "the 'buyer' is now in reality a member and as such he is involved in both the supply and the demand sides, in both production and consumption of organizations' output" (Hirschman, 1970, p. 100). Whereas in neoclassic economics production and consumption are sharply separated, the very nature of being a member in a human community unites elements of consumption and production of collective goods in one and the same person. Every person residing on the territory of a nation-state permanently produces *and* consumes. Illuminating in this context are the parallels of states to clubs as recurrently discussed by Straubhaar (2002, 2003, 2006, see also the spadework of Buchanan, 1965). Similarly to clubs, states provide a bundle of goods, which cannot be provided on a private basis due to the well-known free-rider-problem, for their members and, in also similarly, state members are involved in the production and the consumption of the bundle at the same time. Sinn (1997) has referred to this as "the selection principle". As a result of this, states as clubs are advised to be concerned about the sum of the contributions of the members being sufficient to enable the financing and maintenance of the bundle.[7] From this it follows that exit and therefore the drop-out of a "member of a good quality" immediately leads to a further quality decrease and as a consequence of this to the danger of further exits of "good quality members".[8] "Good quality" or "quality-conscious" members (Hirschman (1970, p. 100) are those who bring a beneficial constellation of consumption and production to the organization. This denotes those members who "over-produce" in the sense that they contribute to the bundle of goods more than they consume from it. In case of an increase of the share of members who "over-consume" and induce net-costs, congestion costs and crowding out-effects appear. In this case we will also use the term "rivalry" in the next sections.

The decision for exit/emigration as a result of individual dissatisfaction with state performance has been interpreted as an exceptional and rare case for a long time. In *Exit, Voice, and Loyalty* a nation-state was considered to be an organization that, in a similar way to a totalitarian party or the family and contrary to companies in a competitive market, has the "ability to exact a high price for exit" (Hirschman 1970, p. 96) and for this reason as quasi-monopolist with regards to the provision of collective goods (Moses, 2005, p. 63). More recent studies also point to limited exit options of state members and assume a general inelastic quality demand for citizenship (Moses, 2005, pp. 66, 72). In microeconomic theory elasticity measures the nature and percentage of the relationship between changes in quantity demanded of a good and changes in its price or quality. Inelasticity thus means that shifts in demand as a reaction to a decreasing quality of membership (or increasing price) are barely existent. The quality of membership depends on the concrete benefits linked to membership and the opportunity costs of switching membership. Moses (2005), however, points to the fact that state membership may not be seen as homogenous and that especially highly skilled members feature a much higher elasticity due to their alternative membership options. Particularly technical innovations such as the "microelectronic revolution", which enabled the maintenance of personal and virtual contacts to the home country despite having exited/emigrated previously,[9] the condensation of transport networks (Straubhaar, 2003, p. 86), and the numerous offers of membership for highly skilled persons (McLaughlan and Salt, 2002) can justify the assumption of differential elasticities within one population. Whereas the demand for membership of low-skilled persons is almost inelastic due to barely existing alternative membership offers and the impossibility of free labour movement (Moses, 2005, p. 72), the elasticity for the highly skilled is much higher. At least for this latter group the state has been losing its former monopolist position as a provider of collective goods. Particularly the "attractive citizen stocks" (Moses, 2005, p. 70), a collective term which summarizes those parts of the population with a favourable constellation of production and consumption and consequentially with a general low propensity of rivalry, easily can respond to a quality decline[10] of the state-provided bundle with exit[11] (see also Hirschman, 1978, pp. 95–96; Sinn, 2002, p. 391). Correspondingly, state governments – in their efforts to provide the bundle of goods and in order to avoid a "large revenue shock" (Moses, 2005, p. 65) and a consequential exit-triggered acceleration of deterioration of the bundle quality – are assumed to exhibit a greater responsiveness to the preferences of this group (Moses, 2005, pp. 66, 69; Straubhaar, 2003, p. 87), because "the revenue-losses from an exiting unskilled labourer might not compare to the anticipated losses of a fleeing CEO" (Moses, 2005, p. 62).

The perception of a decreasing quality of the bundle of state-provided goods particularly among the highly skilled can hazard states, because exit as "a fairly crude, binary response" (Dowding et al., 2000, p. 471) to state performance lapses might induce further exits and further deteriorations and thus might spread into a "circulus vitiosus" or "crippling brain drain" (Hirschman 1978, p. 105), which finally even can jeopardize the existence and operational capability of the state. The former GDR (German Democratic Republic), which, not least because of a sudden simultaneous appearance of exit and voice (Hirschman, 1993), disintegrated within a few months, reacted on emerging exit-spirals in 1961 and "simply closed its frontiers more effectively" (Hirschman, 1978, p. 104; see also Moses, 2005, p. 68).

3. Immigration, rivalry, and the quality of the bundle

I argued earlier that emigration of particularly those members who are endued with attractive alternative locational options (the "quality-conscious" members in Hirschman's terms) might have a negative effect on the quality of the state-provided bundle of goods. This applies particularly to the monetary dimension of the bundle, when the states' "good risks", meaning those individuals who feature a positive fiscal constellation of consumption and production for the state, exercise the option of exit and opt for a membership change by emigrating. Hirschman (1978, p. 105) cites Ireland as an example, which used "as remedy for exit . . . improved economic policy and conditions" and even generalizes the Irish example and recommends "countries worrying about exit . . . to satisfy the basic economic aspirations of their citizens, particularly of the more mobile among them." In addition to the increasing consideration of the preferences of those groups in order to avoid emigration and thus to secure the bundle quality – this being the main argument of Moses (2005, pp. 66, 67) – another option of quality maintenance, which can work as a complement to Moses' argument, might become relevant: the organization of immigration.

Immigration policy systematically means the attraction and admission of "good risks". These are members of other states who are supposed to dispose of a beneficial ratio of consumption to production. In the same way as the avoidance of exit of "attractive citizen stocks" (Moses, 2005, p. 70) by an increasing consideration of their preferences, selective immigration policies, which in Hirschman's words (1978, p. 95) might be described as "pulls from 'superior management' by other bands",[12] might also work as a boost for bundle quality. It thus may not be surprising that the common feature of national immigration policies in the OECD world is an increasing diversification of measures, which barely addresses the general question of whether migrants should be accepted at all, but rather is occupied with the concrete detailed and often technocratic (Boswell, 2004, p. 3) formulation and definition of conditions of access and control.[13] Particularly highly skilled migrants, who – due to their beneficial constellation of production and consumption – feature a greater likelihood of net contribution, can be important factors for bundle improvement. Open societies with a selective immigration policy and a membership approach which pursues the goal of optimizing the bundle that can be used by the stock membership (Straubhaar, 2003, p. 81) have a much better ability to increase the growth potential by accepting non-rivalling members. Immigration and the acceptance of new members can effectively accelerate wealth and improve the quality of the bundle of goods. Immigration policy hence can be understood as a state assessment mechanism that aims at measuring rivalry of potential new members by drawing on their observable, or at least predictable, characteristics. The measurement results provide a basis for the decision to accept or reject the respective applicant. The main goal of immigration policy is to screen for potential new members who – from the perspective of the stock members – feature a beneficial constellation of production and consumption, to convince them to accept the membership offer, and in doing so to realize potentials for the betterment of the bundle, which conversely might curb the propensity of exit particularly for the resident "attractive citizen stocks" (Moses, 2005, p. 70).

4. Highly skilled migrants and bundle improvement

The provision of social security benefits is not the only, but by far the most important, element of the state-provided bundle of goods. Consequentially, a central role in the screening and selection process is occupied by the assessment of whether a migrant can financially contribute to those elements of the bundle that are financed by social security contributions and taxes. A widespread method is to examine the previous occupation or qualifications, which serve as a proxy for the ability to integrate successfully into the national labour market and consequentially for the probability of monetary rivalry. The provision of evidence for non-rivalry in this area, however, does not imply any argument *for* access, only for *not against* access. Nation-states, which are described as providers of bundles of collective goods, organize the task of rivalry assessment in a different manner and apply different definitions and assessment methods. A second element in the state-provided bundle of goods is the production of internal, external, and legal security, which, when compared to social security as a bundle element, has been declining in importance for quite a while. As already indicated, rivalry for this element appears in a monetary form only to a very limited degree. For this element, new members are therefore not asked to provide evidence of being able to provide a positive contribution (over-production) but merely to avoid a negative one (over-consumption). The good-specific rivalry assessment of the state refers to the past of the membership applicant and tries to suggest the probability of the applicant's compliant behaviour, which is understood as behaviour that does not violate the laws of the state, by checking his or her previous criminal record. The executing bodies charged with this task are intelligence services, criminal investigation departments, and secret services, which collect and evaluate information on the applicant's past. In case of having found enough material that justifies the suspicion of good-specific rivalry these bodies might inform the governmental bodies who decide on access (for example, the immigration services) and express their concern about potential rivalry.

A further part of the state-provided bundle of goods can be the provision of a common culture, identity, and traditions. In a more conservative definition this good is incompatible with immigration because rivalry occurs inevitably if potential non-members differ with respect to culture, religion, or ethnicity and by doing so challenge respective expectations of cultural homogeneity of the stock members. The impressive work of Ernest Gellner (1983) describes the ethnically and culturally determined mode of nation-building, in which immigration policy was used as an instrument in state efforts for "reproducing internally homogenous … collectivities, which was achieved by selecting newcomers on the basis of their ethnicity, race, or national origins" (Joppke, 2005, p. 48). The "Chinese Exclusion Act" of the US and the "White Australia" policy are the result of such definitions of rivalry. In this understanding the ability to overproduce is inhered. For quite a while, however, a new understanding of the core of this product and a new definition of rivalry seems to have become accepted. This definition abstains from the consideration of ascriptive group characteristics,[14] outlaws race "as a legitimate ordering principle" (Joppke, 2005b, p. 49), and simply demands the acceptance of and adherence to the political values of the receiving society (democracy, human rights, individual freedom, gender equality, and so on). A good example for this approach is the American oath of loyalty, which demands the willingness of the applicant to: "support and defend the Constitution and laws of the United States of America against all enemies, foreign and domestic". Given this definition, the status of overproducer can be easily achieved by simply adhering to the political and constitutional values of the membership community.

Considering the conditions for an immigration-induced improvement of the bundle quality, the features of immigration policies can be summarized as follows: marketable "skills" are privileged, demonstrating a clear victory of the neutrality and equality principles over the national principle within liberal democratic states. The goal to reproduce historical particularities through immigration has disappeared from the political agendas of most immigration states. Targeted instead are persons with high qualifications, which are used as a proxy for low propensity of rivalry in the range of social security. A second precondition is a clean criminal record as indication for overproduction in the context of internal and external security, while culture-specific preferences are becoming uncommon, since the "normal case" of a mere acceptance of the norms and values of the liberal-democratic state already contributes to specific overproduction. This is the theoretical foil of the mounting body of measures that seek to attract highly skilled migrants.

5. Types of highly skilled recruitment policies

Having answered the question of "who?" what remains to be discussed is the question of "how?" The preceding parts of this chapter show that immigration policy has fundamentally changed so that immigration policy no longer constitutes a tool for nation-building. Instead the organization of admission of new members to a specific territory mainly disregards cultural or religious characteristics of the applicant (Joppke, 2005) and uses as the sole or main decision criterion the ability of the potential new member to contribute to the maintenance or even upgrading of the state-provided bundle of goods (mainly social security). This is the background of a general tendency in the OECD world to enlarge dramatically the possibilities for highly skilled migrants to immigrate and to settle in the country. Although a general liberalization of the entry options for highly skilled migrants depicts a common denominator of most immigration countries, the procedures and methods applied to screen and select applicants for their human capital and qualifications vary considerably among immigration countries. These states dispose of a wide array of different strategies and instruments to screen for highly skilled migrants and to filter good risks. The following section will first propose a categorization for the different attraction schemes and then will discuss some of the most popular instruments and aims for a structuring of these instruments into three general areas of highly skilled attraction policies. In general, admission policies can be broken down into (1) employer-driven procedures, (2) sector-based measures/selection for certain pre-determined skills, and (3) human capital-based instruments. Although most countries rely on a mix of strategies, particularly human capital-based instruments have been gaining in popularity and will therefore be discussed in greater detail. In the following sub-chapters the features of each strategy will be introduced by giving specific examples.

5.1. Employer-driven selection

This strategy of selecting highly skilled migrants prescribes a strong coupling of the recruitment to a concrete job offer of a specific employer. In this respect, the employer is the main actor in the recruiting process and in charge of organizing the procedure and providing the necessary paperwork. The German Aliens Act and the corresponding regulations on "exceptional cases" pertaining to the recruitment ban that were in force until the beginning of 2005, and also the parts of the new rules of the immigration act that came into force in 2005, established a strict coupling between an existing labour contract and the granting of a work permit. Most of the regulations additionally require passing a labour market test in order to demonstrate that there are no eligible workers available locally.

A simplified employer-driven selection procedure has been designed to facilitate the internal labour market allocation of multinational corporations. The importance of cross-border but intra-company movements as immigration channels for highly skilled persons has been disregarded in the literature for quite a while (for a critique see Kolb, 2005b). In this procedure, the otherwise obligatory labour market test (to show that no native workers are available) is not necessary to guarantee a quick and non-bureaucratic way of allocating company members from branch to branch internationally. Regulations have been modified to allow a company to manage its internal workforce in both the German Aliens Act and the new German Immigration Act. Similar regulations for intra-company transfers can be found in many countries. In the US the respective visa-category is the L1-visa, which has become increasingly ubiquitous among US employers in recent years (Hermann and Hunger, 2003). Australia, the Netherlands, and Ireland have also initiated or reformed their legal regulations concerning intra-company movements. In Ireland, for example, intra-company transfer assignments, which only require the submission of a "letter of confirmation" from the home and host employer, are exempt from work permit regulations (McLaughlan and Salt, 2002). The main problem of intra-company transfers, however, is their strong bias in favour of multinational corporations. Since only large enterprises dispose of the necessary internal labour markets, a sheer reliance on intra-company movements would severely constrain the competitiveness of small and medium enterprises. The relative success of the German "Green Card", discussed in greater detail below, therefore, was not simply the advent of experts coming to Germany but the creation of equal opportunities for multinational concerns and small and medium enterprises with regards to their personnel policies (Kolb, 2005b).

One of the best-known employer-driven selection schemes, which does not presuppose the existence of intra-company labour markets, is the so-called H-1B visa in the US. This non-immigrant visa allows US employers to temporarily – up to 3 years, renewable for a total of 6 years – employ highly skilled foreign workers in specialty occupations requiring the attainment of a bachelor's degree or its equivalent as a minimum. The H-1B visa belongs to the group of employer-based selection schemes since the granting of the visa is strictly tied to the confirmation of an employer to employ the attracted persons according to standard wage and labour conditions. This recruitment possibility, however, is subjected to a maximum quota.

The new German Immigration Act features a special and particularly cautious kind of an employer-based recruitment system. In addition to an existing work contract the law features a second and rather strict rivalry check in the range of social security. As a sufficient "safety warranty" concerning rivalry in the area of social security, it requires a gross salary of not less than 64,000 euros or an investment sum of 250,000 euros. A similar construction has been used in Austria for so-called "key employees" and in the Netherlands in the context of the *kenniswerker* recruitment. These persons must demonstrate a gross income of at least 60 per cent of the maximum assessment ceiling in the Austrian social security scheme, or a gross income of about 46,000 euros (or of 34,000 in the case of young applicants under 30 years old) in the Dutch case. Once able to provide such evidence, applicants are deemed to be good-specific overproducers and advance to the next level of the assessment procedure.

These examples of employer-based recruitment schemes for highly-skilled persons are instructive as they illuminate very glaringly how states develop these schemes for a process of rivalry assessment. The most important feature of these instruments is a very strong reliance on the granting of access upon the acceptance of the employer. The establishment of such a connection is intended to eliminate two dangers of rivalry. First and most important, the guarantee of labour market integration, which is the basic precondition for access, minimizes the danger of overuse of the element of social security. In addition, the coupling of an existing labour contract to the residence permit also might be understood as a device to limit the generally existing danger of rivalling in the realm of the good of internal security since non-compliance with the law can lead to dissolution of the labour contract and thus the lapsing of the residence permit. The danger of rivalry in the realm of internal security additionally is minimized by the fact that employer-based recruitment schemes are issued mostly on a temporary basis, which makes the renunciation of the residence permit in the case of good-specific rivalry possible.

5.2. Selection for certain skills determined by government/sector-driven selection

A close relative to employer-based selection procedures is a variety of instruments that limit the recruitment of highly skilled persons (or labour migrants in general) to specific sectors of the economy. One of the best known instruments in this context is the German "Green Card" which was launched at the beginning of the new century in order to ease the recruitment efforts of the – at that time – rapidly growing ICT (Information and Communications Technology) industry. The "Green Card" was designed for foreigners from outside the European Union and targeted those with a degree from a university or polytechnic in the field of information and communication technology, or whose skills warrant an annual salary of at least 51,130 euros. Initially, the government set a quota of 10,000 Green Cards. This quota was then increased to 20,000 within a few months of its introduction. Since the expiration of the Green Card initiative on 1 January 2005, highly skilled migrants can still, under certain conditions, obtain permanent residence under the above-mentioned regulations of the new Immigration Act. Since the residence permits issued on the basis of the Green Card regulations also require a fixed working contract between the highly skilled migrant and the respective employer, the Green Card actually straddles both the categories covered in 5.1 and 5.2. It is an instrument which is reserved for a specific part of the economy and which ties the work permit to the existence of a work contract. The German Green Card has been widely referred to as a major "failure" or "disappointment" because the sheer numbers of issued work permits on the legal basis fell short of the estimations of shortages in the sector. These assessments, however, disregard the fact that the "Green Card" as a new recruitment scheme to a large extent remained irrelevant for multinational corporations, whose main and preferred recruitment channel proved to be intra-company transfers. Contrary to public perception, the "Green Card" in Germany instead was an effective measure to create equal opportunities for small and medium enterprises with regards to the attraction of qualified workers (Kolb, 2005b).

A second German instrument which can be grouped as sector-driven is the so called "shortage diagnosis". This was developed by the members of the government-founded expert council on migration and integration ("Zuwanderungsrat") and is a rather complex two-stage system of identifying sectors and suitable migrants (see for details Sachverständigenrat für Zuwanderung und Integration, 2004; Schäfer, 2004). The first phase of the instruments seeks to identify those sectors that suffer from labour shortages. In the proposal of the "shortage diagnosis" those sectors and occupations qualify for additional recruitment from abroad that have been displaying low unemployment and a high vacancy rate for a certain period of time. The number of foreign workers to be admitted is determined by both the unemployment and the vacancy rate: the lower (higher) the unemployment (vacancy) rate in the specific sectors, the higher the maximum quota of migrants. Admissions terminate when both unemployment and vacancy rates reach an average level. In a second step, the individual qualifications of respective applicants for jobs in sectors qualified for labour migration will be checked. It is proposed that this task is to be conducted by the respective federal offices of labour. The main advantage of this proposal is that sectors that can make use of labour migration need not be formally established in advance but can be identified by the means of a specific shortage analysis. The first disadvantage of this system is that it is rather complicated and time-consuming. A second problem is the result of the strong reliance on the official labour statistics as the main source to calculate sector-specific shortages. The declining tendency of employers to officially register vacancies at the labour offices contributes to a significant inaccuracy in the assessment of shortages (see Kolb, 2006 for more details).

By limiting admissions to a specific part of the labour market, sector-specific procedures organize a prevention of rivalry. These parts must qualify for inflows of labour migrants by severe and enduring labour shortages that make employment likely and consumption of social services and over-consumption of infrastructure unlikely. The specificity of the sector works as proof against over-consumption of the part of the bundle that provides social security. In the realm of internal security over-production – understood as obeying the law – only means non-deviant and thus "normal" behaviour so that additional good-specific checks appear unnecessary. Sector-specific admission schemes, however, generally feature the time-lag problem. The potential for a lot of time to pass between the identification of a sector-specific labour shortage, the organization and implementation of a specific recruitment scheme, and the actual filling of a vacancy reduces the effectiveness of sector-specific measures.

5.3. Human capital selection

In general, immigration policy trends show an increasing emphasis on human capital (McLaughlan and Salt, 2002). Very popular in this context are point systems, which quite often are declared to constitute the master solution for the effective and unbureaucratic recruitment of highly skilled foreigners. The respective mechanism is very simple: contrary to employer-based and sector-specific schemes, no existing labour contract or affiliation to a specific sector of the labour market is required. Instead, only those migrants who have accumulated enough points to pass a defined point threshold are granted access. The point system thus defines a list of point criteria, screens immigrants, and allocates points according to the conformity of the applicants' individual characteristics and the list of point criteria. Among the first to establish a point system was Canada. In the Canadian system applicants first need to prove a clean criminal record – which is understood as an indicator that future rivalry in the realm of internal security will be absent – and a health certificate. Points are allocated for age (privileging youth), language ability, educational level, occupational training, arranged employment, recent work experience, connections with the host country, and personal suitability. Australia pursues a very similar system and takes into account age, language ability, educational level, skills, and recent work experience. Furthermore, potential immigrants must prove the absence of a criminal record and must deliver a health certificate.

Point systems as instruments to check the rivalry of a membership applicant and to organize the decision-making process on membership promise to be more responsive towards the actual needs of a dynamic and changing economy. They dispense with any sector restriction and do not presuppose an existing work contract, but rather enable members of other states with a specific set of human capital characteristics to apply for membership. In the debates in many European countries, point systems are appreciated as superior mechanisms to successfully attract highly skilled migrants. The former expert council on migration and integration in Germany (Zuwanderungsrat, 2004, p. 168) euphorically emphasizes the "transparency, flexibility, openness and sustainability" of a point system, and the UK and the Czech Republic have introduced Canadian-style systems themselves. However, there are mounting concerns that the reputation of point systems exceeds its actual performance (see, for example, Kawano, 2006; Reitz, 1998; van Tubergen, 2004). Schmidtke (2007) correspondingly speaks about a "paradox situation that Canada carefully screens and selects its immigrants according to their skills and qualifications, but then displays very unsatisfying result with regards to the labor market integration." DeVoretz et al. (2003) even report rising levels of remigration of Canadian immigrants due to insufficient compatibility between their qualifications and the needs of Canadian employers. The investment of the state in the respective infrastructure for selection and the investment of the individual migrant in his or her migratory project result in a total loss in this case.

Given this sobering assessment of the point system, human capital-based alternatives become a relevant topic in the debates about the shape and structure of migration regimes. Canada itself, the US, and the UK deserve special attention in this case since these countries have begun to regard the attraction of foreign students increasingly as a major and promising immigration channel (Thränhardt, 2005, p. 7). The highly reputed Ivy League universities in the US have been running recruitment offices in countries with an increasing demand for educational services, such as China and India, for some time. For the Chinese market, the US is the unchallenged market leader, as about 50 per cent of all Chinese students abroad attend an American university (Zhang, 2003, pp. 73–97), but also European universities such as the London School of Economics (LSE) have become active in these countries in recent years and have opened offices there. The number of Chinese students in the UK increased from 10,000 to 80,000 in the past few years (Shen, 2008). The attraction of students appears to be a specific approach in the area of human capital-based recruitment schemes. Under certain conditions, students as immigrants promise to possess those characteristics that the points system only uncovers through its lengthy screening process. This applies first of all to the age of the potential new member, which is particularly relevant for countries with declining fertility rates in Europe. Students as young immigrants automatically exert a (small) mitigating influence on the age composition of the population. More relevant than the demographic argument is the fact that students in most cases already at the beginning of their studies or at the latest during their studies have acquired a sufficient proficiency in the language of the country and thus successful labour market integration is not hampered by poor language skills. In addition, students as potential new members enjoy a high quality and host-country-compatible education, which makes rivalry in the sense of an over-consumption of social security benefits rather unlikely. States that finance their university systems at least partially by charging tuition fees are much less exposed to the danger of educational externalities, because students at least partially pay for the upgrade of their human capital.[15] The economic contribution of foreign students can be significant. A study for the UK quantifies this economic contribution, which largely consists of the tuition fees, of Chinese students at 300 million pounds (Shen, 2008). In the case of an exclusive financing of the university system from the general tax base the danger of *sunk costs* becomes relevant, when highly skilled members who received their education in the country leave the country after graduation. A repayment of the individual training and education costs in this case is omitted (Tietzel, 1995, p. 125). A typical and rigorous example of this problem for a long time was Germany, which until very recently afforded the luxury of offering foreign students a free university education in Germany and afterwards forced them to leave the country after graduation, even in the case of a job offer and work contract. This policy resulting from a bad conscience in the name of development policy did not change until the 2005 Immigration Act came into force, which for the first time gave foreign graduates of German universities the option to remain in the country and look for a job (Kolb, 2005a). Classic immigration countries such as Australia, New Zealand, or Canada, but also the UK, have paid particular attention to the group of students as potential new immigrant members. Sweetman (2005, p. 21) summarizes the background of the increasing attention to students as potential permanent members as follows: "Canadian post-secondary education solves (or at least alleviates) the following barriers to successful labour market integration: acculturation, credential recognition, language, and government administration around screening people." Particularly higher education systems, which provide for an individual contribution of the student as the person who directly benefits from an increasing human capital, can function as efficient mechanisms of rivalry assessment. They do so without lists of defined criteria, which are the core of point systems, but rather by focusing on a specific immigrant group that under certain circumstances possess the exact human capital profile a country needs. A stronger focus on students as immigrants thus might complement point systems as attraction schemes for highly skilled migrants.

The area of human capital-based recruitment schemes also includes strictly market-based mechanisms such as auction or entrance fee systems. Liberal economists such as Becker (1992) and Straubhaar (1992) argue that immigration rights should be made tradable and that a price should be charged for the scarcely issued immigration and residence permits. These proposals maintain immigration restrictions and do not claim an unlimited right for immigration, but organize the restriction in a market economy rather than central planning fashion. Market economy concepts for migration policy, however, do not work without state regulation. For the entrance fee solution, as well as for an auction system, a state authority must be responsible for deciding on either the price that potential migrants are charged for the right to immigrate or on the quantity of permits to be issued. Straubhaar favours the latter approach and proposes a quota that is allocated by an auction process. One basic disadvantage of this proposal, however, is that the maximum quota must be decided on politically in advance. Becker's proposal is the opposite of Straubhaar's. He proposes charging a fixed price for the right to immigrate without the presence of a maximum quota. Although the setting of an entrance fee unrelated to market factors structurally faces the same problems as the political definition of a quota, Becker's proposal seems to be easier to manage because of the presence of various indicators as to the right price, such as the average net-value of social security benefits. Consequently, every applicant willing to pay the price and become subject to a few prerequisites such as not having a terrorist background, criminal record, or contagious disease would be accepted. The main achievement of a market economy approach on immigration would be increased effectiveness and efficiency. The former would be met automatically, because a market-based system capitalizes on the infinite knowledge possessed by each individual actor. Immigrants willing to pay the required entrance fee would automatically have various characteristics that destination countries seek in their entrants. Proponents of a market-based system underline that the migration process can be understood as an investment decision.[16] Individuals will decide to immigrate to a particular country only if they anticipate receiving more than they invest. The total amount to be invested in this case should equal the entrance fee plus other transaction and adjustment costs. Correspondingly, only those individuals who expect a return from the residence permit that exceeds the total costs would seek entrance. As a result individuals striving for entrance would have a favourable age profile since young adults would gain more from migrating because they would receive higher earnings over a relatively longer time period. Furthermore, they would need to be rather skilled, high earning and ambitious to afford the entrance fee. In general it can be assumed that the introduction of a market-based system would induce a positive self-selection of immigrants. In addition to an increased effectiveness, efficiency should also be enhanced because the entrance fee system does not require points systems, lengthy hearings, and an extensive immigration bureaucracy. The necessary organizational infrastructure would simply require a small public authority to screen for terrorist background and criminal record while processing the fee. Though far from entertaining serious chances of implementation, market-based systems of immigration control are an alternative to the established human capital-based immigration systems such as the point system. The money paid or vouched for by an individual migrant in these systems serves as a proxy for their human capital and as security proof against over-consumption of parts of the state-provided bundle of goods.

6. Conclusion: Immigration policy as rivalry assessment for states' human resources policies

The aim of this chapter has been to demonstrate that immigration policy increasingly emerges as a policy field that is exposed to the challenge of developing procedures and methods for the optimization of access of new members in a way that optimizes the quality of the bundle of goods that can be used by the stock members. In order to exploit the potentials of bundle upgrading that are linked with immigration as the attraction of new members, and in order to avert the threat of a "slack organisation" (Maurer, 2006, p. 72), new applicants are subjected to a rivalry control that refers to the state-provided bundle of collective goods. Membership is only granted if the rivalry assessment procedure in every control area diagnoses the absence of rivalry/over-consumption and threat of quality losses. Within the bundle, a shift with regards to the importance of the single components can be observed in recent years. Particularly the element of social security and respective efforts to avoid "immigration into the social systems" have gained importance, whereas the "cultural" component which for quite a while was the expression of an ethno-cultural self-understanding of nationhood has been undergoing a major process of transformation and now appears as an element which only demands the acceptance of procedural political and constitutional values. Not least because of the demographic development in many OECD countries, it can be expected that the policy field of immigration policy, which for a long time seemed to be "reserved for immigration lawyers and charity organisations" (Santel, 1996, p. 9) will increasingly become relevant for economic policy considerations. Immigration policy and the associated regulation of membership in a nation-state can be interpreted as an important option for state human resource development. In a similar manner as the prevention of exit of quality-conscious members described by Hirschman (1970), the attraction of "good risks" can be utilized for efforts to increase the state-provided bundle of goods. Particularly the "classic" countries of immigration such as the US, Australia, and Canada have a long history of utilizing immigration for quality improvements of membership (see, for example, the papers in Thränhardt and Hunger, 2003). One common feature among all immigration countries thus is the further liberalization and specification of attraction schemes for highly skilled migrants. In this area particularly human capital-based recruitment and screening schemes have been gaining in importance over recent years, since they promise the greatest flexibility and smoothest organization of the admission process.

Notes

1. Doomernik's (2006) proposal of a regime of "Open Borders, Close Monitoring" at first glance seems to deviate from the conclusion above that all liberal welfare states must be alert to the danger of over-consumption of the welfare bundle by immigrants. This concept, however, reintroduces the threshold of inequality, which in most other migration regimes is based on border control and selective admission policies, by excluding immigrants from the usage of welfare benefits.
2. It is worth noting, however, that in this context the problems linked with migration are by no means specific problems of migration, but rather general problems of the welfare state (Straubhaar, 2002, p. 60).
3. For a long time, restrictive immigration preferences of the electorate have been demonstrated by opinion polls in many countries. See for the US Simon and Lynch (1999, pp. 455–467) and for Germany, Winkler (2003, pp. 33–38).
4. The divergence between the electorate's restrictive preferences concerning immigration policy and the liberal policy outcomes has been discussed in migration research for quite a while. Debates about the so-called "gap-hypothesis" initiated a fruitful theoretical competition between neo-institutionalist studies (Hollifield, 1992; Soysal, 1994) and political economy approaches (Freeman, 1995; Money, 1999).
5. Contrary to the opinion of Hirschman (1970), many proponents of the competitive market paradigm of neoclassic economics are convinced that – at least as long as there are some outside options available – the strategy of exit generally is of superior nature compared to voice. Milton Friedman (1955, 1962) describes the political process and the institutionalization of voice as "cumbrous" and "cumbersome" and stresses the advantages of exit.
6. The main exceptions are from Hirschman himself (1978, 1993), Tietzel and Weber (1993), and Tietzel (1995). Hirschman (1978, p. 91) regrets that he "had neglected the possible role of exit in the analysis of political behaviour" in his book *Exit, Voice, and Loyalty*.

7. For a detailed discussion of the structural differences between states and clubs, see Kolb (2008).
8. At this stage parallels to the Tiebout-model (1956) of a mobility-induced competition among jurisdictions become apparent.
9. Huge parts of the literature on "transnationalism", a school of thought that has been mushrooming in migration research for the last decade, supply multifaceted descriptions of this phenomenon.
10. Hirschman assumes this deterioration to be exogenous and to occur for any number of reasons.
11. Of course, it is a gross simplification to assume general free exit as it is done in the paper. Basically the right to exit from a country is guaranteed by international law. This right proves to be quite unfruitful because of the absent corresponding right of free entry into other countries. See Weiner (1995, pp. 444–445) for a description of various exit regulations.
12. See Preuhs (1999) for an empirical application. He investigates the effects of state policy on American net interstate migration and finds "states with low taxation levels, high investment-consumption ratios, and more liberal ideologies relative to other states... to experience more population growth via interstate migration."
13. For a highly informative description on the influential role of the bureaucracy on the formulation of migration policy see Guiraudon (2000).
14. The only exception in this context is family reunification between children and parents. This is "couched as an individual right and carried by a consensus that the family is the fundamental building block of society" (Joppke, 2005b, p. 2).
15. Becker/Becker (1998, p. 98) refer to the high rate of returns of a college education in the US, which amounts to an annual return rate of more than 10 per cent.
16. See also the early work of Sjastaad (1962, p. 83) who argues that migration must be understood "as an investment increasing the productivity of human resources, an investment which has cost and which also renders returns".

References

Becker, G. (1992) "Eintrittspreise für Immigranten. Plädoyer für einen moderaten Liberalismus in der Einwanderungspolitik", in *Neue Züricher Zeitung*, 21.10/1.11, pp. 41–42.

Becker, G. and Becker, G. N. (1998) *Die Ökonomik des Alltags. Von Baseball über Gleichstellung zur Einwanderung: Was unser Leben wirklich bestimmt* (Tübingen: Mohr Siebeck).

Bommes, M. and Halfmann, J. (eds.) (1998) *Migration in nationalen Wohlfahrtsstaaten. Theoretische und vergleichende Untersuchungen* (Osnabrück: Rasch).

Borjas, G. J. (1999) "The Economic Analysis of Immigration", in Ashenfelter, O., and Card, D. (eds.), *Handbook of Labor Economics*. Vol. 3 (Amsterdam: Elsevier Science), pp. 1679–1769.

Boswell, C. (2004) *Knowledge Transfer and Migration Policy Making*. Special Lecture on Migration (Geneva: International Institute for Labour Studies).

Buchanan, J. M. (1965) An Economic Theory of Clubs, *Economica*, 125, pp. 1–14.

DeVoretz, D., Ma, J., and Zhang, K. (2003) "Triangular Human Capital Flows: Empirical Evidence from Hong Kong and Canada", in Reitz, J. G. (ed.), *Host Societies and the Reception of Immigrants* (La Jolla: University of California Press), pp. 469–492.

Doomernik, J. (2006) *Open Borders, Close Monitoring*. Paper Presented at the Conference "Innovative Innovative Concepts for Alternative Migration Policies", Vienna: ICMPD, 24/25 March.

Dowding, K., John, P., Mergoupis, T. and Van Vugt, M. (2000) "Exit, Voice and Loyalty: Analytic and Empirical Developments", *European Journal of Political Research*, 37, pp. 469–495.

Freeman, G. P. (1995) "Modes of Immigration Politics in Liberal Democratic States", *International Migration Review*, 29, 4, pp. 881–902.

Friedman, M. (1955) "The Role of Government in Education", in Solo, Robert A. (ed.), *Economics and the Public Interest* (New Brunswick: Rutgers University Press), pp. 123–144.

Friedman, M. (1962) *Capitalism and Freedom* (Chicago: Chicago University Press).

Gellner, E. (1983) *Nations and Nationalism* (Ithaca, N.Y.: Cornell University Press).

Guiraudon, V. (2000) *Les politiques d' immigration en Europe* (Paris: L'Harmattan/Logiques politiques).

Hermann, V. and Hunger, U. (2003) Die Einwanderungspolitik für Hochqualifizierte in den USA und ihre Bedeutung für die deutsche Einwanderungsdiskussion, in Hunger, U. and Kolb, H. (eds.), *Die deutsche "Green Card": Migration von Hochqualifizierten in theoretischer und empirischer Perspektive*, Vol. 22 (Osnabrück: IMIS-Beiträge), pp. 81–98.

Hillman, A. L. (1994) "The Political Economy of Migration Policy", in Siebert, H. (ed.), *A Challenge for Europe* (Tübingen: Mohr Siebeck), pp. 263–282.

Hirschman, A. O. (1970) *Exit, Voice, and Loyalty. Responses to Decline in Firms, Organizations, and States* (Cambridge, MA: Harvard University Press).

Hirschman, A. O. (1978) "Exit, Voice, and the State", *World Politics*, 1, pp. 90–107.

Hirschman, A. O. (1993) "Exit, Voice, and the Fate of the German Democratic Republic. An Essay in Conceptual History", *World Politics*, 2, pp. 173–202.

Hollifield, J. F. (1992) *Immigrants, Markets and States. The Political Economy of Postwar Europe* (Cambridge, MA: Cambridge University Press).

Joppke, C. (2005) "Exclusion in the Liberal State: The Case of Immigration and Citizenship Policy", *European Journal of Social Theory*, 43, pp. 43–61.

Joppke, C. (2005b) *Selecting By Origin: Ethnic Migration in the Liberal State* (Cambridge, MA: Harvard University Press).

Kawano, Y. (2006) *Social Determinants of Immigrant Selection. The United States, Canada, and Australia* (New York: LFB Scholarly Publishing).

Kolb, H. (2005a) "Die Green Card: Inszenierung eines Politikwechsels", *Aus Politik und Zeitgeschichte*, 27, pp. 18–24.

Kolb, H. (2005b) "Germany's Green Card in Comparative Perspective", in: Henke, H. (ed.). *Crossing Over: Comparing Recent Migration in the United States and Europe* (Oxford: Lexington), pp. 303–318.

Kolb, H. (2006) "Internationale Mobilität von Hochqualifizierten – (k)ein Thema für die Migrationsforschung", in Swiaczny, F. and Haug, S. (eds.), *Neue Zuwanderergruppen in Deutschland (Materialien zur Bevölkerungswissenschaft)* (Wiesbaden: BiB, 2006), pp. 159–174.

Kolb, H. (2008) "States as Clubs? The Political Economy of State Membership", in Kolb, H. and Egbert, H. (eds.), *Migrants and Markets. Perspectives from Economics and the Other Social Sciences* (Amsterdam: Amsterdam University Press), pp. 120–146.

Kolb, H. and Fellmer, S. (2008) Abwanderung, Einwanderung und Mitgliedschaftsqualität: Zur politischen Ökonomie von Migrationspolitik, *Wirtschaftspolitische Blätter*, 55, 2, pp. 277–288.

Martin, P. (1992) "Germany: Reluctant Land of Immigration", in Cornelius, W. A., Martin, P., and Hollifield, J. F. (eds.), *Controlling Immigration. A Global Perspective* (Stanford: Stanford University Press), pp. 189–226.

Maurer, A. (2006) Abwanderung und Widerspruch: Grenzüberschreitungen zwischen Soziologie und Ökonomie, in Pies, I. and Leschke, M. (eds.), *Albert Hirschmans grenzüberschreitende Ökonomik*, (Tübingen: Mohr Siebeck), pp. 67–85.

McLaughlan, G. and Salt, J. (2002) *Migration Policies Towards Highly Skilled Foreign Workers* (London: Report to the Home Office).

Moch, L. P. (1992) *Moving Europeans: Migration in Western Europe since 1650* (Bloomington: Indiana University Press).

Money, J. (1999) *Fences and Neighbors: The Political Geography of Immigration Control* (Ithaca, N.Y.: Cornell University Press).

Moses, J. W. (2005) "Exit, Vote and Sovereignty: Migration, States and Globalization", *Review of International Political Economy*, 1, pp. 53–77.

Pfister, D. (2006) "Exit, Voice and Mobility", *BSIS Journal of International Studies*, 3, 43–58.

Pies, I. (1995) Kommentar zu Manfred Tietzel: Zur politischen Ökonomie der internationalen Migration, *Jahrbuch für Neue Politische Ökonomie*, 14, pp. 151–153.

Preuhs, R. (1999) "State Policy Components of Interstate Migration in the United States", *Political Research Quarterly*, 52, pp. 527–547.

Reitz, J. G. (1998) *Warmth of the Welcome: The Social Causes of Economic Success for Immigrants in Different Nations and Cities* (Boulder, CO: Westview Press).

Rokkan, S. (1974) "Politics Between Economy and Culture", *Social Science Information*, 13, 1, pp. 27–38.

Santel, B. (1996) *Migration in und nach Europa: Erfahrungen, Strukturen, Politik* (Opladen: Leske und Budrich).

Sachverständigenrat für Zuwanderung und Integration (2004) Migration und Integration – Erfahrungen nutzen, Neues wagen (Berlin: Sachverständigenrat).

Salt J. (1992) "Migration Processes among the Highly Skilled in Europe", *International Migration Review*, 26, 2, pp. 484–505.

Schäfer, H. (2004) Möglichkeiten der qualitativen und quantitativen Entwicklung von Zuwanderung in Teilarbeitsmärkten in Deutschland – Grundlagen einer Indikatorik für eine arbeitsmarktbezogene Zuwanderung', Expert Report (Bonn: Sachverständigenart für Zuwanderung und Integration).

Schmidtke, O. (2007) Errungenschaften und Herausforderungen der kanadischen Immigrations- und Integrationspolitik: ein Beispiel für Deutschland?' in Thränhardt, D. (ed.), *Entwicklung und Migration. Jahrbuch Migration – Yearbook Migration 2006/2007* (Münster: LIT Verlag), pp. 128–152.

Shen, W. (2008) "Chinese Student Migration in Europe: A Migration That Nobody Objects To?" in Kolb, H. and Egbert, H. (eds.), *Migrants and Markets – Perspectives from Economics and the Other Social Sciences* (Amsterdam: Amsterdam University Press), pp. 147–167.

Simon, J. (1989) *The Economic Consequences of Immigration* (Oxford: Blackwell).

Simon, R. J. and Lynch, J. P. (1999) "A Comparative Assessment of Public Opinion Toward Immigrants and Immigrations Policies", *International Migration Review*, 33, 2, pp. 455–467.

Sinn, H.-W. (1997) "The Selection Principle and Market Failure in Systems Competition", *Journal of Public Economics*, 66, pp. 247–274.

Sinn, H.-W. (2002) Der neue Systemwettbewerb, *Perspektiven der Wirtschaftspolitik*, 3, pp. 391–407.

Sjastaad, L. (1962) "The Costs and Returns of Human Migration", *Journal of Political Economy*, 70, pp. 80–93.

Soysal, Y. (1994) *Limits of Citizenship. Migrants and Postnational Membership in Europe* (Chicago: Chicago University Press).

Stichweh, R. (1991) *Der frühmoderne Staat und die europäische Universität. Zur Interaktion von Politik und Erziehungssystem im Prozeß ihrer Ausdifferenzierung (16–18. Jahrhundert)* (Frankfurt am Main: Campus).

Stichweh, R. (1998) Migration, nationale Wohlfahrtsstaaten und die Entstehung der Weltgesellschaft, in Bommes, M. and Halfmann, J. (eds.), *Migration in nationalen Wohlfahrtsstaaten. Theoretische und vergleichende Untersuchungen* (Osnabrück: Rasch), pp. 49–61.

Stichweh, R. (2005) Migration, Weltgesellschaft und Weltkommunikation. Zur strukturellen Einbettung von Migration in Entwicklungsphasen der Weltgesellschaft, in Stichweh, R. (ed.), *Inklusion und Exklusion. Studien zur Gesellschaftstheorie* (Bielefeld: Transcript), pp. 145–160.

Straubhaar, T. (1992) "Migrationspolitische Instrumente aus ökonomischer Sicht", in Kälin, W. And Moser, R. (eds.), *Migrationen aus der Dritten Welt. Ursachen –Wirkungen –Handlungsmöglichkeiten* (Bern: Haupt), pp. 275–300.

Straubhaar, T. (2002) *Migration im 21. Jahrhundert* (Tübingen: Mohr Siebeck).

Straubhaar, T. (2003) Wird die Staatsangehörigkeit zu einer Klubmitgliedschaft, in Thränhardt, D. and Hunger, U. (eds.), *Migration im Spannungsfeld von Globalisierung und Nationalstaat* (Wiesbaden: VS Verlag), pp. 76–89.

Straubhaar, T. (2006) Herausforderungen und Perspektiven der Migration im makroökonomischen Kontext, 3–1 (Hamburg: HWWI Policy Paper of the HWWI Kompetenzbereichs Migration).

Sweetman, A. (2005) "Canada", in Niessen, J. and Schibel, Y. (eds.), *Immigration as a Labour Market Strategy – European and North American Perspectives* (Brussels: MPG), pp. 13–46.

Thränhardt, D. (ed.) (1992) *Europe – A New* Immigration Continent. *Policies and Politics since 1945 in Comparative Perspective* (Münster: LIT).

Thränhardt, D. (2005). Entwicklung durch Migration: ein neuer Forschungs-ansatz, *Aus Politik und Zeitgeschichte*, 27, pp. 3–11.

Thränhardt, D. and Hunger, U. (eds.) (2003) *Migration im Spannungsfeld von Globalisierung und Nationalstaat* (Wiesbaden: VS Verlag).

Tiebout, C. (1956) "A Pure Theory of Local Expenditure", *Journal of Political Economy*, 5, pp. 416–424.

Tietzel, M. (1995) Zur politischen Ökonomie der internationalen Migration, *Jahrbuch für Neue Politische Ökonomie*, 14, pp. 117–142.

Tietzel, M. and Weber, M. (1993) Autokratische Mobilitätspolitik. Zur Politischen Ökonomie der Berliner Mauer und des Eisernen Vorhangs, *Ordo, Jahrbuch für die Ordnung von Wirtschaft und Gesellschaft,* 44, pp. 291–305.

Van Tubergen, F. (2004) *Integration of Immigrants in Cross-National Perspective* (Utrecht: Utrecht University Press).

Weiner, M. (1995) *The Global Migration Crisis* (New York: HarperCollins).

Winkler, J. (2003) Ursachen fremdenfeindlicher Einstellungen in Westeuropa, *Aus Politik und Zeitgeschichte,* 26, pp. 33–38.

Zhang, G. (2003) "Migration of Highly Skilled Chinese to Europe: Trends and Perspective", *International Migration,* 41, 3, pp. 73–97.

Zolberg, A. (1992) "Labour Migration and International Economic Regimes: Bretton Woods and After", in Zolberg, A. (ed.), *International Migration Systems: A Global Approach* (Oxford: Clarendon Press), pp. 316–319.

Zuwanderungsrat (2004) Migration und Integration – Erfahrungen nutzen, Neues wagen (Berlin/Nürnberg: BAMF).

5
Trade Unions and Migrant Labour in the "Global Age": New Alliances or Old Antagonisms?

Torben Krings

At the beginning of the twenty-first century, European trade unions are at a crossroad. In most countries unions struggle to adapt to contemporary processes of global change that have strengthened the position of capital *vis-à-vis* labour. While unions are still primarily organized at the national level, multinational companies are increasingly organized as global production networks that show little regard for national boundaries (Castells, 2000). As a result of globalization and EU enlargement, trade unions face a two-fold challenge. On the one hand, they are confronted by the relocation of parts of production to Eastern Europe and Asia in the name of "competitiveness" (or the threat of it to keep wages down). On the other hand, the inflow of migrant workers into service industries that cannot be "offshored" can fulfil a similar purpose of reducing wage costs (Menz, 2005). While the challenges that unions face in the light of economic internationalization and the growing mobility of transnational companies features in quite a number of publications (cf. Ferner et al., 2006; Hoffmann, 2002; Rigby et al., 1999), relatively little research has been carried out on trade union responses to the recent increase in cross-border mobility of people (for some exceptions see Haus, 2002; Watts, 2002). This may come as a surprise as "immigration is in important respects a matter of labour" (McGovern, 2007, p. 231).

The last two decades have seen an increase in population movements. Not only is South–North migration on the rise, but also since 1989 and the demise of the Eastern Bloc, East–West migration (Castles and Miller, 2003; Favell and Hansen, 2002). In spite of assumptions that "post-industrial" societies would no longer have a need for migrant labour, Western European countries continue to rely on foreign workers to fill labour-intensive jobs that are poorly paid, confer little prestige, and are often shunned by domestic workers (Piore, 1979). Although many unskilled and semi-skilled manufacturing jobs have been exported to lower wage countries, there are limits to the export of low-skilled jobs. As Castles (2006, p. 7) argues, "[t]he manufacture of cars, computers and clothing could be shifted to China, Brazil or Malaysia, but the construction industry, hotels and restaurants, hospitals and many other service enterprises could not". Migrant employment in the "global age", however, is not confined to less-skilled positions as there is also a growing demand for highly skilled migrants to fill positions such as financial analysts and ICT (Information and Communications Technology) specialists (OECD, 2007).

How do trade unions respond to this "new" immigration? It is often assumed that trade unions would oppose new labour migration as structural unemployment has become a feature of many Western European countries (Penninx and Roosblad, 2000). However, some writers have recently challenged this "conventional wisdom" (Watts, 2002, p. 1) by arguing that under the conditions of globalization, unions are not necessarily predisposed towards a restrictive stance. As unions acknowledge that the movement of people is part of the transnationalization of labour markets, they increasingly view "zero immigration" policies as neither desirable nor feasible (Haus, 2002; Milkman, 2006; Watts, 2002). However, as the latter studies are mainly confined to the US and the Mediterranean countries, there is a need for more comparative research on the immigration preferences of unions in the "global age" (Haus, 2002, pp. 159–160).

To shed further light on the immigration policies of organized labour, this chapter examines union responses to immigration in four Western European countries, Austria, Germany, Ireland, and the UK. By drawing on empirical research in the four countries, I specifically examine their policy positions in relation to non-EU immigration. I show that the immigration preferences of unions is best captured by the concept of "managed migration" that opens up avenues for legal immigration from outside the European Economic Area (EEA).[1] This should entail the option of permanent residence from the very beginning and should be accompanied by policies that facilitate the integration of the newcomers. In their preferences for long-term immigration, however, unions face the dilemma that there is a renewed commitment by policy-makers to temporary migrant worker programmes at the national as well as the European level.

1. Trade unions and immigration

Generally, trade unions in the industrialized world have an ambiguous relationship with migrant labour that can be situated "on a continuum ranging from exclusion to inclusion" (Kahmann, 2006, p. 186). While the labour movement has a tradition of international solidarity, established workforces have often displayed hostilities towards the inflow of new workers (Castles and Kosack, 1973; Milkman, 2006). The economic rationale for such exclusionist attitudes is to limit the number of workers to keep wages high as "this ensured an artificial scarcity of their specific category of labour so that the 'higgling of the market' operated in their favour" (Hyman, 2001, p. 7). On the other hand, a surplus of workers on which employers can draw tends to have a depressing effect on wages. Furthermore, an untapped pool of non-unionized workers weakens the bargaining position of organized labour. Moreover, employers are often among the most vocal supporters of immigration in their quest for a more "flexible" workforce. Thus, it is assumed that an inflow of migrant labour inevitably strengthens the position of employers *vis-à-vis* organized labour (Avci and McDonald, 2000, pp. 118–119; Goldthorpe, 1984, p. 330).

The recruitment of workers from abroad adds not only to the quantitative supply of labour but also brings about qualitative changes in the workforce. Historically, employers frequently deployed immigrants as strike-breakers which undermined the possibility of effective industrial action (Milkman, 2006, p. 118). As many immigrants are from countries with lower wages and living standards, they tend to be more willing to accept lower wages which in turn could undercut the wages of indigenous workers (Waldinger and Lichter, 2003). Furthermore, as a result of labour migration the workforce becomes more fragmented due to language and cultural differences between native and migrant workers. These differences can be exacerbated by the hostile behaviour among sections of the domestic workforce towards the newcomers. This may lead to a situation in which migrant workers who often come from countries with no strong tradition of trade unionism may be even less inclined to join unions (Castles and Kosack, 1973, p. 128).

1.1. Unions and labour recruitment after World War II

In the light of such concerns, unions generally were less than enthusiastic when most Western European countries began to recruit foreign labour in the 1950s and 1960s. It was not only concerns about their bargaining position but also the fact that unions were part of the "imagined national community" that led them to show some reservations towards an inflow of foreigners (Penninx and Roosblad, 2000). Whatever the reservations held by many unions, it became obvious that resisting the inflow of immigrants was not a viable option. During the "golden age" of capitalism after 1945, most Western European countries experienced an acute shortage of labour as unemployment was at historically low levels. As indigenous workers developed growing aspirations in times of rising educational and living standards, they were less willing to take up low-skilled menial jobs. Hence the import of additional labour became a necessity to sustain continuous economic growth (Kindleberger, 1967).[2]

It is against this background that unions in most countries transformed their initial reservations towards labour migration into a position that if immigration takes place, it should not harm labour relations and employment standards. Hence, unions demanded that migrants should receive the same pay and working conditions as indigenous workers (Castles and Kosack, 1973).[3] Apart from this core demand, trade union responses towards immigration varied considerably across Europe. In some countries unions began to promote the integration of immigrants in the workplace and wider society, but in others they took no initiatives to improve the situation of foreign workers (Cachón and Valles, 2003; Penninx and Roosblad, 2000).

The official labour recruitment programmes came to a halt in 1973 at the time of the oil crisis and ensuing economic recession. Notwithstanding expectations that the "guestworkers" would return to their home countries, a sizeable section of them stayed, brought their families over, and eventually settled down in the host countries (Castles and Miller, 2003). The termination of recruitment programme was supported by unions across Europe. Indeed, in relation to new labour migration, although not necessarily in relation to other forms of migration such as family reunification and asylum-seekers, most trade union movements adopted a rather restrictive stance as unemployment began to rise in the mid-1970s (Penninx and Roosblad, 2000). However, there is some evidence to suggest that more recently, in the context of globalization and EU enlargement, unions have re-examined their position on new labour migration.

1.2. Unions and new immigration in the "global age"

Processes of globalization are not only characterized by an increase in cross-border flows of capital, goods, services, and information but also by more people crossing boundaries (Held et al., 1999). This, as some writers argue, is increasingly accepted by the representatives of organized labour. As there is a growing realization that the movement of people is an inextricable part of globalization, "zero immigration" is no longer regarded as a feasible or, for that matter, desirable policy option. Instead unions place greater emphasis on the organization of migrants as "an alternative strategy to restrictionism for improving wages and work conditions" (Haus, 2002, p. 7; see also Avci and McDonald, 2000; Milkman, 2006; Watts, 2002).

The change in union policy came along for both ideological and strategic reasons. As unions are "value-rational organizations" (Frege et al., 2004, p. 143), they are in part driven by ideological convictions that are open to change. Haus (2002), for instance, argues that more inclusive policies towards immigrants are linked not only to processes of economic globalization but also to the internationalization of human rights. The latter have led unions to show "greater normative concern for the rights of migrants in their role as human beings than did their counterparts in the early twentieth century" (Haus, 2002, p. 37). These concerns for the rights of immigrants are not necessarily confined to migrants "at work", as some trade unions have been increasingly critical of aspects of restrictive government policies on asylum-seekers as well (Kühne, 2000, p. 53). Overall, unions have become more receptive to issues of racial discrimination which has led many trade union movements in Europe to adopt policies on anti-racism (Avci and McDonald, 2000; ETUC, 2003).[4]

However, it is not only ideational change within trade unionism that has led them to reconsider their immigration preferences. As trade unions are reflective actors who aim to pursue the best interests of their members, they have to make "strategic choices" (Kochan et al., 1986) about new challenges. As there is a growing sense of the inevitability of immigration, some union officials no longer believe that their interests are best served by restrictive immigration policies. Such policies may channel even more migrants into the underground economy, which would further undermine established labour standards (Avci and McDonald, 2000; Watts, 2002). The following statement by the European Trade Union Confederation (ETUC) is emblematic of this thinking:

In recent years many EU member states have adopted very restrictive asylum policies and *"zero immigration"* policies especially with regard to low-skilled workers and as a result offered European Citizens a false sense of protection. In doing so, they have *increased the pressure* at the EU's external borders and the number of illegal immigrants...in EU labour markets.

(ETUC, 2005, pp. 3–4, emphasis in original)

In particular the accession of eight countries from Central and Eastern Europe to the EU in 2004 has created a new dynamic of labour migration in Europe (Tamas and Münz, 2006). In such circumstances, the continuation of transitional restrictions in some Western European countries may simply lead to an increase in rather precarious forms of migration including posted workers, "bogus" self-employment, and irregular work as alternative means of accessing labour markets, as some trade union leaders are well aware (Krings, 2009).

Restrictive immigration policies may not only channel migrants into more precarious employment which in turn could undermine existing labour standards, but may be also detrimental to the aim of organizing migrants (Watts, 2002). As unions face the decline of their traditional core membership, they increasingly aim to organize new sections of the workforce that have not featured as prominently on the radar of the labour movement in the past. These previously untapped groups of employees include, besides the young and women, migrant workers. Previous assumptions about the inherent impossibility of unionizing migrants have given way to the view that if unions adjust their organizing campaigns to the needs of migrant workers, such campaigns can be quite successful (Bronfenbrenner et al., 1998; Milkman, 2006). Thus, unions are in their greater emphasis on the organization of migrant workers not only driven by normative concerns but also by self-interest: the organization of migrant workers could stop a decline in union membership and offer protection against the further erosion of labour standards.

These studies shed some important insights on the changing immigration preferences of unions in the "global age". However, as the research is mainly confined to the US and the Mediterranean countries, the generalizability of the argument is somewhat limited. To further explore whether union attitudes towards immigration have changed, I now examine trade union responses to migrant labour in Austria, Germany, Ireland, and the UK. By drawing on qualitative interviews with union representatives as well as documentary analysis (Table 5.1), I show that "zero immigration" is no longer regarded as a viable policy option. This view, however, does not make unions favour "open door" policies. Instead their immigration preferences are best captured by the concept

Table 5.1   List of consulted trade unions

Austria
ÖGB *Österreichischer Gewerkschaftsbund*
GBH *Gewerkschaft Bau-Holz*
HGPD *Hotel, Gastgewerbe, Persönlicher Dienst* (now Vida)
GMT-N *Gewerkschaft Metall-Textil-Nahrung*

Britain
TUC Trades Union Congress
TGWU Transport and General Workers Union (now Unite)
GMB
UCATT *Union of Construction, Allied Trades and Technicians*
USDAW *Union of Shop, Distributive and Allied Workers*

Germany
DGB *Deutscher Gewerkschaftsbund*
IG BAU *Industriegewerkschaft Bauen, Agrar und Umwelt*
IG Metall
Ver.di *Vereinigte Dienstleistungsgewerkschaft*
NGG *Nahrung-Genuss-Gaststätten*

Ireland
ICTU *Irish Congress of Trade Unions*
SIPTU *Services, Industrial, Professional and Technical Union*
Mandate
UCATT *Union of Construction, Allied Trades and Technicians*

---

of "managed migration" that opens up avenues for legal immigration from outside the EEA.

2. Trade union responses to non-EEA immigration

2.1. Britain

In Britain, immigration policy has been comprehensively overhauled with the introduction of a points-based system as part of the Government's "managed migration" approach. The new system which came into force in 2007 is based on a five-tier framework. The first two tiers aim to attract highly skilled migrants who have unrestricted access to the labour market upon arrival and the prospect of permanent residency after 2 years as well as skilled workers with a job offer in the UK who may qualify for settlement after 2 years. In turn, tiers three to five (low-skilled workers, students, youth mobility, and temporary migrants allowed to work for primarily non-economic reasons) are designed to foster temporary migration where migrants are expected to leave the UK after a certain period of stay (Home Office 2006).

The British trade union movement, while stressing that "migrant workers make a major contribution to Britain's economic and cultural life", agrees that there is a "need for an objective system for determining whether people are allowed to enter the UK to work, in the interests of migrant workers and the wider community" (TUC, 2007a). It therefore supports a system of "managed migration", but is adamant that such a system "should ensure equal rights for people at work whether they are indigenous or migrant workers" (TUC, 2005, p. 2). While welcoming parts of the new points-based system, the TUC expressed concerns about those measures that are seen as counter-productive to a rights-based approach to migration. Particular concerns have been expressed about "any managed migration scheme that restricts workers to a particular employer or sector as it may leave them more vulnerable than indigenous workers who have no such restrictions" (TUC, 2005, p. 7).

Furthermore, the TUC has expressed concern about the distinction made between high-skilled migrants who are offered a route towards permanent settlement and low-skilled migrants who are allowed in only on a temporary basis under tier three of the new scheme. According to the TUC, "[t]he condition that tier 3 workers should have no dependents is offensive – this is a 'guest-workers' scheme – and contradicts concepts of family reunification" (TUC, 2005, p. 8). Such measures would "deter integration and contribute to a two-tier workforce" (TUC 2005, p. 8). Instead, the TUC demands "better measures to aid integration into the UK for migrant workers" (TUC, 2005, p. 10) which should not be confined to non-EU migrants but should also be open to migrants from the new EU member states in particular.

In this regard, unions attach particular relevance to the issue of language training as John Hannett, General Secretary of the USDAW, points out: "Improving language skills at no cost is without doubt one of the keys to fully integrating migrants into their workplaces and also into the wider community in which they and their family live" (USDAW, 2006). Hence unions were particularly opposed to plans to scrap the availability of free English lessons for Speakers of Other Languages (ESOL):

> We have got a particular battle on at the moment about the languages that used to be automatically free to workers and the Government has just announced that will no longer be the case. We have been using ESOL and access to ESOL as part of our organizing campaigns in that people need to be able to read about their rights in order to exercise them. So we are very concerned that the removal of that free entitlement will disadvantage especially lower-paid migrant workers.
>
> (Interview, TUC, 2006)

Thus, the issue of integration is often linked to work-related matters. It is perhaps less of a surprise that for unions the issue of integration and work feature quite prominently. This is not confined to migrant workers but also extends to other groups of immigrants such as asylum-seekers. At its annual conference in 2004, the TUC agreed "to continue to press for asylum seekers to be granted the right to work legally in the UK while their applications are being processed. This right would bring valuable benefits to society and the economy, as well as to asylum seekers themselves" (TUC, 2004). This position should be seen in the context of the particular situation of asylum-seekers whose cases often go on for years and who sometimes engage in irregular work during this time. Instead, unions prefer asylum-seekers to be allowed to work regularly which is seen as the best way to ensure that established labour standards are not undermined. Furthermore, the TUC committed itself "to the human right of those fleeing persecution to seek refuge and condemns those governments, including the UK Government, who impose increasingly restrictive immigration and asylum legislation" (TUC, 2004).

Thus, the British trade union movement advocates a rights-based approach to the management of migration and recognizes that the UK will continue to require immigration at different skill levels due to a skill and labour shortage in some employment sectors. At the same time, however, the TUC stresses that in some instances "the labour shortages which exist are due to the low levels of pay and conditions on offer" (TUC, 2005, p. 3). Thus, there is clearly a belief that if working conditions are improved, domestic workers would be quite willing to take on more jobs in the low-wage sectors which are currently difficult to fill. Moreover, unions are adamant that migration alone cannot be a solution to skill shortages in sectors such as construction. According to a UCATT representative:

> There has been an underinvestment in training in the UK workforce for a number of years, the apprenticeship scheme is not as strong as it was twenty to thirty years ago. We believe that this is contributing to the reason why construction companies are turning to migrant workers today. So we think it is a short-term solution, there can't be a guarantee that the workers working in the UK today will be here tomorrow.
>
> (Interview, UCATT, 2006)

In spite of these reservations about *how* migrant labour is utilized by some employers to drive down working conditions or to abdicate training responsibilities, British unions have repeatedly stressed the benefits, economic and otherwise, that migration brings to the UK. Indeed, in a statement on the "Economics of Migration" the TUC has been quite emphatic that:

> immigration does not have a negative impact: overall levels of employment and wages are slightly higher as a result of immigration, and migrant workers pay more in taxes than the value of the public services they receive... the old accusations of the extreme right, that immigrants take native workers' jobs or are a drain on the welfare state, are as false as they have ever been.
>
> (TUC, 2007b, p. 28)

The British trade union movement recognizes that the UK will continue to need immigration not only from within the enlarged EU but also from further afield. If migration takes place, unions prefer a form of migration that is based on equal rights for migrant workers to prevent the emergence of a two-tier workforce. Further, British unions have repeatedly taken a stance against anti-immigration forces in society and have pointed to the positive impact of immigration upon the UK.

2.2. Ireland

As in Britain, Ireland has recently seen a comprehensive overhaul of immigration legislation, pertaining to both economic migration and other aspects of immigration including asylum and residency rights. With the 2006 Employment Permits Act, Ireland has introduced a "Green Card scheme" for occupations where, according to Minister Micheál Martin, "we have strategically important high level skills shortages" (DETE, 2007). At the same time, the new Act limits work permits to a restricted list of occupations. Thus, the expectation among the Irish government is that future non-EEA immigration should be mainly of the high-skilled variety whereas demand for less-skilled jobs should be met by migrants from within the enlarged EU (NESC, 2006). Furthermore, in 2008 the Immigration, Residence and Protection Bill has been published which replaces previous immigration legislation and sets out the terms and conditions under which foreign nationals can enter the state, their entitlements as well as residency rights (DJELR, 2008).

The Irish trade union movement was broadly welcoming of the attempt by the Irish government to introduce a policy of "managed migration". As unions had long demanded an "end to the work permit system held by the employer, which is no better than bonded labour or slavery" (ICTU, 2005, p. 5), they welcomed in particular provisions in the Employment Permits Act which allow migrants to apply and reapply for their own permit. At the same time, unions have expressed disappointment that the new legislation does not provide for a proper Green Card system. Although, as mentioned, the Employment Permits Act introduces a "Green Card scheme", the ICTU notes that "[p]ermanent residence, on entry to the country, is the essential feature of a green card. There are no provisions whatsoever... to support the introduction of such a scheme" (ICTU, 2008, p. 7).[5] In relation to the Immigration, Residence and Protection Bill, the ICTU demands that migrants should be eligible to apply for a long-term residence permit after two instead of 5 years as currently provided by the legislation. The main rationale for this is to ensure that migrants are less vulnerable at work:

> It is likely that workers conscious of the need to remain in work on the permit, will cooperate with any and all request of the employer, no matter how unreasonable. Workers will be reluctant to speak out as their access to the Long Term Residence Permit will rely on the ongoing renewal of their employment permit.
>
> (ICTU, 2008, p. 8)

Thus, the Irish trade union movement favours immigration policies which offer the option of permanent residence for immigrants. This should be combined with an emphasis on integration where, according to a SIPTU representative, the government

> ha[s] to do a lot more to help people integrate into Irish society and make sure that they avoid ghettoizing people... If they come, we should make every effort to make them welcome, to help them to integrate into Irish society, to help them with language skills and so on.
>
> (Interview, SIPTU, 2006)

In this regard, unions expressed some disappointment that the new Immigration, Residence and Protection Bill does not include provisions for family reunification. This is regarded as important for a successful integration process as "immigration is fundamentally a human activity and the decision to admit migrant workers is closely associated to admitting family migrants" (ICTU, 2006, p. 7). The issue of integration has also acquired more prominence as part of the social partnership process. Not only have the social partners, notably the ICTU and the Irish Business and Employers Confederation, been involved in initiatives such as the "Anti-Racism Workplace Week" that aim to promote an intercultural workplace, but also the partnership agreement *Towards 2016* includes some integration measures such as the provision of extra language support teachers (Department of the Taoiseach, 2006, p. 43). Furthermore, the ICTU demands easier labour market access for asylum-seekers:

> The Irish Congress of Trade Unions strongly supports…the right to work after six months for asylum seekers whose applications remain unprocessed. To force human beings, who are strangers in need, to remain idle for an indeterminate period of time is a denial of their fundamental human rights.
>
> (Irish Refugee Council, 2001)

Thus, Irish unions promote a "rights based immigration system" (ICTU, 2008, p. 3) which includes, perhaps less surprisingly from a trade union perspective, the right to work. In spite of an acknowledgement that non-EU immigration is likely to continue into Ireland, unions are anxious that immigration should not be utilized by employers to drive down wages and employment conditions. In that regard unions demand a more rigorous labour market test to establish labour shortages. To ensure that employers do not prefer migrant to indigenous workers, the ICTU demands that the job to be filled is "advertised at the 'going rate for the job' and with established conditions and skill levels" (ICTU, 2008, p. 4). Thus, migrant workers should only be recruited into those sectors that have a genuine labour shortage. This would require "sector-specific strategies to manage migration that involve trade unions, employers and Government" (ICTU, 2008, p. 4). The Irish trade union movement therefore promotes a system of managed migration that tries to open up possibilities for legal immigration from non-EEA countries while at the same time trying to ensure that migrants are not recruited to drive down conditions of employment. In this, unions try to balance the economic needs of Ireland with an emphasis on the human rights of migrants including those of asylum-seekers and irregular migrants.

2.3. Germany

In Germany, trade unions were part of the Independent Commission on Immigration which proposed a new immigration and integration policy at the turn of the century. In its final report, the Commission unambiguously stated that Germany has long been a country of immigration, in spite of official denials. It also found that Germany will continue to need immigration for both economic and demographic reasons (Unabhängige Kommission "Zuwanderung", 2001). The proposals of the Commission for a new immigration policy, however, were watered down in the eventual 2005 Immigration Act. For instance, while the Commission on Immigration had proposed a points-based system akin to the one in Canada, the new Act only allows for the permanent immigration of some categories of highly skilled immigrants.

While welcoming aspects of the Act, trade unions were critical that it does not herald "a change of perspective in migration policies" (DGB, 2004, p. 5).[6] Unions were particularly critical that the new Act does not allow for a new politics of labour migration, as it leaves the official recruitment stop of 1973 in place. At first glance, such a critique may come as a surprise, taking into account that at the time of the enactment of the recruitment stop, unions were one of its supporters. However, while unions continue to insist that the "reduction of unemployment and further education have to have priority over the recruitment of labour" (DGB, 2003, p. 2), there is increasingly an unease about the official recruitment stop. On the one hand, an analysis of the ageing of German society and the social security systems has led to a more open attitude towards new immigration in light of a declining working population (DGB, 2001). On the other hand, a DGB representative pointed out that the recruitment stop has increasingly proven to be impractical and ineffective:

> The recruitment stop with its many rules of exception (*Ausnahmeverordnungen*) hasn't delivered on what we thought it would at that time. Instead the recruitment stop led to measures linked to the legal position of foreigners which, we believe, are rather detrimental not least for trade unions... If you look at the options (for migration, T.K.) today, you will see that the main focus is not on the immigration of employees and their families, but on the temporary deployment of employees, whereby family reunification and a permanent stay is not possible.
>
> (Interview, DGB, 2006)

As the number of temporary labour migrants who entered Germany as contract workers, seasonal workers, or as part of the EU freedom of services significantly grew during the 1990s,[7] the DGB increasingly talked about the "fiction of the recruitment stop" (DGB, 2004, p. 8). Moreover, what became an issue of particular concern to unions was that some of these new forms of labour migration, particularly the temporary posting of workers, were linked to incidents of wage dumping and job displacement (interview, IG BAU, 2006; interview, NGG, 2006). It is against this background that unions re-evaluated their immigration preferences in favour of a system of managed migration that should entail the right to a permanent stay from the very beginning: "The trade unions and the German Trade Union Confederation stand for a policy of managed immigration. They prefer regular, permanent immigration to the temporary deployment of posted employees" (DGB, 2001). Thus, unions view a form of long-term immigration that offers the prospect of integration in the workplace and wider society as preferable to temporary labour migration during which migrants do not become integrated in the workforce on par with domestic workers.

Such a new immigration system, unions are adamant, has to be managed "to avoid negative consequences for the employment of domestic workers" (*Arbeitsmarktinländer*), whereby the DGB defines domestic workers as "all persons who have equal access to the labour market, including, among others, German citizens, EU citizens and third-country nationals with a status of permanent residency" (DGB, 2001). Unions are particularly anxious that employers do not utilize migrant labour from abroad at the expense of vocational training and qualification in Germany. To some extent, this can provide a dilemma to unions as one DGB representative reasons:

> In light of significant unemployment and a lack of apprenticeship particularly for people with a background of migration, how do we get business to live up to its training responsibilities, and do not provide them with tools in the form of immigration through which they can compensate for a decline in vocational qualification in the domestic labour market.
>
> (Interview, DGB, 2006)

Hence the main criteria for a system of managed migration should be the middle- to long-term prospect of the labour market. To establish the number of labour migrants on the basis of a points-based system, it is suggested that the government should consult with the social partners (DGB, 2003, p. 2). What is of particular importance for unions is that immigration should be accompanied by measures that facilitate the integration of migrants, whereas integration is understood as "the comprehensive participation in political, social and working life" (IG Metall, 2007, p. 6). The view that "immigration requires integration" has been articulated in a joint statement by the DGB and the Confederation of German Employer Associations (BDA) in which the social partners demand, among other things, an increase of language support for migrants and easier access to the labour market (DGB and BDA, 2004).

Unions are keen to stress that integration measures such as language training and educational and vocational support should not be confined to new immigrants but should also be open to long-term foreign residents. As regards the latter, unions demand that all migrants who have been in Germany for longer than 5 years, regardless of their status, should be granted permanent residence. As for those migrants who have been in Germany for longer than a year, they should be entitled to a limited residence permit "which should include equal access to the labour market" (DGB, 2004, p. 6). The DGB is adamant that this should also apply to asylum-seekers and, consequently, demands that a general ban on paid employment for the latter group should be abandoned (DGB, 2003, p. 2). Further, unions argue that the need to continue to provide asylum to people fleeing war or political persecution should be viewed separately from any discussion on possible quotas for labour migration. Hence unions demand adherence to the 1951 Geneva Refugee Convention including protection in the case of non-state and gender-specific persecution (DGB, 2003; IG Metall, 2007). Thus, the German trade union movement combines a relatively liberal policy on asylum-seekers and refugees with support for a policy of managed labour migration that should create opportunities for long-term immigration as opposed to the temporary posting of workers.

2.4. Austria

In contrast to Germany, debate in Austria on a new immigration and integration policy has so far featured less prominently. In spite of a substantial immigrant population which accounts for over 13 per cent of the population, Austria continues to see itself as not being a country of immigration (NCPA, 2003). In terms of labour migration, the Austrian "guestworker system", based on the principle of "rotation", was strongly defended by the Austrian trade union movement in the past. It is only since the 1990s that unions have increasingly recognized that a settlement process has gradually taken place. This was also the time when unions began to talk about the need for integration measures, without necessarily pushing this issue to the top of their agenda in the social partnership process which has a considerable influence on the formulation of Austrian social policy (Bauböck and Wimmer, 1988; Gächter, 2000).

In recent years, unions have become critical of temporary labour migration programmes, arguing that such programmes are lacking an integration perspective. According to one representative of the HGPD, "we were extremely opposed to the seasonal labour rules because these do not facilitate the integration at the workplace. At a time when Switzerland has abolished the seasonal labour rules, Austria has introduced them!" (interview, HGPD, 2006). Such sentiments have been echoed by the ÖGB when commenting on a set of new proposed EU directives on labour migration:

> These regulations – geared towards temporary migration – could potentially lead to an increase in precarious employment relations. Models of migration which are based on the principle of rotation and only entail short- to middle-term residence stand in opposition to an effective policy of integration.
>
> (ÖGB, 2007, p. 13)

Thus, as in other countries, Austrian unions are increasingly uneasy with temporary migrant worker programmes, arguing that such programmes lack an integration perspective. However, in contrast to other countries, the Austrian trade union movement has so far provided few proposals on how to open up avenues for long-term immigration from outside the EU. While it is clear that unions have become more outspoken about the rights of long-term foreign residents, the impression remains that they have retained a rather defensive approach towards new immigration. Unions are adamant that the training and qualification of the domestic workforce has to have priority over the recruitment of foreign labour and have therefore repeatedly rejected calls by employer associations to increase the quota for qualified labour from abroad: "To support and train Austrian labour has to be the first step to ameliorate the shortage of qualified labour, before an increase in the labour contingent from abroad can be considered" (GBH, 2006). While unions agree that immigration is likely to continue, they have few policies in place on how to open up avenues for legal immigration beyond a recognition that it is likely that most of the future labour migration to Austria will issue from the new EU member states from Central and Eastern Europe (interview, ÖGB, 2007; interview, GMT/N, 2007).

In terms of policies on asylum, a representative of the ÖGB is adamant that "we don't want 'Fortress Europe'. We can have as many war ships in the Mediterranean Sea as we like to displace those guys from Senegal, that is not the solution of the problem" (interview, ÖGB, 2007). Hence the trade union confederation demands asylum and refugee policies that are in "accordance with humanitarian principles and the rule of law", including easier access to the labour market for asylum-seekers (ÖGB, 2007, p. 19). Thus, the trade union movement in Austria has become more receptive to the rights of long-term immigrants and asylum-seekers. Moreover, trade unions, in conjunction with employer associations and other stakeholders have published policy proposals on the integration of long-term immigrants, among which language support for foreign residents and their children feature prominently (ÖGB 2008). This is quite an important development, taking into account that in "corporatist Austria" the issue of foreign labour did not feature prominently on the social partnership agenda in the past (Bauböck and Wimmer, 1988). At the same time, however, the Austrian trade union movement has come up with few policy proposals that could open up possibilities for legal immigration for people from outside the EEA. While there is no longer an appetite for temporary "guestworker" programmes which are seen as counter-productive to integration, there are few ideas on how to actively "manage" a system of non-EU immigration. Hence the impression remains that Austrian unions have largely adopted a defensive approach to new immigration.

3. Conclusion: Trade unions, "managed migration" and the quest for integration

This chapter has examined union responses to immigration from outside the EEA. Across Europe, there is a growing recognition among unions that even in the wake of EU enlargement, Western European countries will continue to require non-EU immigration, not only for economic reasons but also increasingly because of the demographic development in Europe. This view does not make unions favour "open door" policies. Instead the immigration preferences of the British, German, Irish, and indeed most other European trade union movement is best captured by the concept of "managed migration" that opens up avenues for legal immigration from outside the EEA (Pajares, 2008). Such a system should ensure that labour migration takes place in response to genuine skill and labour shortages to avoid a situation in which employers could prefer migrants to domestic workers and abdicate their training responsibilities.

The concept of "managed migration" as promoted by unions goes hand in hand with an emphasis on employment and other political and social rights for migrants, including asylum-seekers. If migration takes place, unions prefer a form of rights-based immigration that should be accompanied by policies that facilitate the integration of the newcomers. The main rationale for this, it seems, is that migrants who become integrated in the workplace and wider society are less likely to undermine labour standards and may be more willing to join trade unions. Consequently, unions demand that immigration should be accompanied by family reunification and integration measures such as language training. Indeed, unions are adamant that such integration support should also be open to EU migrants and long-time foreign residents who sometimes are not included in official integration policies.

Thus, trade unions promote a rights-based form of "managed migration" that should entail the option of permanent residency from the very beginning. However, in their preference for long-term immigration unions face the dilemma that there is a renewed commitment by policy-makers to temporary migrant worker programmes (TMWPs). Throughout the 1990s, many Western European countries have introduced new TMWPs to meet the demand for additional labour, both skilled and less-skilled (Castles, 2006). At the European level, the EU Commission has published its "Policy Plan on Legal Migration" in 2005 which proposes four new EU directives covering different aspects of labour migration (European Commission, 2005). With its emphasis on circular migration, this policy initiative creates a new framework for temporary labour migration.

It therefore appears that the ability of unions to influence migration policy both at the European and the national level is limited. This is due in part to the declining political clout of unions. In a country like the UK the political influence of unions has been in decline for quite some time. However, even in "neocorporatist" Austria where until recently unions had considerable input in the political process, their ability to influence public policy issues outside of the area of collective bargaining is waning (Blaschke, 2006). Further, although unions in most countries now support a system of "managed migration", they do not regard this as an issue to which they would attach particular importance (Menz 2009, p. 263). This might be due to the fact that although unions recognize that population movements are a part of globalization and EU enlargement, a certain ambiguity towards new immigration remains, particularly in times of rising unemployment. To conclude, it seems likely that in the years ahead a system of "managed migration" will be established at the level of the EU. However, whether such a system will reflect the policy preferences of unions for a rights-based migration policy that opens up new channels for permanent immigration remains more doubtful.

Notes

1. The EEA encompasses all EU countries as well as Iceland, Norway, and Liechtenstein. For a comparative analysis of union policies in relation to intra-European migration in the context of recent EU enlargement see Krings (2009).
2. It should be noted however that not all countries opted for a "guestworker" strategy to increase the labour force during the post-World War II period of economic growth. Social democratic welfare states such as Sweden implemented policies, in particular childcare policies, to encourage higher female labour force participation (Naumann, 2005).
3. In reality, however, immigrants usually worked in the lower, or lowest segments of the labour market with little prospect of upward mobility. Nevertheless, their social rights in the workplace where often more advanced than their political rights particularly in countries like Germany where the reformed *Betriebsverfassungsgesetz* (Works Constitutional Act) of 1972 enshrined the principle of equal treatment regardless of descent, religion, nationality, or ethnic origin (Hunger 2001, p. 42).
4. However, Jeffrey and Ouali (2007) point out that there is often a gap between these policies agreed on at the national level and the often only half-hearted implementation of them at the workplace level.
5. Under the Irish scheme, a Green Card is initially issued for 2 years after which a recipient has the right to apply for permanent residence.
6. All citations from union documents and interviews with German and Austrian unions have been translated into English by the author.
7. The number of these temporary migrants, who entered Germany as part of the *Anwerbestoppausnahmeverordnung* (Regulation on the exception from the recruitment stop) averaged 350,000 annually at the beginning of the twenty-first century (Tamas and Münz 2006, p. 140).

References

Avci, G. and McDonald, C. (2000) "Chipping away at the fortress: unions, immigration and the transnational labour market", *International Migration*, 38(2): 191–213.

Bauböck, R. and Wimmer, H. (1988) "Social partnership and 'foreigners policy': On special features of Austria's guestworker system", *European Journal of Political Research*, 16(6): 659–681.

Blaschke, S. (2006) "Restructuring as a reaction to growing pressure on trade unionism: the case of the Austrian ÖGB", *Industrial Relations Journal*, 37(2): 147–163.

Bronfenbrenner, K., Freidman, S., Hurd, R., Oswald, R.A., and Seeber, R.L. (eds.) (1998) *Organizing to Win: New Research on Union Strategies* (Ithaca, NY: ILR Press).

Cachón, L. and Valles, M.S. (2003) "Trade Unionism and immigration: Interpreting old and new dilemmas", *Transfer*, 12(3): 469–482.

Castells, M. (2000) *The Rise of the Network Society*, 2nd edn (Oxford: Blackwell).

Castles, S. (2006) *Back to the Future? Can Europe Meet its Labour Needs through Temporary Migration?* IMI Working Paper No. 1. (Oxford: International Migration Institute).

Castles, S. and Kosack, G. (1973) *Immigrant Workers and Class Structure in Western Europe* (London: Oxford University Press).

Castles, S. and Miller, M.J. (2003) *The Age of Migration: International Population Movements in the Modern World*, 3rd edn (Basingstoke/New York: Palgrave Macmillan).

Department of Enterprise, Trade and Employment (DETE) (2007) "Address by Minister for Enterprise, Trade and Employment Mr. Micheál Martin, T.D. at the launch of the New Employment Permits Arrangements including the Green Card Scheme", available at http://www.entemp.ie/press/2007/20070124a.htm (accessed October 2008).

Department of Justice, Equality and Law Reform (DJELR) (2008) "Launch of new Immigration Bill", available at http://www.justice.ie/en/JELR/Pages/Launch%20of%20new%20Immigration%20Bill (accessed October 2008).

Department of the Taoiseach (2006) *Towards 2016: Ten-Year Framework Social Partnership Agreement 2006–2015* (Dublin: Stationary Office).

DGB (2001) "Grundsätze des Deutschen Gewerkschaftsbundes für die Regelung der Einwanderung", available at http://www.dgb.de/themen/migration/dokumente/zuw-grunds.pdf (accessed October 2008).

DGB (2003) *Kernforderungen des Deutschen Gewerkschaftsbundes für einen Perspektivenwechsel in der Einwanderungs- und Integrationspolitik* (Berlin: Deutscher Gewerkschaftsbund).

DGB (2004) "Eine unendliche Geschichte: Das Zuwanderungsgesetz: Ein Rückschritt in der Einwanderungs- und Integrationspolitik?", available at http://www.dgb.de/themen/migration/dokumente/stllgn_gesetz.pdf (accessed October 2008).

DGB and BDA (2004) "Gemeinsame Erklärung von Michael Sommer, Vorsitzender des Deutschen Gewerkschaftsbundes (DGB) und Dr. Dieter Hundt, Präsident der Bundesvereinigung der Deutschen Arbeitgeberverbände (BDA): Miteinander statt Nebeneinander – Integration durch Fördern und Fordern", available at http://www.dgb.de/themen/themen_a_z/abisz_doks/g/gem_erkl_integration.pdf (accessed October 2008).

European Commission (2005) *Policy Plan on Legal Migration*, COM (2005) 669 final, Brussels, 21.12.2005.

ETUC (2003) *Migrant and Ethnic Workers: Challenges to Trade Unions* (Brussels: European Trade Union Confederation).

ETUC (2005) "Towards a Pro-active EU Policy on Migration and Integration: ETUC response to the Commission's Green paper on a EU Approach to Managing Economic Migration", available at http://www.etuc.org/a/1159 (accessed October 2008).

Favell, A. and Hansen, R. (2002) "Markets against politics: Migration, EU enlargement and the idea of Europe", *Journal of Ethnic and Migration Studies*, 28(4): 581–601.

Ferner, A., Quintanilla, J., and Sánchez-Runde, C. (eds.) (2006) *Multinationals, Institutions and the Construction of Transnational Practices* (Basingstoke/New York: Palgrave MacMillan).

Frege, C., Heery, E., and Turner, L. (2004) "The new solidarity? Trade union coalition-building in five countries", in Frege, C. and Kelly, J. (eds.) *Varieties of Unionism: Strategies for Union Revitalization in a Globalizing Economy* (Oxford: Oxford University Press).

Gächter, A. (2000) "Austria: Protecting indigenous workers from immigrants", in Penninx, R. and Roosblad, J. (eds.) *Trade Unions, Immigration, and Immigrants in Europe, 1960–1993: A Comparative Study of the Attitudes and Actions of the Trade Unions in Seven West European Countries* (Oxford: Berghahn Books).

GBH (2006) "GBH Bundesvorstand: Auf neue Bundesregierung warten zahlreiche wichtige Aufgaben: Politik der sozialen Kälte wurde abgewählt, nun ist Politik für Arbeitnehmer gefragt", available at http://www.oegb.at/servlet/ContentServer?pagename=OEGBZ/Page/OEGBZ_Index&n=OEGBZ_9.1.a& cid=1165837175178 (accessed April 2007).

Goldthorpe, J.H. (ed.) (1984): *Order and Conflict in Contemporary Capitalism* (Oxford: Clarendon).

Haus, L.A. (2002) *Unions, Immigration, and Internationalization: New Challenges and Changing Coalitions in the United States and France* (New York/Basingstoke: Palgrave Macmillan).

Held, D., McGrew, A., Goldblatt, D., and Perraton, J. (1999) *Global Transformations: Politics, Economics and Culture* (Cambridge: Polity).

Hoffmann, J. (ed.) (2002) *The Solidarity Dilemma: Globalisation, Europeanisation and the Trade Unions* (Brussels: European Trade Union Institute).

Home Office (2006) *A Points-Based System: Making Migration Work for Britain*, available at http://www.homeoffice.gov.uk/documents/command-points-based-migration?view=Binary (accessed October 2008).

Hunger, U. (2001) "Betriebliche Exklusion von Migranten in der Bauwirtschaft. Ein neues Modell der Ausländerbeschäftigung für Deutschland?" in Hunger, U. and Hinken, G. (eds.) *Inklusion and Exklusion: Migrantinnen und Migranten auf dem deutschen Arbeitsmarkt. Drei Fallstudien: Metallindustrie, Bauwirtschaft, IT-Sektor* (Münster: Arbeitsstelle Interkulturelle Pädagogik).

Hyman, R. (2001) *Understanding European Trade Unionism: Between Market, Class and Society* (London: Sage Publications).

ICTU (2005) *Migration Policy and the Rights of Workers* (Dublin: Irish Congress of Trade Unions).

ICTU (2006) *Observations and Recommendations on the Application of Transitional Measures on the Accession of Bulgaria and Romania to the EU on 1st January 2007* (Dublin: Irish Congress of Trade Unions).

ICTU (2008) "Observations and Recommendations on the Immigration, Residence and Protection Bill 2008", available at http://www.ictu.ie/download/pdf/immigration_bill_apr_08.pdf (accessed October 2008).

IG Metall (2007) "Migrationspolitisches Forderungs- und Arbeitspapier der IG Metall", available at http://www.igmetall.de/cps/rde/xbcr/internet/docs_ig_metall_xcms_25502__2.pdf (accessed October 2008).

Irish Refugee Council (2001) "The right to work = the right to dignity", available at http://www.irishrefugeecouncil.ie/press01/righttoworkdignitypr.html (accessed October 2008).

Jeffrey, S. and Ouali, N. (2007) "Trade unions and racism in London, Brussels and Paris public transport", *Industrial Relations Journal*, 38(5): 406–422.

Kahmann, M. (2006) "The posting of workers in the German construction industry: Responses and problems of trade union action", *Transfer*, 12(2): 183–196.

Kindleberger, C.L. (1967): *Europe's Postwar Growth* (Cambridge: Harvard University Press).

Kochan, T., Katz, H.C., and McKersie, R.B. (1986) *The Transformation of American Industrial Relations* (New York: Basic Books).

Krings, T. (2009) "A race to the bottom? Trade unions, EU enlargement and the free movement of labour", *European Journal of Industrial Relations*, 15(1): 49–69.

Kühne, P. (2000): "The Federal Republic of Germany: Ambivalent promotion of immigrants' interests", in Penninx, R. and Roosblad, J. (eds.) *Trade Unions, Immigration, and Immigrants in Europe, 1960–1993: A Comparative Study of the Attitudes and Actions of the Trade Unions in Seven West European Countries* (Oxford: Berghahn Books).

McGovern, P. (2007) "Immigration, labour markets and employment relations: Problems and prospects", *British Journal of Industrial Relations*, 45(2): 217–235.

Menz, G. (2005) *Varieties of Capitalism and Europeanization: National Response Strategies to the Single European Market* (Oxford: Oxford University Press).

Menz, G. (2009) *The Political Economy of Managed Migration: Nonstate Actors, Europeanization and the Politics of Designing Migration Policies* (Oxford: Oxford University Press).

Milkman, R. (2006) *L.A. Story: Immigrant Workers and the Future of the U.S. Labour Movement* (New York: Russell Sage Foundation).

National Contact Point Austria (NCPA) (2003) *The Impact of Immigration on Austria's Society* (Vienna: International Organization for Migration/European Migration Network).

National Economic and Social Council (NESC) (2006) *Migration Policy* (Dublin: NESC).

Naumann, I.K. (2005) "Child care and feminism in West Germany and Sweden in the 1960s and 1970s", *Journal of European Social Policy*, 15(1): 47–63.

ÖGB (2007) *Internationales und Europapolitik (Angenommene Anträge, beschlossen am 16. ÖGB Bundeskongress)* (Vienna: Österreichischer Gewerkschaftsbund).

ÖGB (2008) "Vorschläge für ein Maßnahmenpaket der Bundesregierung zur Integration", available at http://www.oegb.at/servlet/ContentServer?pagename=OEGBZ/page/OEGBZ_Index&n=OEGBZ_1.a&cid=1214133034306 (accessed April 2008).

Organisation for Economic Co-operation and Development (OECD) (2007) *International Migration Outlook 2007* (Paris: OECD).

Pajares, M. (2008) "Foreign workers and trade unions: The challenges posed", *Transfer*, 14(4): 607–624.

Penninx, R. and Roosblad, J. (eds.) (2000) *Trade Unions, Immigration, and Immigrants in Europe, 1960–1993: A Comparative Study of the Attitudes and Actions of the Trade Unions in Seven West European Countries* (Oxford: Berghahn Books).

Piore, M.J. (1979) *Birds of Passage: Migrant Labour and Industrial Societies* (Cambridge: Cambridge University Press).

Rigby, M., Smith, R., and Lawlor, T. (eds.) (1999) *European Trade Unions: Change and Response* (London/New York: Routledge).

Tamas, K. and Münz, R. (2006) *Labour Migrants Unbound? EU Enlargement, Transitional Measures and Labour Market Effects* (Stockholm: Institute for Future Studies).

TUC (2004) "Congress Decisions 2004 Resolutions carried", available at http://www.tuc.org.uk/congress/tuc-8810-f0.cfm (accessed October 2008).

TUC (2005) *Making a Rights-Based Migration System Work: TUC Response to the Home Office Consultation Document "Selective Admission: Making Migration Work for Britain"* (London: TUC).

TUC (2007a) "Congress 2007: Resolutions carried", available at http://www.tuc. org.uk/congress/tuc-13720-f0.cfm (accessed October 2008).

TUC (2007b) *The Economics of Migration: Managing the Impacts* (London: TUC).

Unabhängige Kommission "Zuwanderung" (2001) *Zuwanderung Gestalten – Integration Fördern* (Berlin: Bundesministerium des Innern).

USDAW (2006) "MPs back USDAW campaign to keep ESOL lessons free for migrant workers", available at http://www.usdaw.org.uk/politics/news/ 1166009420_869.html (accessed October 2008).

Waldinger, R., and Lichter, M. (2003) *How the Other Half Works: Immigration and the Social Organization of Labor* (Berkeley: University of California Press).

Watts, J. (2002) *Immigration Policy and the Challenge of Globalization* (Ithaca/ London: Cornell University Press).

Section II
The Effects of Europeanization

6

Crossing Over, Heading West and South: Mobility, Citizenship, and Employment in the Enlarged Europe

*Ettore Recchi and Anna Triandafyllidou**

1. Introduction: From the iron curtain to rights of free movement

Except for Europe, no part of the globe can claim to have a borderless space between 27 sovereign states. This is even more striking in a continent where for centuries so many wars have been fought to defend or move state boundaries. European citizenship – which has its cornerstone in the right of free movement – permits one to reside in any EU member state, enjoying the same entitlements as nationals. This constitutes quite a unique regime, which can still be qualified as *international* migration, though it operates under the conditions of *internal* migration. To stress this novelty semantically, in their documents EU institutions tend to designate any cross-state transfer of European citizens as "mobility", whereas "migration" is used to refer to third country nationals only. "Mobility" means first class migration, without the fatigue of controls, visas, permits of stay, and the overall risk that marks traditional migrants' typical travel and settlement experiences.

From its early and timid formulation in 1951 (with the Treaty establishing the European Coal and Steel Community), the right of visa-free crossing and settlement among EEC (and then EU) member states widened its scope as well as the pool of potential recipients – from miners and steelworkers in the 1950s to all workers after 1968, to virtually any EU citizen from the 1990s, and even EU long-term residents after 2004 (settlement being still conditioned on either work, study, or economic self-sufficiency). The legal impact of the almost universal expansion of free movement and settlement rights in the EU is remarkable, especially because it entails access to social rights on a transnational scale. Hence, it contributes indirectly to the creation of a European welfare system, eroding an important area of member state sovereignty, and pushing forward political integration (Favell and Recchi, 2009). To place this into context, even free movement across US states was only fully acknowledged as a constitutional right in the 1940s (Giubboni, 2007).

Thus, in the last half-century the rights of free movement and settlement have *deepened*, but at the same time they have also *enlarged*. This was seen most spectacularly in 2004 and 2007, when 12 new member states joined the EU – ten being in the Eastern and formerly Communist side of the continent that had been separated from the West by armed borders for about 40 years. From an iron curtain to free movement between the Atlantic and the Urals – this was hardly imaginable less than one generation ago. What for citizens of Communist regimes was a forbidden dream (at the cost of exile, imprisonment, or even death when crossing a wall) has now become a subjective right as simple as buying a train ticket in any small-town railway station of Silesia or Bucovina.

This chapter presents both a statistical outline and a qualitative analysis of movements of Central and Eastern Europeans to Western and Southern EU member states in the last 20 years. We consider migrant numbers, duration of stay, and the motivations for relocating. We thus seek to outline the overall pattern of intra-EU mobility between new and old member states. We also investigate the more concrete experiences of those who moved, notably whether they moved legally or without documents, and how (and if) they managed to regularize their status. For this purpose we propose a distinction between three periods of East to West/South migration within the EU, notably the early period during the 1980s when movement was mainly politically motivated, an intermediate period during the 1990s until 2001, and the most recent period since 2001 (when visas began to be waived for the citizens of Central-Eastern European countries) encapsulating the accessions of 2004 and 2007. This chapter focuses on the second and third period and discusses the migration status and employment experiences of new intra-European movers and how these have changed over the years. We also briefly discuss their understanding and experience of becoming EU citizens even if this is still a recent and less-studied phenomenon.

The chapter draws mainly on Eurostat and EU Labour Force Survey data for its statistical outline. For the qualitative part of the analysis, we look into the broader literature on the topic and particularly draw on two recent studies, one on Polish migration in Europe (Triandafyllidou, 2006) and the second on new European citizens in Greece (Triandafyllidou and Maroukis, 2010) from which the bulk of interview excerpts have been taken. Overall, the picture emerging from both the quantitative and qualitative evidence shows the prevailingly market-driven nature of these migration flows and the persistent channelling of intra-EU migrants from NMS (New Member States) to the low-wage sector of the labour market, where ultimately working conditions and wages do not really change much, even once the employees in these sectors become newly minted EU citizens.

In the concluding section of the chapter we discuss the distinction between migration and mobility within the EU and the relationship between citizenship and migration, outlining future prospects and policy issues for intra-EU migration from Central Eastern European countries.

2. The return of intra-European migration: A statistical overview

In the final 5 years of the twentieth century, net migration into the EU15 amounted to about 600,000 persons per year – that is, half the amount of the US. In the following 5 years, this figure almost doubled. For the first time, immigration flows became larger in Europe than in the US (especially as US immigration policy tightened after 9/11). The peak was reached in 2003, when net migration to the EU15 reached 2 million persons (Eurostat, 2009, p. 54). Such migration flows have been notably asymmetric. In absolute terms, the highest numbers have been recorded in Spain, Germany, the UK, and Italy. Without precedent, in Spain and Ireland (as well as Cyprus and Luxembourg, small states experiencing vigorous immigration), newcomer rates have been as high as 15–20 per thousand residents (Herm, 2008, p. 2).

To a large extent, this migration boom was fed by the 2004 and 2007 enlargements. On average, between 2004 and 2008 the yearly net increase of immigrants in the EU15 amounted to about 250,000 persons from A8 (mainly Poland) and about 300,000 persons from A2 (mainly Romania) (Brücker et al., 2009, pp. 23, 27). At the peak of out-migration from Central-Eastern Europe, in 2006, three-quarters of all new immigrants in the EU originated from the 2004 and 2007 accession countries.

Interestingly, Eastern enlargement triggered East-West/South population movements even before it took place, as migrants moved West somewhat earlier in anticipation of being automatically legalized and "upgraded" once their home country joined the EU. For instance, 40 per cent of the A8 citizens who requested a work permit in the UK in 2004 were already residing there pre-enlargement (European Commission, 2008, p. 11). Movements were even more rapid and proportionally larger (given the size of the countries of origin) immediately preceding and soon after the second enlargement. By the end of 2007, the stock of registered Romanians and Bulgarians living in EU15 had equalled that of movers from the 2004 enlargement countries: 1.9 million persons.

Contradicting many projections,[1] the rise of the Central-Eastern European population that re-settled in the EU15 in the first 8 years of the new century was robust and uninterrupted. Most spectacularly, Romanians in "old" Europe were seven times more numerous in 2007 than in 2000, while Lithuanians and Slovaks were five times more numerous. Even nationals of the countries with the lowest outflows, that is, Slovenia and Hungary, increased by more than 50 per cent over this period (Table 6.1).

Overall, Eurostat calculates that in 2007 the EU27 member states hosted 29.1 million foreign citizens, among whom 10.6 million were intra-EU migrants (European Commission, 2008, p. 115). EU movers formed 2.1 per cent of the EU population and 2.6 per cent in the EU15. About 40 per cent were citizens of new member states (NMS), the majority being Romanian (1.6 million), Polish (1.3 million), and Bulgarian (310,000). This means that an astounding 7.2 per cent of Romanians, 4.1 per cent of Bulgarians, and 3.4 per cent of Poles exercise their free movement rights to live out of their country as EU citizens. Out-migration has been remarkably high in Lithuania and Cyprus as well, as over 3 per cent of the working age population moved abroad in Europe up to 2007.[2] Even these impressive figures grossly underestimate the real size of the mobile population, as they do not include temporary, seasonal, and shuttle migrants who move back and forth across home and host(s) countries and thus escape statistical registration (either in local or national censuses, permits of stay, or official surveys). They also fail to include returned movers, who have made use of their EU citizenship rights in the past.

Among the receiving countries, Britain and Ireland stand out, due to the dynamism of their economies and the open door policies they adopted immediately after the 2004 enlargement (no transitional measures were introduced in Sweden either, but without a comparable

Table 6.1   Growth in the stocks of NMS citizens legally resident in EU15 (2000–2007, 2000 = 100)

	2000	2001	2002	2003	2004	2005	2006	2007
Czech Rep	100	125	137	168	148	168	215	246
N	*42,379*							
Estonia	100	113	123	145	145	166	178	199
N	*18,458*							
Hungary	100	112	116	111	108	120	125	156
N	*84,976*							
Latvia	100	89	102	113	111	152	194	196
N	*21,713*							
Lithuania	100	151	172	222	218	353	473	531
N	*24,154*							
Poland	100	112	114	121	127	159	208	272
N	*476,229*							
Slovak Rep	100	147	155	174	208	324	363	525
N	*25,195*							
Slovenia	100	129	131	150	136	146	144	151
N	*23,814*							
Total A8	100	115	120	129	132	167	210	266
Total N	*716,917*							
Bulgaria	100	144	197	233	285	307	357	434
N	*71,437*							
Romania	100	131	179	254	333	405	493	714
N	*217,669*							
Total A2	100	134	183	249	321	380	459	645
Total N	*289,106*							

Source: Authors' calculations from Brücker et al. (2009, p. 32), on the basis of Eurostat and EU LFS.

appeal among A8 movers). Almost 70 per cent of A8 citizens who migrated in Europe settled in these two countries alone (Brücker et al., 2009, p. 23). In Britain, 27 per cent of registered workers from NMS in 2007 lived in London and East Anglia, but the attractiveness of London – perhaps due to the cost of living – has declined (Dobson, 2009). In Ireland, Poles and Lithuanians (the latter in smaller absolute numbers, but proportionally higher) have altered the demographic profile of the country: in 2007, 5 per cent of working age residents were A8 citizens who arrived in the last 4 years. On the other hand, the preferred destinations of mobile Romanians were in fact Southern European countries: half of them have settled in Spain, and a quarter in Italy, while the remaining quarter went elsewhere in Western and Central Europe.

Men and women are equally represented among citizens of A8 countries, while women constitute a slightly larger portion of the Romanian and Bulgarian contingent, perhaps because of the strong demand for domestic workers from these countries in EU15. Further, it is no surprise that the new opportunities of mobility created by EU enlargements have been seized most by the youngest cohorts of workers. More than three-quarters of the NMS citizens who moved in 2007 were under 35 years of age.

Partly due to their younger age, the proportion of university graduates among Central-Eastern European movers is only slightly below that of native workers in the EU15. In fact, the share of NMS movers with an upper secondary degree is higher than among natives in the EU15 workforce. This means that the human capital of those who moved West/South after the enlargements is heavily under-utilized. Wage differentials between the old and the new member states have fostered a mobility that is channelled to traditional sectors of migrant work. At least in a first stage of migration, Western and Southern Europe have exacted somewhat of a brain-drain upon the new member states – to the point that countries like Poland and Romania suffer from labour shortages in some occupations (noticeably, health care), forcing them to launch schemes to retain or recall their qualified workers (Kaczmarczyk and Okolski, 2008).

Central-Eastern European workers have found work mostly in industry, construction, hotels, restaurants, and as domestic caregivers. This places them at the bottom of the occupational hierarchy, with more than 35 per cent classified by Eurostat as holding low-skilled manual employment (European Commission, 2008, p. 130). In stark contrast, EU mobile workers from Western Europe are over-represented (compared to natives) among managers (more than 10 per cent), professionals (more than 25 per cent), and other high prestige occupations (ibid.). While EU15 citizens who relocate in another EU member state are more likely than those who stay at home to get jobs at the upper end of the socioeconomic hierarchy, A8 and A2 movers' occupational fate in Western and Southern Europe is less stellar than that of their sedentary co-nationals (Figure 6.1). Plant or machine operators and non-qualified manual workers make up 20 per cent of the workforce of A8 countries, but constitute almost 50 per cent of A8 citizens working abroad in Europe. Equally, almost 40 per cent of all A2 migrant workers are employed in elementary occupations,[3] as opposed to only 11 per cent in their countries of origin. Since "most of the data indicates

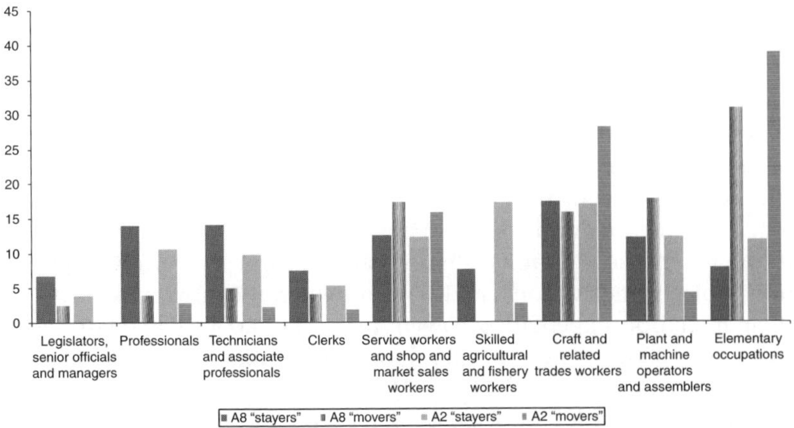

Figure 6.1 Occupation of A8 and A2 workers in their home countries and in other EU member states, 2007 (in % of total employment by group)
Source: Authors' elaboration from European Commission (2008, p. 130), based on EU LFS.

that there is a positive selection of emigrants from the NMS with regard to education" (Brücker et al., 2009, p. 92), we can conclude that Westbound and Southbound migration from the countries of the 2004 and 2007 enlargements has ended up following – at least in its early years – a downward social mobility path. Possibly even more than in other migration systems, a higher salary abroad was exchanged with a decline in social status. From the viewpoint of migrants themselves, the odd combination of such social status degradation and political status upgrading as EU citizens has nurtured frustration and disillusionment about European integration. The experience of mobility, therefore, tends to be stripped of any political meaning, becoming reduced to the economic maximization logic of traditional migration (for example, Anghel, 2008a; Morawska, 2008).

The large differences of occupational destinations of intra-EU movers from the "old" and "new" Europe have eventually become mirrored in their collective representations in the EU15. While they are European citizens, public opinion views Poles and Romanians as "immigrants", to the point that they are sometimes even confounded with third country nationals in the press, whereas Germans, Britons, or Spaniards can circulate as "mobile Europeans" with little exposure to discrimination (Recchi and Favell, 2009).

3. Migration within an enlarged EU: From third country nationals to becoming EU citizens

The individual migration projects[4] of citizens from the new member states are influenced by a number of factors, most notably economic need (low salaries, high unemployment rates, decline of specific industrial sectors, deregulation of labour markets, implosion of welfare systems), but also an overall desire to improve their lives and ensure a better future for their children. Qualitative studies suggest a variety of migration projects, motivations, and ways in which migrants make sense of their migration experiences (Favell and Nebe, 2009; Kassimati, 2003; Lazarescu, 2009; Maroufof, 2009 and 2010; Nikolova, 2009; Meardi, 2009; Metz-Göckel et al., 2008; Triandafyllidou, 2006). Hereafter, we draw on these studies for evidence and examples.

While economic motivations remain central for most if not all citizens of the new member states who have migrated to EU15, the importance of these motivations in comparison to other motivations such as maintaining or increasing one's social or professional status or enjoying a family life can vary. Thus, we may distinguish along a continuum between two extremes: at one pole we find people who moved because they could not earn a living in their place of origin, while at the other end of the continuum we find people who moved to improve their future, buy a house, fund their children's education, accumulate capital to start a business, or simply experience work and life "in the West". Of course, these are the two opposite ends of a continuum and real biographies and experiences lie somewhere in between.

Motivations and the level of economic need may differ, but all migrants from new to old member states have had to adapt their projects to changes in their countries of origin and in the migration policy of other EU countries. Thus, a better understanding of migration projects and how they have evolved over time can be achieved if we acknowledge the different phases of East–West migration within Europe (and now within the EU). These different phases are shaped by political and economic developments in countries of origin as well as by the development of EU migration and mobility policies with regard to the citizens of these countries. In the following sections we focus on three of the most mobile nationalities, notably Poles, Romanians, and Bulgarians, to suggest a phasing of their intra-EU migration and to analyze their experiences as regards employment before and after accession, as well as their understanding of EU citizenship and/or European identity.

3.1. Phases of migration and migration projects

A tentative periodization of migration and mobility in the wider European space before and after the 2004 and 2007 enlargements distinguishes three main periods. The first period refers to migration that took place in the 1980s, before the fall of the Communist regimes. The initial political refugees from Romania, Bulgaria, and Poland to Western Europe were people who had been politically active and who fled oppression in their countries of origin. In many cases these early refugees either relocated further to the US, or after 1989 returned to their countries of origin. However, in most cases they established the path of migration to specific countries and created the community infrastructure that helped those who moved later, tempted by the prospects of better employment opportunities (Lazaridis and Romaniszyn, 1998; Maroufof, 2009 and 2010). A further component of these early migrations included those who moved because they married foreign students (for example, Western students temporarily enrolled in Eastern European universities) or other non-nationals (for example, Greek political refugees who had moved to Poland after the Greek civil war in the late 1940s). Within this first period one would not refer to any irregular migration since political refugees from the East were welcome in Western Europe.

A second phase of migration from East to West started in 1990 after the implosion of the Communist regimes and ended with the waiving of visa requirements for the EU in 2001. This second phase of migration varies in intensity of movements for the different countries investigated here. Thus, Bulgarians moved mostly at the end of the 1990s, following the major economic crisis that the country faced in 1997, while Romanians and Poles have moved since the early 1990s when they experienced the first economic and political crisis that followed the political change of 1989.

A Romanian interviewee in Greece summarizes the main events and the context of that period:

> From 1990 and 1995 on, when the transformations in Romania started, a large mass of Romanians left the country in search for a better life. At the time, Greece was in a deep need (and it continues to be so up to this day) for low skilled labour. More specifically, workers are needed in constructions, in agriculture for collecting olives and oranges, as well as in restaurants. In other words, it needed low skilled people.
>
> (Interview 6, cit. in Lazarescu, 2010)

During this second phase, migration took place largely through irregular channels. People travelled as tourists, overstayed their visas, and engaged in employment, or, alternatively, they crossed the borders with false documents or through unguarded points of entry. In the case of Southern Europe, this meant traversing the mountainous borders between Bulgaria and Greece or Slovenia and Italy. In the case of Poles and Romanians, the passage involved counterfeiting visas, travelling West by bus, facing time-consuming and humiliating checks at the borders, and/or eventually resorting to some petty bribe for the night-time border guards (Anghel, 2008b).

In Britain there were opportunities for regularizing their stay and working as professionals or small business founders. Renata, a middle aged Polish woman who migrated to England in the mid-1990s with her husband, is a case in point. She worked as a cleaner and her husband was a construction worker. They had migrated with a tourist visa, but when faced with the prospect of entering into irregular status, they sought immigration advice and filed a successful small business permit application:

> Before our first six month visa expired we found out [about a possibility of getting a business visa] from a mate Darius worked with at a building site. When you apply for a business visa you need to have a valid tourist visa, so, because ours were about to expire we went to France and back. We also started contacting people who could help in submitting business visa applications. It took us four months to get all the papers together and apply for that visa. Firstly we talked to a man who presented our possibilities to us. He was a [Polish] accountant.
>
> (Düvell, 2006, p. 72)

In Southern European countries, opportunities arose for legalizing migrants' stay through occasional amnesties or regularization programmes. However, some migrants who applied to such programmes had difficulty renewing their permits or even struggled to demonstrate the required conditions. Although pathways for acquiring legal status existed in Southern European countries, their impact on migrants' plans and working/living experiences should not be overstated (see also Psimmenos and Kassimati, 2006; Triandafyllidou and Kosic, 2006).

Of course, the situation was more complicated in countries like Germany where those who moved clandestinely remained undocumented throughout their stay, as labour markets were tightly regulated and there were no *ad hoc* regularization programmes. Testimonies presented in Cyrus and Vogel (2006) show that the impossibility of achieving a regular immigration status discouraged Polish migrants in Germany from settling down and rather obliged them to keep going back to Poland, especially in the case of accident or illness. Yet, comparison to interviews with Polish undocumented migrants in Germany and Britain in the early 2000s demonstrates that both groups felt insecure and considered returning to Poland, although their stories did prove that for many going back home was not an economically viable option. Indeed, the wages back home or the difficulties of finding a job were important discouraging factors. Derek, a young Polish man living in England at the turn of the century (late 1990s/early 2000s), gives an eloquent account of the dilemma that Central-Eastern European immigrants faced at that time:

> I haven't got a visa any more. So if I get caught, I get caught. They will send me to Poland, and what can I do?…If I'm caught at work it'll not matter if I have visa or not. I never knew about any possibility of legally extending my visa….I will stay here till December. In December I will take First Certificate exam. And then I'll go back, 'cause I'm slowly having enough of getting up at 5:40am. I'm a person who graduated from university. I cannot keep hoovering for the rest of my life. Cleaners are the lowest layer, the lowest caste of working people…. After going back I'll have a rest for three months and then I'll get myself a ticket to England. No, no I'm joking. It's a joke. But that's what people do. They go back to Poland saying they would never come back. Stay there for a month, spend the money they've saved here. That's what people do very often.
>
> (Düvell, 2006, p. 67)

The third phase covers the period starting in 2001, that is, the period between the suspension of the entry visa for Romanian, Polish, and Bulgarian nationals travelling within the Schengen area and the three countries' accession to the EU, which took place in 2004 for Poland and in 2007 for the other two countries. The main forms of migration included either legal migration through preferential channels offered by old EU member states to citizens of the accession countries or, more commonly, through entry without visa and engagement in informal employment.

The waiving of entry visas for citizens of the accession countries made it easier for migrants to enter legally and then settle for a shorter or longer period of time in other EU countries. Since irregular stay and informal work were widespread especially in Southern Europe, the governments of these member states once again implemented regularization programmes that allowed for a large number of Central-Eastern Europeans to become legal migrants.

The situation shifted again in 2004 for Poles, and in 2007 for Romanians and Bulgarians, when they became fully-fledged EU citizens. Even if the two-year transition period was applied by all but three (Britain, Ireland, and Sweden) EU countries towards A8 citizens, and by all EU countries for Romanians and Bulgarians, the accession of these three countries to the EU meant that their citizens were entitled to move and reside freely – although not permitted to take up employee jobs – within the entire Union. Thus, many who had migrated without papers to EU15 before 2004 and 2007 found an opportunity to indirectly regularize their stay even if they could not legalize their working status. The stay permit they obtained did not correspond to their real situation on the market.

A telling assessment of the latest developments in intra-EU mobility is the following remark of the chief editor of a Romanian newspaper in Greece:

> I remember the interviews we used to take at the travel agent offices. The number of buses coming from Romania was increasing significantly, while the buses were full of people who had bought a one way ticket, in search of the chimera of economic prosperity.
>
> (Interview 2, cit. in Lazarescu, 2010)

3.2. Employment

The employment situation of citizens of the "new" EU member states has changed during these different phases of migration, albeit not always in the ways one would expect. In the first phase, employment was legal and numbers rather small. During the second phase, irregular entry and stay was accompanied by irregular employment in the shadow economy. Men were predominantly employed in construction, agriculture, and other manual jobs, and women in the care and cleaning sectors. While in Northern European countries, such as Britain or France, those who obtained a permit of stay usually managed to also obtain legal employment (see, for instance, the experience of Poles in Britain: Düvell, 2006), in Southern Europe emergence from irregularity to legal status and work was often temporary and not at all straightforward (Baldwin-Edwards and Arango, 1999; Kosic and Triandafyllidou,

2006; Triandafyllidou and Kosic, 2006). Frequently the impossibility of finding work with a proper contract and welfare contributions prevented legalized migrants from renewing their permits, leading some to fall back into irregular status.

The third phase has been characterized by legal stay often coupled with informal employment. Paradoxically in many cases, being freed from the requirement to obtain and renew a stay permit for work purposes as third country nationals, and hence having a legal stay status, NMS citizens found it more difficult to secure legal employment. As Nikolova's (2010) and Lazarescu's (2010) recent research on Bulgarians and Romanians in Greece reveals, they often offer to work without a proper contract or without overtime and weekend pay so as to be competitive in the labour market – emphasizing to employers that their EU citizen status had released them from the "unnecessary" burden of welfare insurance.

3.2.1. Mobility and flexibility

EU movers from the new member states show a high level of mobility and flexibility in the labour market. Not only do they work for periods of varying duration in the shadow economy, they also adapt to market demands by changing employers, places of work, and sectors of employment frequently. In large numbers, EU movers from NMS fall prey to the shady practices of some temporary work agencies. In the UK, about a third of workers from the new member states obtained their first job through such agencies (Meardi, 2009, p. 109). A perception of exploitation and discrimination is widespread from these experiences, which do however reflect employers' actual view of Eastern workers as hyperflexible and disposable, as well as the migrants' own need for easily accessible, ready-made employment.

Already in the late 1990s and early 2000s, it was unusual for a Polish migrant worker to stay in the same job for a period as long as 18 months, especially if the position was one's first job upon arrival. Almost every Eastern European worker in Britain experienced job instability, but this is generally framed as mobility rather than insecurity (Düvell, 2006). By contrast, Cyrus' (2006) study of Berlin during the same years testifies more to the anxiety of securing long-term employment as well as the difficulty in finding employment when one's social capital (that is, insertion into other migrants' networks) was relatively low.

More recent studies suggest that, after 2004 and 2007, this is more common among men. Nikolova (2009) notes that Bulgarian men are particularly dynamic in changing jobs as well as specialization when their work is no longer available or when they seek higher pay or better employment conditions:

> I have worked in a Chinese restaurant, in a company that was transporting electric appliances, as porter at the harbour, as decorator. I have changed several professions to make ends meet. To take care of my family. Nothing more.
>
> (Interview 3, man, 37 years old, cit. in Nikolova, 2010)

> [I have changed jobs] more than 50 times. I worked at a restaurant in the kitchen, I have picked up oranges, olives, I trimmed trees in the streets, I worked in public construction works for the Olympic Games. My life could be the scenario for a movie. [You have to] change jobs, to match [the demand]. And because you are hard working none will send you away.
>
> (Interview 6, man, 49 years old, cit. in Nikolova, 2010)

Similar accounts are also provided by Lazarescu (2010) as regards Romanian workers. As one shop owner explains:

> I have changed many jobs. I used to hand out leaflets, I worked in a gas station, I also worked in a snack bar, so I've tried a lot of things.
>
> (Interview 7, cit. in Lazarescu, 2009)

Contrary to men, women appear to be trapped in the cleaning and domestic care sector with few possibilities for transition into other occupations. Some women note that they prefer working for cleaning firms, although worse paid than cleaning or caring privately for families, because they can receive some welfare contributions and because these are more stable jobs. Many women who left Romania, Bulgaria, and Poland arrived initially as live-in maids, either through chain migration (through the recommendation or as replacement of a relative or friend) or through specialized employment agencies that arranged for their arrival and employment without a permit. Many women who began as live-in maids later sought jobs as external cleaners or caregivers. However, several qualitative studies show that in comparison, women are more likely to remain in the care and cleaning sectors and show less mobility than men in terms of sectors of employment and places of work (Catanzaro and Colombo, 2009; Lazarescu, 2010; Metz-Göckel et al., 2008; Nikolova, 2010; Triandafyllidou and Maroufof, 2009). They do however change employer in search of better pay, working hours, or working conditions.

For both men and women from NMS living in the EU15, their home countries' accession to the EU has not translated immediately into an improvement in their labour market position. If they were subjected to the 2-year transition period such improvement was impossible because of their restricted access to the labour market. Indeed, the policy of restriction has led to the creation and proliferation of semi-compliance practices (that is, legal stay, but irregular employment status). Moreover, these restrictions, in combination with discretionary practices in the implementation of the law, contribute to the development of a small industry of employment and legal counselling offices that "help" immigrants obtain official documents and also offer them "solutions" to various legal issues.

Following the recent abolition of labour market access restrictions, the employment situation of Romanians, Bulgarians, and Poles does not seem to have improved substantially, especially in Southern Europe, as their opportunities for employment remain confined in the low-skill low-pay low-status segments of the labour market.

3.2.2. Emergence of ethnic entrepreneurship

Self-employment seems to be one of the few possibilities of social mobility for intra-EU migrants who have settled for longer periods and who have thus managed to achieve a better position in the labour market. More specifically, as a Romanian interviewee in Greece explains:

> When the specialization level is rather low one may say that the image held is not positive. Up to now there are no Romanians who came to Greece after 1990 and who made it to a higher status level in the social hierarchy. Those who work for the public sector or for a research institute come from the old Romanians [here the respondent refers to the Romanians who belong to the pre-1989 migration wave]. I believe that there is a social stratification also among the Romanians who have arrived to Greece recently. For instance, besides the owners of shops and restaurants, there are individuals who passed the stage of construction wage-worker and now have their own team made of other Romanians and they contract work by themselves.
>
> (Interview 6, cit. in Lazarescu, 2009)

While ethnic solidarity creates opportunities for Central Eastern European migrants to overcome glass ceilings in the workplace – a frequent experience in spite of their EU citizenship status – it is also often linked to exploitation and circumvention of labour laws, as found in many other contexts (Light and Bonacich, 1988). It is also true for NMS citizens living in Western and Southern Europe that ethnic entrepreneurship is directly related to the duration of their settlement in the host society (Barberis, 2008; Pajares, 2007, pp. 197–199). Possibly due to their earlier arrival and acquisition of EU citizenship, self-employment and entrepreneurship rates are thus higher among Poles than among Romanians and Bulgarians in Spain and Greece, albeit not in Italy (Caritas/Migrantes 2009, p. 277ff.; Viruela Martinez, 2009, p. 84). In Greece, for instance, data from the Commercial Chamber of Athens suggest that while Poles account for only 1.1 per cent of the country's immigrant population, they own 3.8 per cent of the foreign firms in town. The bulk of these firms are directly related to the occupations where Poles are employed most often: construction and cleaning. However, there is also a significant and growing number of catering establishments such as restaurants, cafés, bars, and grocery shops that import and sell Polish products. Business around Polish migration has flourished particularly in Britain where the obstacles to establishing a new enterprise are fewer (Eade et al., 2006). Qualitative research shows that these migrant enterprises mainly serve their co-nationals' demand (Rabikowska and Burrell, 2009; Ram and Jones, 2008). As a study of Poles' entrepreneurship in Berlin suggests, transnationalism is the most appropriate frame of the bulk of such economic activities (Miera, 2008).

3.3. Issues of identity and citizenship rights

Recent studies point out that migrants view their countries' accession to the EU positively, but at the same time it creates some confusion about their legal status (Lazarescu, 2009; Nikolova, 2009). Apparently there are still many Romanians and Bulgarians who believe that becoming European citizens frees them from the obligation of acquiring a stay permit. Local authorities and civil servants' varied practices in the old member states seem to have contributed to misinformation about the duties and rights of EU citizenship. Furthermore, especially Polish interviewees (since Poles were the first group to become EU citizens) note a high level of discretion as some civil servants wield their own personal interpretation of the law and for a period failed to recognize the rights of some migrants as EU citizens.

Research on Bulgarians and Romanians in Greece (Lazarescu, 2010; Nikolova, 2010) shows that the accession of their countries to the EU triggered little change in the everyday dealings of Poles, Romanians, and Bulgarians with the Greek state. When asked directly, Bulgarian and Romanian residents noted that attaining European citizenship did not make a difference to them apart from the practical fact that the process of renewing their stay permits had become much easier or indeed they no longer had to register with the authorities at all. Most of all, they have lost their fear of being deported. However, in accounts about their travelling back and forth to their country of origin they noted how much easier the border controls had become for them and how positive they felt about it. Indeed this same feeling of liberation was also manifested in earlier research on Poles in Italy and Britain (Kosic and Triandafyllidou, 2006; Morawska, 2008; Triandafyllidou and Kosic, 2006).

4. Conclusion: EU enlargements as generators of migration

A question looms large in EU studies dealing with migration: Does the EU have a migration policy at all? Most scholars argue that the answer is basically "no". In fact, while we acknowledge that the EU has not inspired consistent regulations of migration flows and integration measures in member states, there is an EU policy (and a related discourse) that has shaped the ways population movements are managed in the Union: EU citizenship and its underlying distinction between "migration" (for third country nationals) and "mobility" (for EU citizens).

This is a meta-policy with long-standing factual outcomes, ultimately granting a priority of access to immigrant labour markets for workers originating from the East of the continent over those crossing the Southern borders (or even further away). Such a policy reinvigorates the continental character of migration in the EU15. Immigration is welcomed if it is the immigration of neighbours – particularly if they come from the same side of the street (that is, the continent).

Even if at times "old" Europe's public opinion seemed reluctant – to say the least – about an open-door migration policy for citizens of the new member states (as it was during the Polish plumber campaign in France in 2004–2005 and the anti-Romanian demonstrations in Italy in 2007–2008), overall this solution turned out to be the least conflictive compromise between the economic demand for immigrant labour and voters' hostility towards migrant minorities. All in all, Polish plumbers – especially after the ironic and sexy undertone of the Polish tourist agency's advertisements – still make better co-workers than

Pakistanis, Algerians, and Chinese in the eyes of many citizens of the EU15.

When inventing European citizenship, member states "upgraded" intra-EU migrants and opted, in the long run, for the creation of a global region of self-feeding population movements. Enlargements to the East, even if not primarily justified in terms of migration needs for Western economies, reiterated this logic: *Europe as a continent produces a sufficient workforce for its overall development needs.* As a consequence, Central-Eastern Europeans are the primary candidates for immigrant labour in the rest of the continent. The preference for these "immigrants-turned-into-movers" stems from twin expectations of: (a) higher cultural compatibility with (Western) European culture and lifestyle, and (b) easier re-incorporation into their countries of origin, in the case of excess labour demand or economic expansion in those same countries. In sum, it is assumed that Central-Eastern EU citizens form a more adaptable and reversible factor of production compared to non-European potential immigrants.

The first of these hypotheses is almost self-fulfilling. An easier adaptation is inherent in the concession of citizenship status, which removes many conditions of marginality for immigrants (possible refusal of permits of stay and labour, denied access to health care, no right to unemployment benefits). The second hypothesis – postulating a strong reversibility of migration choices of moving EU citizens – is, in fact, still to be tested.

Recent studies on the current economic recession suggest that the bulk of intra-EU migrants from the new member states adopt a strategy of wait-and-see rather than returning home (for example, Cingolani, 2009; Schneider and Holman, 2009). Some also accept lower wages, keeping their complementary rather than antagonistic position even in contracting labour markets. Though reduced in magnitude, the East-West flow has not ceased: "During the first quarter of 2009, the number of applications approved under the WRS [Workers' Registration Scheme of the UK] was 21,275, considerably down from the 46,645 approved in the first quarter of 2008. However, an inflow continuing to run at around 7,000 per month, though less than half of that a year ago, does not necessarily lend support to there being a net outflow brought on by labour market conditions" (Dobson et al., 2009, p. 17).

The attractiveness of the EU15, and the UK in particular, as a destination of migration projects from the new member states seems hardly at stake (Blanchflower and Lawton, 2010). Converging evidence is found in the sending countries. Polish survey data show that "the crisis has not triggered large-scale returns. Only a small portion of the emigrants are coming back to Poland [...] The main strategy [of Poles working abroad] is to wait the crisis out as emigrants" (Baczynska, 2009, based on a report by the Centre for International Relations in Warsaw). Most significantly, "many of the Poles who returned home said they were hoping to move abroad again in the future" (ibid.). Possibly some of them will pack their suitcases again after the final lifting of transitional measures in Germany. The complete opening of the German and Austrian labour markets to NMS citizens in 2011 (for nationals of A8 countries) and 2014 (for nationals of A2 countries) may mark another milestone in the history of intra-EU migration, fostering the emergence of a truly supernational labour market spanning across Central and Eastern European countries that lie at the opposite ends of workforce demand and supply in the continent.

This chapter has shown that the effect of EU enlargement on East-West/South migration has been twofold. As EU accession and European citizenship has automatically "regularized" citizens of the new member states who had migrated to the old member states previously under irregular conditions (and/or were employed in the informal labour market), it has broadened their migration options within the EU. Thus, they can choose to settle permanently in their destination countries or to return to their country of origin, or – as was and is extremely common – move back and forth, adapting to changing personal and contextual conditions. However, they seem to have reacted to these new opportunities mainly as a function of job openings and cost of living rather than in relation to their new citizenship. By contrast, EU citizenship seems to remain for many only an instrumental device that they know little about beyond that it secures their "papers", and not an identity.

Secondly, obtaining EU citizenship virtually opened up additional possibilities for occupational and social mobility through intra-EU migration. However, such mobility is, for the time being, hard to come by as employment opportunities largely remain in the same low-pay low-skill sectors of the economy as before accession. Moreover, in Southern European countries for men and in all countries for women in particular, the jobs available are mostly in the informal labour market. Thus, legal status has not translated into legal jobs or into social mobility as automatically as one might have thought. While prospects and experiences are better now than previously, labour market conditions continue to override citizenship rights, paradoxically "re-converting" mobile EU citizens into migrants.

Notes

*This chapter was conceived jointly by its authors. However, Ettore Recchi wrote Sections 1 and 2, while Anna Triandafyllidou wrote Section 3. Section 4 was written together.

1. In particular, on the basis of a sophisticated neoclassical econometric model, a report for the UK Home Office concluded that "net immigration from the AC-10 to the UK after the current enlargement of the EU will be relatively small, at between 5,000 and 13,000 immigrants per year up to 2010" (Dustmann et al., 2003, p. 59). Whether because it unquestioningly obeyed some "orderly aesthetic assumptions" of migration projections (Pijpers, 2008) or because it neglected the effect of a differential application of transitional measures among EU member states, this forecast could hardly have been more wrong.
2. A less known, but still relevant, out-migration is that from Portugal: 1.2 per cent of the Portuguese left their home country for another EU member state in 2003–2007. In terms of stocks, given the movements in the past decades, Portugal and Ireland are the countries with the largest proportion of citizens residing in another EU member state: 9 per cent and 8.2 per cent respectively.
3. In ISCO-88, "elementary occupations" (major group 9 of the classification) include manual employments of the lowest socioeconomic status, requiring minimal skills, such as cleaners, door-keepers, transport labourers, freight handlers, and construction workers (cf. http://www.ilo.org/public/english/bureau/stat/isco/isco88/publ4.htm).
4. The expression "migration project" is used here to refer to the plan that a migrant consciously makes before moving and during the migratory experience. The migration project may be realized or not and often changes during the move. The expression denotes that it is a conscious decision of the migrant, even if not necessarily a rational one, motivated by some factors and taking into account others. Naturally, eventually migration projects are shaped both by the agency of the individual migrant and her or his family as well as by structural factors such as migration laws, labour markets, or welfare services.

References

Anghel, R. G. (2008a) "Changing Statuses: Freedom of Movement, Locality and Transnationality of Irregular Romanian Migrants in Milan", *Journal of Ethnic and Migration Studies*, 34, 787–802.

Anghel, R. G. (2008b) "Come hanno fatto i rumeni ad arrivare in Italia" in A. Colombo and G. Sciortino (eds.) *Stranieri in Italia: Trent'anni dopo* (Bologna: Il Mulino).

Baczynska, G. (2009) "Few Poles Returning Home despite Crisis – Survey", Reuters, 29 May, available at www.reuters.com (accessed 29 May 2009).

Baldwin-Edwards, M. and Arango, J. (eds.) (1999) *Immigrants and the Informal Economy in Southern Europe* (London: Frank Cass).

Barberis, E. (2008) *Imprenditori immigrati. Tra inserimento sociale e partecipazione allo sviluppo* (Rome: Ediesse).

Blanchflower, D. G. and Lawton, H. (2010) "The Impact of the Recent Expansion of the EU on the UK Labour Market" in M. Kahanec and K. F. Zimmermann (eds.) *EU Labor Markets After Post-Enlargement Migration* (Berlin: Springer).

Brücker, H., Baas, T., Beleva, I., Bertoli, S., Boeri, T., Damelang, A., Duval, L., Fihel, A., Hauptmann, A., Huber, P., Iara, A., Ivlevs, A., Jahn, E. J., Kaczmarczyk, P., Krisjane, Z., Landesmann, M., Mackiewicz-Lyziak, J., Makovec, M., Monti, P., Nowotny, K., Okólski, M., Richter, S., Upward, R., Vidovic, H., Wolf, K., Wolfeil, N., Wright, P., and Zylicz, A. (2009) *Labour Mobility within the EU in the Context of Enlargement and the Functioning of the Transitional Arrangements*, final report (Nuremberg: European Integration Consortium).

Caritas/Migrantes (2009) *Immigrazione. Dossier statistico 2009* (IDOS: Rome).

Catanzaro, R. and Colombo, A. (eds) (2009) *Badanti & co. Il lavoro domestico straniero in Italia* (Bologna: Il Mulino).

Cingolani, P. (2009) *Romeni d'Italia. Migrazioni, vita quotidiana e legami transnazionali* (Bologna: Il Mulino).

Cyrus, N. and Vogel, D. (2006) "Polish Migrants in Germany" in A. Triandafyllidou (ed.) *Contemporary Polish Migration in Europe. Complex Patterns of Movement and Settlement* (Lewiston, NY: Edwin Mellen Press), pp. 91–136.

Dobson, J. R. (2009) "Labour Mobility and Migration within the EU Following the 2004 Central and East European Enlargement", *Employee Relations*, 31, 121–138.

Dobson, J. R., Latham, A. and Salt, J. (2009) *On the Move? Labour Migration in Time of Recession*, Policy Network Paper (London: Policy Network).

Dustmann, C., Casanova, M., Fertig, M., Preston, I., and Schmidt, C. M. (2003) *The Impact of EU Enlargement on Migration Flows*, Home Office Online Report 25/03, London, available at http://eprints.ucl.ac.uk/14332/1/14332.pdf (accessed 20 February 2010).

Eade, J., Drinkwater, S. and Garapich, M. (2006) *Class and Ethnicity. Polish Migrants in London*, Final Project Report, available at http://www.surrey.ac.uk/Arts/CRONEM/polish/POLISH_FINAL_RESEARCH_REPORT_WEB.pdf (accessed 18 February 2010).

European Commission (2008) *Employment in Europe 2008* (Luxembourg: Office for Official Publications of the European Communities).

Eurostat (2009) *Key Figures on Europe. 2009 Edition* (Luxembourg: Office for Official Publications of the European Communities).

Favell, A. and Nebe, T. (2009) "Internal and External Movers: East-West Migration and the Impact of EU Enlargement" in E. Recchi and A. Favell (eds.) *Pioneers of European Integration: Citizenship and Mobility in the EU* (Cheltenham: Elgar).

Favell, A. and Recchi, E. (2009) "Introduction" in E. Recchi and A. Favell (eds.) *Pioneers of European Integration: Citizenship and Mobility in the EU* (Cheltenham: Elgar).

Giubboni, S. (2007) "Free Movement of Persons and European Solidarity", *European Law Journal*, 13, 360–379.

Herm, A. (2008) "Recent Migration Trends: Citizens of EU-27 Member States Become Ever More Mobile while EU Remains Attractive to Non-EU Citizens", *Eurostat – Statistics in Focus*, 98/2008, available at http://epp.eurostat.ec.europa.eu/cache/ITY_OFFPUB/KS-SF-08-098/EN/KS-SF-08-098-EN.PDF (accessed 11 October 2009).

Kaczmarczyk, P. and Okolski, M. (2008) *Economic Impacts of Migration on Poland and the Baltic States*, FAFO Paper no. 1/2008, Oslo, available at http://www.fafo.no/pub/rapp/10045/10045.pdf (accessed 11 October 2009).

Kassimati, K. (2003) "Female Immigration from Albania and Poland – Occupations and Differences" in K. Kassimati (ed.) *Immigration Policies and Integration Strategies. The Case of Albanian and Polish Migrants* (Athens: Gutenberg).

Kosic, A. and Triandafyllidou, A. (2003) "Albanian Immigrants in Italy: Migration Plans, Coping Strategies and Identity Issues", *Journal of Ethnic and Migration Studies*, 29, 997–1014.

Kosic, A. and Triandafyllidou, A. (2006) "Polish and Albanian Workers in Italy: Between Legality and Undocumented Status" in Franck Düvell (ed.) *Illegal Migration in Europe: Beyond Control?* (Basingstoke: Palgrave-Macmillan), pp. 106–136.

Lazarescu, D. (2009) Ρουμάνικη μετανάστευση στην Ελλάδα: Άτυπα μεταναστευτικά δίκτυα, working paper, ELIAMEP, available at http://www.eliamep.gr/default-category/diktia-ke-diadromes-epta-metanasteftikon-omadon-stin-ellada/ (accessed 20 February 2010).

Lazarescu, D. (2010) "Ρουμάνικη μετανάστευση στην Ελλάδα: Άτυπα μεταναστευτικά δίκτυα πριν και μετά την ένταξη στην Ευρωπαϊκή Ένωση" in A. Triandafyllidou and T. Maroukis (eds.) *Η μετανάστευση στην Ελλάδα του 21ου αιώνα* (Athens: Kritiki), pp. 207–257.

Lazaridis, G. and Romaniszyn, K. (1998) "Albanian and Polish Undocumented Workers in Greece: a Comparative Analysis", *Journal of European Social Policy*, 8, 5–22.

Light, I. and Bonacich, E. (1988) *Immigrant Entrepreneurs: Koreans in Los Angeles, 1965–1982* (Los Angeles: University of California Press).

Maroufof, M. (2009) Πολωνική μετανάστευση στην Ελλάδα, working paper, ELIAMEP, available at http://www.eliamep.gr/default-category/diktia-ke-diadromes-epta-metanasteftikon-omadon-stin-ellada/ (accessed 20 February 2010).

Maroufof, M. (2010) "Οι Πολωνοί μετανάστες στην Ελλάδα" [Polish migrants in Greece] in A. Triandafyllidou and T. Maroukis (eds.) *Η μετανάστευση στην Ελλάδα του 21ου αιώνα* (Athens: Kritiki, in Greek) [Migration in 21st Century Greece], pp. 309–339.

Meardi, G. (2009) "A Suspended Status: The Puzzle of Polish Workers in the West Midlands" in H. Fassmann, M. Haller and D. Lane (eds.) *Migration and Mobility in Europe: Trends, Patterns and Control* (Cheltenham: Elgar).

Metz-Göckel, S., Morokvasic, M., and Senganata Munst, A. (2008) (eds.) *Migration and Mobility in an Enlarged Europe: A Gender Perspective* (Leverkusen: Budrich).

Miera, F. (2008) "Transnational Strategies of Polish Migrant Entrepreneurs in Trade and Small Business in Berlin", *Journal of Ethnic and Migration Studies*, 34, 753–770.

Morawska, E. (2008) *East European Westbound Income-seeking Migrants: Some Unwelcome Effects on the Sender- and Receiver-Societies (A report on a Study in Progress)*, paper presented at the conference "The impact of 1989 on Europe: structural integration but ideational divergence?" European University Institute, Fiesole, 8 November.

Nikolova, M. (2009) Βουλγαρική μετανάστευση στην Ελλάδα, working paper, ELIAMEP, available at http://www.eliamep.gr/default-category/diktia-ke-diadromes-epta-metanasteftikon-omadon-stin-ellada/ (accessed 20 February 2010).

Nikolova, M. (2010) "Οι Βούλγαροι στην Ελλάδα" in A. Triandafyllidou and T. Maroukis (eds.) Η μετανάστευση στην Ελλάδα του 21^{ου} αιώνα (Athens: Kritiki).

Pajares, M. (2007) *Inmigrantes del Este: procesos migratorios de los rumanos* (Barcelona: Icaria).

Pijpers, R. (2008) "Problematising the 'Orderly' Aesthetic Assumptions of Forecasts of East-West Migration in the European Union", *Environment and Planning A*, 40, 174–188.

Psimmenos, I. and Kassimati, K. (2006) "Polish Workers and Flexible Service Work" in A. Triandafyllidou (ed.) *Contemporary Polish Migration in Europe. Complex Patterns of Movement and Settlement* (Lewiston, NY: Edwin Mellen Press), pp. 291–316.

Rabikowska, M. and Burrell, K. (2009) "The Material Worlds of Recent Polish Migrants: Transnationalism, Food, Shops and Home" in K. Burrell (ed.) *Polish Migration to the UK in the "New" European Union: After 2004* (Farnham: Ashgate).

Ram, M. and Jones, T. (2008) "Ethnic-Minority Businesses in the UK: A Review of Research and Policy Developments", *Environment and Planning C: Government and Policy*, 26, 352–374.

Recchi, E. and Favell, A. (eds.) (2009) *Pioneers of European Integration: Citizenship and Mobility in the EU* (Cheltenham: Elgar).

Schneider, C. and Holman, D. (2009) *Longitudinal Study of Migrant Workers in the East of England. Interim Report* (Cambridge and Chelmsford: Anglia Ruskin University).

Triandafyllidou, A. (ed.) (2006) *Contemporary Polish Migration in Europe: Complex Patterns of Movement and Settlement* (Ceredigion, Wales and Washington, D.C.: Edwin Mellen).

Triandafyllidou, A. and Kosic, A. (2006) "Polish and Albanian Workers in Italy: Between Legality and Undocumented Status" in F. Düvell (ed.) *Illegal Migration in Europe: Beyond Control?* (Basingstoke: Palgrave-Macmillan).

Triandafyllidou and Maroufof (2009) Η εγκατάσταση των Μεταναστών στην Ελλάδα. Δυναμικές ένταξης και προβλήματα καταγραφής [Migrant Settlement in Greece. Dynamics of integration and problems of registration] in A. Takis (ed.) Μετανάστευση, ετερότητα και θεσμοί υποδοχής στην Ελλάδα. Το στοίχημα της κοινωνικής ένταξης [Migration, otherness and reception institutions in Greece. The bet of social integration], Thessalonike: Sakkoulas, pp. 39–81, in Greek.

Viruela Martinez, R. (2009) "Europeos del Este en el mercado de trabajo español: un enfoque geografico", *Revista CIDOB d'Afers Internacionals*, 84, 81–103.

7
Labour Immigration in the EU Through the Back Door? The Free Provision of Services as a Facilitator of Migration Flows

Vassilis Hatzopoulos

1. Introduction

It is quite uncommon to associate migration with the rules on services trade. Indeed, all economic definitions of services insist on their immaterial nature and on the increased possibility of trading them "virtually" over networks or else, without any physical movement of the parties involved. Somehow this "immaterial" nature of services reflects on their providers/recipients which seem to be "invisible". Even though most services still require the physical contact of the provider with the recipient[1] and, when provided over national borders, do entail migration, service providers and/or recipients are rarely dealt with under the usual migration policy tools. This may be due to the fact that they enter the foreign territory with a specific aim and, once this aim is accomplished, move back to their state of origin; technically they only qualify as short-term non-cyclical migrants and are of little interest to policy-makers. A second reason may be that both service providers and recipients are economically desirable: the former are typically highly skilled and trained professionals and the latter are well-off "visitors", increasing consumption in the host state. A further reason may be that it is quite impossible to quantify the phenomenon: while it is absolutely impossible to know, at any given time, the number of service providers/recipients making use of their Treaty freedoms (especially given that all tourists travelling in other member states are service recipients),[2] it is also very difficult to make any approximate estimation concerning the number of workers posted from one member state to another, for the purpose of performing some service.[3]

The legal definition of services in Article 57 of the Treaty on the Functioning of the European Union (TFEU, ex 50 of the EC Treaty) further nourishes this idea about service providers/recipients not being migrants: the relevant Treaty rules only apply when the provisions on free movement of workers and freedom of establishment – themselves clearly linked to migration – do not apply. This distinction has been clarified by the Court of Justice of the European Union (CJEU, as the European Court of Justice – ECJ – has been renamed by the Lisbon Treaty; both terms and acronyms are used interchangeably, depending on whether reference is made to the past – ECJ – or to the future – CJEU) which has consistently held that the distinction between the rules on establishment, on the one hand, and the rules on services, on the other, lies on duration (see below, 2.1). Indeed, all EU manuals state four types of service provision falling under the EU Treaty: (a) where the service provider moves to the recipient's state, for a short period of time (longer stay would amount to establishment), (b) where the service recipients themselves move to the state where the service is offered (that is, for medical care, education, tourism, and so on), (c) where both service providers and recipients move together in another member state (that is, a tourist guide accompanying a group travelling abroad), and (d) where the service itself is provided across the borders (typically through the use of Information and Communication Technologies – ICTs). None of these situations would typically qualify as migration.

The above "dissociation" between services and migration has been gradually weakened in the recent years. Indeed, migration is increasingly connected to the transnational provision of services. This is the result of three kinds of factors: developments in the ECJ's case law; legislative initiatives in the EU; and the General Agreement on Trade in Services (GATS). Each one of these is considered in some detail below.

The aim of the analysis which follows is to show the extent to which (legislative and judicial) policies aimed at the free provision of services actively affect migration conditions – especially what can be termed "service migration" – within the EU. The EU rules on the provision of services primarily affect the movement of EU nationals. As it will be shown below, however, third country nationals (TCNs) may also claim the benefits of the rules on services, either as recipients thereof or as employees of some EU undertaking which is providing services in another member state (posted workers) or, lastly, as nationals of the WTO states which have signed the GATS.

2. The ECJ extension of rules on services to cover migration

In these last years the ECJ has applied quite extensively the Treaty rules on services (Hatzopoulos, 2000; Hatzopoulos and Do, 2006). Some aspects of this case law have provoked vivid – occasionally violent – reactions, while others have gone quite unnoticed. In the former category, the recent cases concerning posted workers have not only aggrieved trade unions and surprised lawyers specializing in labour and social law, but they have even prompted some of the most prominent EU scholars to ask for disobedience to the Court (Scharpf, 2009). In the latter category, the extensive application of the rules on services in cases where a long-term establishment is involved, has only been noticed by few scholars – and has been welcomed by many of them. Both these developments are highly relevant as means of opening up further migration.

2.1. Rules on services to apply on long-term establishment

According to the black letter of Article 56 TFEU (ex 49 EC), it is supposed to apply to situations where no other Treaty freedom applies; it has a subordinate character. In this respect, services (Article 56) were traditionally distinguished from establishment (Article 49 TFEU, ex 43 EC) by virtue of their temporary nature.[4] This made commentators conclude that service provision must be of an "episodic" or "irregular" nature.[5] In its most recent case law, however, the Court seems to be abandoning the temporal criterion in favour of a more economic one. Indeed, the Court seems ready to treat economic activities which qualify as services under Article 56 TFEU, irrespective of their duration. In *Schnitzer*[6] a German national was pursued in Germany for having employed a Portuguese construction company for 3 years, without it being registered in conformity with the German legislation. Such omission would be illegal if the Portuguese company were deemed to be established in Germany, but not necessarily if it were considered to be a mere service provider.[7] The Court found that "services within the meaning of the Treaty may cover services varying widely in nature, including services which are provided over an extended period, even over several years".[8] Not only did the Court make it clear that it is the economic nature – and not the duration – of the activity that constitutes the main criterion for its legal classification, it also creates a presumption in favour of the application of Article 56 TFEU in all service situations. This is so, according to the Court, since the nature of the activity is readily ascertainable and can safely lead to legal qualifications, while its duration, periodicity, and so on, are not.[9] The (r)evolution of the concept of services catalyzed by the judgement in *Schnitzer*, largely unnoticed by the doctrine,[10] was confirmed by the Court some months later in a case against Portugal concerning private security firms.[11] The Portuguese legislation at stake only concerned undertakings offering private security services within Portugal for longer than a calendar year, and the question arose whether the said legislation could be judged by reference to Article 56 TFEU. Here, again, in view of the economic nature of the activity concerned and the impossibility to determine in advance the duration of trans-border provision, the Court replied in the affirmative.

In this way, the concept of service under the EC Treaty is brought into line with that under the WTO agreement and the GATS (for which see below Section 4). Moreover, logic and coherence are introduced in the way that EC Treaty provisions apply, since the legal category of services is *prima facie* made to coincide with the economic one. Henceforth, the rules on establishment which exist under the EC Treaty (in contrast to the GATS, where no such rules exist) ought to apply only in those cases where the service provider genuinely and permanently moves to another member state.

It therefore becomes clear that any EU national wishing to exercise an economic activity that qualifies as a service in another member state may henceforth invoke the rules on services, even if such service provision entails a (temporary?) migration. Under any kind of classification of migrations (King, 2002; Triandafyllidou and Gropas, 2007; Triandafyllidou et al., 2007), a delocalization for a period of one – or several – years in another state does qualify as migration and, indeed, long-term migration. Therefore, all the rules on services – including the Services Directive – become relevant for intra-EU migration.

This is not a purely theoretical development, but has serious practical consequences. While the Treaty provisions on the free movement of workers and freedom of establishment are based on the idea that migrants should, in principle, comply with all the requirements of the host state, the service providers are allowed, to a large extent, to rely on their home state regulatory framework while offering their services abroad. Through the imposition of extensive mutual recognition obligations and administrative cooperation, the Court has put into place an imperfect (and unspoken) country of origin principle (CoOP) (Hatzopoulos, 2008a). This translates into some kind of regime portability: all qualifications, guarantee deposits, other authorization requirements examined by the home state, safety and security regulations complied with in the home state, and so on, should be given full effect in the host state (Hatzopoulos, 1999; Hatzopoulos, 2008b). In the recent cases concerning posted workers (for which see below Section 2.2) the Court went as far as recognizing that this regime portability covers, under certain circumstances, also the employment legislation and collective agreements in force in the home state.

It is clear that this regime portability enhances the mobility of service providers across the borders. Therefore, the extension *ratione temporis* of the scope of application of the rules on services to cover periods extending to several years may have positive impact on intra-community migration; it may, thus, qualify as a facilitator.[12] While, on the face of it, such a facilitator only concerns EU nationals, in the following paragraphs it will be shown that TCNs are also to a large extent favoured in their migration plans by such a development.

2.2. Posted workers

The starting point in the Court's case law concerning posted workers are cases *Evi v Seco*, *Rush Portuguesa*, and *Vander Elst*.[13] The first concerned a French undertaking using third country nationals in railway repairs in Luxembourg, the second a Portuguese undertaking deploying Portuguese nationals (at a time when they did not yet benefit from free movement) in railway construction in France, and the third, a Belgian undertaking deploying Moroccan workers in construction (read: demolition) works in France. Read together, these three cases broadly settled the issue of posted workers, along with three key principles: (a) a service provider may move from one member state to another with his own personnel, irrespective of their nationality, without having to satisfy supplementary administrative requirements linked either to immigration or to labour market regulations; (b) a service provider may, nonetheless, be required to comply with the legislation (collective agreements, arbitral sentences, and so on) of the host State concerning minimum remuneration and other working conditions and all national measures reasonably suited to enforcing/monitoring such a requirement are acceptable;[14] (c) a service provider may not be required to comply with all the social security obligations and linked formalities for workers who are already covered in his (home) state of establishment, unless such burdens actually add up to the protection of workers. These basic principles, especially in relation to minimum pay, were later "codified" by Directive 96/71.[15] All three principles above were consequently confirmed in *Arblade and Leloup*, which concerned two French undertakings who had been employing their own personnel (the nationality of which is not specified in the Court's judgement) in Silo constructions in Belgium and were required to pay supplementary social security contributions for them.[16] It is also worth noting that, following the adoption of Directive 96/71 and while the above judgements were still pending, in February 1999 the Commission tabled a draft directive on the posting of workers who are third country nationals for the provision of cross-border services,[17] but this initiative did not receive the support of member states and was subsequently dropped from the Commission's agenda.

It is in the last 10 years, however, that developments in the area of posted workers have been spectacular; in at least two respects. For one thing, the Court has cut down on national administrative requirements concerning entry and working conditions of TCNs (Section 2.2.1.). More importantly, the Court has somehow curbed the principle that posted workers should be fully subject to working and pay conditions of the host country (Section 2.2.2.). While the former development makes it easier for TCNs to integrate the EU job market, the latter confers on them (or gives them back) a clear competitive advantage over indigenous workers.

2.2.1. *Softening up administrative requirements for entry and work*

Already in *Vander Elst*[18] the Court had held that it was enough for TCNs legally resident and employed in Belgium and temporarily posted to France to comply only with the migration requirements of the latter state and that no individual working permits could be required by the French authorities. Similarly, in *Commission v. Luxembourg, posted workers I*,[19] EU rules on services were found to be breached by a measure requiring service providers deploying non-EU personnel in Luxembourg to obtain individual or collective working permits. From the above case law it stems that TCNs may work in a member state without having the required working permit, as long as such work is provided in the framework of an employment contract with an undertaking based in any other member state.

In *Commission v. Germany, posted workers*,[20] the regulation at stake required foreign workers to be in possession of an entry and work visa, which was only delivered to posted workers provided *inter alia* that they were already employed with the posting firm for at least a year. The Court found this requirement – and in general the visa regime – in violation of Article 56 TFEU. Again, a declaration obligation imposed on the posting undertaking would suffice for the protection of the reasons invoked by Germany. In a subsequent case, however, even a notification obligation, was held to violate Article 56 TFEU, because it contained "ambiguities" that were able to "dissuade undertakings wishing to post workers to Luxembourg from exercising their freedom to provide services."[21]

2.2.2. *Wage and social rights portability*

2.2.2.1. Inroads to the full applicability of host state legislation. Concerning minimum pay, the Court has shown clear signs of departure from full and automatic application of the host state legislation. In *Mazzoleni*[22] the question arose whether the personnel of a French security company occasionally deployed in sites in Belgium should be paid at the higher tariffs applicable in Belgium. The Court held that the application of the host country legislation may become, under certain circumstances, neither *necessary* nor *proportional*.[23] The necessity test requires the host state authorities to verify whether their national legislation is needed to ensure an "equivalent" level of remuneration for workers, taking into account fiscal and social charges applicable in the states concerned.[24] Even if the necessity test is satisfied, the application of the host state legislation may still be countered if it entails disproportionate administrative burdens for the service provider or inequalities between its employees (proportionality test).[25] A few months later in *Portugaia Construcoes*[26] the Court held that the host State's collective agreement on salaries could be applied only if it contributed in a "significant way" to the employees' social protection.[27] Therefore the sacrosanct principle of the respect of host state minimum pay requirements becomes conditional on (a) significantly increasing the employees' revenue and (b) not disproportionally burdening the employer (!).[28] Broadly the same principles above apply in relation to social security contributions in the host state, following the Court's judgement in *Finalarte*.[29]

2.2.2.2. Portability of home state legislation? It is, however, with its infamous judgements in *Laval*, *Viking* and *Rüffert*,[30] that the Court has administered a decisive blow to the applicability of host state minimum wages and rules of social protection, and has opened the way for some kind of regime portability for posted workers. These judgements are extremely important in many respects and have aroused excitement among trade unions, practitioners, and academic writers (Ashiagbor 2009; Barnard, 2008; Blanpain, 2009; Cremers et al., 2007; Dashwood, 2008; Deakin, 2008; Hös, 2009; Malmberg and Sigeman, 2008). In *Laval* and *Viking* the main question raised was that of the legality of industrial action undertaken by trade unions in high-wage countries (Sweden and Finland, respectively) in order to impose their own wage requirements on low-wage posted workers (from Latvia and Estonia, respectively, at a time when such workers enjoyed no right to work on their own). The Court held that industrial action by trade unions (in high-wage countries) should be exercised in accordance to the Treaty fundamental freedoms (such as the freedom of establishment and the free provision of services) and only be the source of restrictions which are proportional to the aims pursued: only if the level of protection afforded to posted workers under the legislation of their (low-wage) state was inadequate would industrial action be justified. Failure to take into account the level of protection ensured under the home state legislation is not merely a hindrance to the enjoyment of the fundamental freedoms, but discrimination proper: it is one of the rare situations where discrimination lies in the application of the same rules to different situations, the difference being that foreign service providers are already subject to their home rules on workers' protection. In other words, the failure to apply the principle of mutual recognition (of social and other charges) amounts, in this case, to discrimination![31]

The need to take into account the level of protection already offered by the legislation of the home state has been further confirmed in very strong words in both cases. Thus, in *Laval* one bit of Swedish legislation was condemned since it failed "to take into account, irrespective of their content, collective agreements to which undertakings that post workers to Sweden are already bound in the Member State in which they are established".[32]

The Posted Workers Directive 96/71 for its part, which was supposed to ensure that basic employment regulations of the host state apply to all workers posted there,[33] has been seriously undermined by the Court in *Laval*, and even more so in the subsequent *Rüffert* and *Commission v Luxembourg* cases,[34] in four ways. First, the scope of measures which the host member state may impose on posted workers has been drastically circumscribed, while the list of issues on which the host state may apply its own legislation, has been construed as being an exhaustive one.[35] Second, the possibility of the host state to impose measures justified by public order considerations, is also seriously restricted and controlled by the Court.[36] Third, contrary to a clear statement in recital 17 and Article 3(7), whereby the Directive's terms "shall not prevent application of terms and conditions which are more favourable to workers", the Court has transformed the "floor" into a "ceiling" by striking down more favourable national arrangements.[37] Fourth – and this is the development having the most far reaching consequences – the Court in the most recent *Commission v Luxembourg, posted workers II* case, discretely opens the way for using the Directive against its very objective, in order to pre-empt the host state from imposing its own measures on posted workers: for issues which are subject to a minimum harmonization and are, as a matter of law, secured by all member states, the host member state may not impose its own (more demanding) conditions.[38]

Therefore, the Court transforms what was initially thought of as a guarantee against social dumping and as a safe harbour from the application of the country of origin principle to quite the contrary: a presumption of regime portability. Such portability stems from Articles 49 and 56 TFEU and may, on some occasions, be orchestrated by virtue of the very directive that was supposed to prevent it.

Such a result may seem far-fetched and even absurd in the light of the considerations above. From a migration point of view, however, it may not be as undesirable an outcome. Indeed, it may be said that the Court's recent case law is informed from the neoclassical analysis of migration.[39] The Court tacitly acknowledges wage differentials as the main driving force behind economic migration and, through the above case law, creates the conditions for wage competition and self-regulation through the labour market. Increased supply of labour in high-wage countries will cause wages to drop, while at the same time wages in the sending countries will rise as a consequence of labour shortages there. Eventually, wages in the sending/receiving countries will converge and the motivation to migrate will decline; by the same token real convergence of member states economies will have been achieved. From such a perspective the Court's case law on posted workers makes perfect sense: in the short term it enhances migration and, hence, free movement, while in the medium to long term it contributes towards "an ever closer Union" since it brings wages and other market conditions closer.

This pro-migration stance of the Court of Justice is not new. Indeed, the Court has constantly lent its support to migrant workers, since the beginnings of the Community. Not only has the Court supported European workers, but also TCNs associated with some European undertaking. In the latter case, instead of the rules on the free movement of workers and freedom of establishment, the Court had to ground its findings on the rules on services. It is also no secret that the Posted Workers Directive corresponds to the member states' effort to circumscribe the Court's early case law on TCNs as posted workers (Davies 1997; Meyer 1998).

On the other hand, it may not be said that the Court has been unaware of the risks of regulatory competition stemming from its pro-migration stance. Already in *Vander Elst* the Court found that "the application of the Belgian system in any event excludes any substantial risk of workers being exploited or of competition between undertakings being distorted".[40] This consideration, however, has been forgotten in subsequent case law and, in any event, does not hold true after the 2004 and 2007 enlargements and the accession in the Community of low-wage countries. Therefore, it could be said that the Court privileges migration, integration, and effective equalization of working conditions in the medium term, at the price of permitting short-term regulatory competition. Such an approach – if it does exist – makes sense where European nationals are concerned, but much less so in relation to TCNs. In the Court's case law, however, such a distinction cannot be identified. Based on Article 56 TFEU and the nationality of the employer/service provider – not that of the employee/posted worker – the Court's case law benefits European and non-European workers alike. It is true that the recent enlargements temporarily shifted the focus from the latter to the former, but the path there has also been opened for migrant workers from third countries.[41]

3. EC legislature facilitating foreign service provider activity

3.1. The services directive 2006/123 – enhancing service provision

The Services Directive does not concern migration; it is primarily concerned with the intra-EU provision of services. Its main focus, therefore, are Community nationals, not TCNs (Section 3.1.1.). Moreover, the few provisions of the (Bolkestein) draft directive which affected posted workers have been dropped from the final text. TCNs, nevertheless, may be the indirect beneficiaries of various provisions of the Services Directive, in at least three ways (Section 3.1.2.). Indeed, to the extent that this directive will actually facilitate the cross-border provision of services, it will also increase migration pressures.

3.1.1. *Facilitating the establishment of EC service providers*

One of the main inputs of the Services Directive – and the one least discussed by legal writers – is the extent to which it simplifies the establishment of service providers. Chapter III of the Directive (Articles 9–15) constitutes the first piece of legislation of a horizontal nature (that is, not sector-specific, such as the TV without frontiers Directive) to align the economic with the legal concept of services (see above Section 2.1.

for the corresponding case law) and to regulate the establishment of service providers.

Service providers wishing to establish themselves in another member state, have, in principle, to comply with the host state legislation. This requirement has been tempered, by the Court, through the imposition of the general principles of non-discrimination, necessity, proportionality, and mutual recognition. Chapter III of the Directive codifies the relevant case law of the Court in two sections, one concerning authorization procedures and the other all other measures restricting establishment.

Such codification does offer some clear added value. First, the codification of the case law into the text of a directive – and its transcription into national law – does away with the case-specific character of the principles developed by the Court and brings them closer to both service providers and to member states' administrations. Second, these principles shift from being *ex post* remedies for service providers into *ex ante* obligations for national administrations. Third, the Directive goes beyond mere principles and offers practical details about their application, something the Court may only rarely do. Fourth, member states' discretionary powers are circumscribed, to the extent that states are subject to reporting obligations on the restrictions maintained/imposed both to one another and to the Commission (Article 39 of the Directive).

3.1.2. Enhancing service provision – to the benefit of EC and TC nationals

3.1.2.1. The provision of information – for prospective service providers. One of the major innovations introduced by the Directive – and the most daunting task for national administrations – is the institution of "points of single contact" (Article 6) which should be able to (a) deal with all the necessary applications and documents for taking up the relevant economic activity, (b) assist prospective service providers with their applications, and (c) provide them with all the necessary information. This information should include (Article 7(1)):

(a) requirements applicable to providers established in their territory, in particular those requirements concerning the procedures and formalities to be completed in order to access and to exercise service activities;
(b) the contact details of the competent authorities enabling the latter to be contacted directly, including the details of those authorities responsible for matters concerning the exercise of service activities;

(c) the means of, and conditions for, accessing public registers and databases on providers and services;
(d) the means of redress which are generally available in the event of dispute between the competent authorities and the provider or the recipient, or between a provider and a recipient or between providers;
(e) the contact details of the associations or organizations, other than the competent authorities, from which providers or recipients may obtain practical assistance.

Such information should be "easily accessible at a distance and by electronic means and that they are kept up to date" (Article 7(3)).

As soon as such information becomes available on the web, it is to be expected that private initiative and entrepreneurship will complete it with extra information on the kind of services already available on the market, practical requirements and tips for the provision of services, data on demand of various services, and other packages of electronic data concerning (mainly) professional services. Such information will be primarily aimed at EU service providers. It will, however, also be available to TCNs, to whom it will be equally valuable.

Indeed, one of the main reasons migration pressures are rendered fuzzy and unpredictable – and thus immigration policies are condemned to failure – is the erratic dissemination of information about the market conditions pertaining in the host state (Triandafyllidou, 2009). Greater availability of information is expected to attract more and more suitable migrant workers, both Community nationals and TCNs. Next to this quantitative leap, a qualitative one is also to be expected: since the information provided online will essentially concern service (that is, essentially white-collar) activities, qualified migration is likely to benefit from the whole transparency process. Further (third), and in relation to the previous point, the desire of member states to attract migrant workers qualified in specific service areas, such as IT services, may lead to further simplification of the requirements for the take up of the relevant activities; such simplified requirements may be seen as completing the "Blue Card" system put in place by Directive 2009/50.[42] In this respect, migration concerns may act as catalysts of reducing red tape and rationalizing the provision of services.

3.1.2.2. Consumer protection – for service recipients. Service provision also covers the movement of recipients to meet the providers of their choice – and such movement may constitute migration: studying abroad or receiving long-term medical treatments may take several years. In this respect the Services Directive innovates by introducing rules in favour of service recipients. In a short section consisting of three articles the Directive prohibits restrictions imposed by the *home* state (Article 19), condemns discriminatory measures liable to be adopted by the *host* state (Article 20), and offers "assistance to recipients" (Article 21).

To be more precise, the recipient's home state may neither impose any authorization or declaration requirement nor put limits on the financial aid to which the recipient is entitled, just because they have opted for receiving a given service in another member state. Clearly, the principles established in *Kohll*, *Smits and Peerbooms*, and *Vanbraekel* underpin Article 19 of the Directive.[43] Similarly, the Court's judgements in *Trojani*, *Collins*, and *Bidar*,[44] seem to transcend Article 20 which prevents the host state from introducing any discriminatory measure against foreign service recipients. It has to be stressed that – unlike Article 16 of the Directive – the two provisions on service recipients do not exclude services of general economic interest. Hence, they may be invoked by nationals of one member state in order to secure access to services having a social character in other member states: henceforth, mobile students or patients will be able to invoke these provisions in order to gain access to grants offered in the "host" member state or refunds, and the like, secured by their home state.

These same provisions may also be invoked by TCNs legally established in a member state. The Court, already in *Svensson and Gustavsson*[45] has held that, as long as there is a service flowing from one member state to another, it matters little that the recipient of such service is a TCN. The Services Directive itself, in Article 4(3), defines as recipient "any natural person who is a national of a Member State or who benefits from rights conferred upon him by Community acts...who, for professional or non-professional purposes, uses, or wishes to use, a service." More interestingly, it may be that Article 20 of the Services Directive, which requires states to "ensure that the recipient is not made subject to discriminatory requirements based on his nationality or place of residence" and that providers established in their territory do not discriminate on those grounds, is the first EC text explicitly to extend to TCNs the principle of non discrimination on grounds of nationality.[46]

The final provision on service recipients aims at making information accessible to recipients and at building up confidence in services offered within other member states: electronic means of communication, single points of contact, simple guides, and so on, are all available to the service recipients in their home state. This information is different from – and adds up to – that provided under Article 7 (above), as it does not concern the conditions for the provision of services, but rather the opportunities for receiving services in other member states.

3.1.2.3. Administrative cooperation. The creation of one or more "liaison points" in every member state responsible for the exchange of information between national authorities will certainly help the application of the Directive (Article 28). In addition, a "European network of Member States" authorities' will run an alert mechanism whenever it "becomes aware of serious specific acts or circumstances relating to a service activity that could cause serious damage to the health or safety of persons or to the environment" (Article 32). An electronic system for the exchange of information (Article 34(1)) and some rules on the respective competences of the home and host state complete the rules on cooperation.

All the above are ways to rationalize and adapt the way that national administrations work in order for them to cope more efficiently with the increased mobility of service providers and recipients. The Court's extended case law shows that the areas in which administrative cooperation is highly deficient are the ones directly connected with individual rights affected by free movement: pension, and health care rights,[47] as well as recognition of professional qualifications (for which see below Section 3.4).

These should be seen, together with the SOLVIT system, put into place by the Commission as a means of extra-judicial settlement of disputes related to the internal market.[48] This system consists of a network of online dispute resolution available both to undertakings and to consumers. The "plaintiffs" contact the SOLVIT point of contact in their country. If the complaint is within the "tasks" of the SOLVIT network, this contact point registers it within an electronic database and contacts the SOLVIT point in the member state where the problem has occurred. The latter SOLVIT point, together with the authorities of the state concerned, tries to resolve the problem. This system, after a hesitant start, has gained in credibility and the number of disputes settled increases year after year.[49] There are, however, two limitations to SOLVIT's potential. It is competent to intervene on a limited number of issues.[50] Moreover, SOLVIT has only vertical but no horizontal action: it may mediate only between an individual and a state authority, not between two individuals.

Direct administrative cooperation together with cooperation through SOLVIT are means deemed to facilitate the movement of persons within the internal market. They are liable, however, by their very logic and by the dynamism they entail, to lead to the rationalization and simplification of the regulatory environment in general, to the further benefit of TCNs.

3.2. The modification of the social security regulation 1408/71 – extending (home state) regime portability

Regulation 1408/71 on the coordination of social security systems puts into place a system of portability of pension and health care rights. This Regulation has been modified at least 30 times, the last important modification extending its personal scope to cover TCNs legally residing within the EU.[51] This extension was indirectly prompted by the Court's earlier judgement in *Khalil*,[52] where it held that the personal scope of the Regulation lawfully extended to refugees and stateless people established within the EU.

Regulation 1408/71 has been codified and repealed by Regulation (EC) 883/2004[53] which entered into force on 1 March 2010. The new Regulation does not radically depart from the previous one, but does prolong the period during which employees may remain subject to their home state social security system from 12–24 months. One further innovation is the abolition of "Annex VII situations", whereby a person may exceptionally be subject to two social security schemes. Henceforth, a person, who works as an employee as well as a self-employed person in several countries at the same time, will automatically be subject to the social security scheme for self-employed persons of the state which is already competent for the employed activities (with regard to the totality of his activities). Both modifications strengthen the workers' links with their home countries and should be read together with the Court's case law, discussed above, which recognizes a "regime portability" for posted workers.

3.3. The long-term migrants directive – The Blue Card Directive: mobility of TCNs as service providers/recipients

The Long-Term Residence Directive[54] foresees a privileged status for those TCNs who have legally remained within the EU for over 5 years. This directive is said to institute some kind of "civil citizenship" for integrated TCNs, running parallel to the European citizenship.[55] It gives migrants two broad categories of rights. First, the directive gives to long-term migrants a very secure status: life-long right to stay in the member state where they have legally remained for 5 years (Article 8), automatic issuance and renewal of residence permits (Article 8), protection against expulsion even where public order is at stake (Articles 9–10 and 12), treatment "similar"[56] to that of nationals of the member state concerned (Article 11) in respect of professional life, access to health care social benefits, schooling, pensions, and so on.

Second, and more importantly from the point of view of the present study, the Directive grants TCNs the right to free movement within the entire EC, broadly on the same terms as this right is recognized to EC nationals. Therefore, TCNs may (a) on the basis of their long-term permit travel in any other member state for a period not exceeding 3 months and (b) move (together with their families) temporarily or permanently in any other member state in an employed or self-employed capacity (Article 14). Therefore, they may easily travel abroad as service recipients and, more importantly, may move to other member states in order to offer services there.[57]

A similar right to freely move to other member states and become established there for shorter or longer periods is instituted by the Blue Card Directive 2009/50[58] in favour of the Blue Card holders, after only 18 months of legal residence in one member state (Article 18). Contrary to the Long-Term Residents Directive, however, the Blue Card Directive specifically provides that this right may only be exercised "for the purpose of highly qualified employment there", therefore excluding self-employed activities. Hence, from a legal point of view it may not be said that Blue Card holders have a right to the free provision of services, since the main feature distinguishing a service provider from an employee is economic independence. In economic terms, however, Blue Card holders will, in the absolute majority of cases, be providing services. Moreover, as any other TCN, Blue Card holders may travel to other member states for short periods not exceeding 3 months on the basis of their residence card.

Although it is true that Article 56 TFEU and the Services Directive (Article 4(2)) only contemplate the provision of services by EC nationals, they do cover TCNs as service recipients. Moreover, it is difficult to see how the above categories of professionals (long-term residents and Blue Card holders) providing services will, in practice, be deprived of the benefits of the said rules. Therefore, it may safely be said that the directives on Long-Term Residence and the Blue Card – two migration legislative instruments par excellence – will have a double effect on service provision within the EU: for one thing there will be an increased offer and demand of services and, presumably, greater service mobility; this, in turn, will trigger the application of the rules on the free provision of services in situations for which they were not contemplated.

3.4. The new "general system" on professional qualifications

Mutual recognition of diplomas and professional experience has always been one of the objectives of the Treaty. What is now Article 53 TFEU (ex 47 EC) has grounded the issuance of numerous "transitory" measures of recognition of professional qualifications already since 1964,[59] followed by the issuance of the sector specific directives for six health professions, architects, and lawyers in the 1970s and 1980s and, finally, the General Systems in the 1990s.[60] All these legal instruments have now been either repealed or consolidated and extended by Directive 2005/36.

Directive 2005/36 innovates in at least three ways. First, it is much more flexible than the pre-existing General Systems in that it foresees five different levels for the recognition of equivalence (Article 11), starting from the mere "attestation of competence" delivered as proof of a simple training course, 3 years experience or general primary and secondary education and going up to a "diploma" certifying at least 4 years post-secondary education. Second, in doing so, it allows more extensively for professional experience to be taken into account. Third, it also allows for qualifications and professional experience acquired in non-member states to be taken into account. Article 3(3) expressly states that "evidence of formal qualifications issued by a third country shall be regarded as evidence of formal qualifications if the holder has three years professional experience in the profession concerned on the territory of the Member State which recognized that evidence of formal qualifications". Article 14(5), on the other hand, deals with professional experience and foresees that "if the host Member State intends to require the applicant to complete an adaptation period or take an aptitude test, it must first ascertain whether the knowledge acquired by the applicant in the course of his professional experience in a Member State or in a third country, is of a nature to cover, in full or in part, the substantial difference".

All three innovations are important for EC nationals. They are also extremely important for TCNs since their qualifications are likely to have been achieved in non-member states and will be more difficult to compare with "equivalent" levels of study in the member states. Moreover, the fact that experience acquired in third countries may be "validated" *ex post*, after 3 years of exercising the corresponding profession, is extremely valuable to TCNs.

Formally, the scope of Directive 2005/36 seems to be contemplating EC nationals as being the only beneficiaries of the rights it organizes. However, the Long-Term Resident's Directive foresees that "[l]ong-term residents shall enjoy equal treatment with nationals as regards: [...] c) recognition of professional diplomas, certificates and other qualifications in accordance with the relevant national procedures".[61] A similar clause is foreseen in favour of the Blue Card holders by the relevant directive.[62] In an oblique, yet clear, way the scope of the General System for the mutual recognition of professional qualifications is being extended to cover TCNs who fall within the scope of these two directives. By the same token, the provisions of the General System briefly presented above become all the more important for encouraging (qualified) TCNs' migration into the EU.

4. The impact of the GATS

4.1. Introducing the GATS

In the GATS, the WTO signatory states have, for the first time, agreed on a basic framework for the free trade of services. The GATS covers all services, subject to exceptions. It covers all kinds of service trade across the borders. These are typified under four modes. *Cross-border provision* (mode 1), whereby a service provided in one state is used by a recipient in another state, typically making use of ICTs; *consumption abroad* (mode 2), where the recipient moves towards the provider's state, there to receive the services offered (typically tourism, health, education); *commercial presence* (mode 3), whereby the provider establishes, for example, a branch or subsidiary in another state, in order to provide services; and *presence of natural persons* (mode 4), whereby service providers move to another state themselves or post their personnel. The GATS concerns measures which affect trade in services in one of the above ways, provided they emanate from governments and public authorities – but it does not cover "private measures". Measures affecting trade in services are essentially non-tariff ones and, typically, are not imposed at the border. They follow increasingly more sophisticated policy objectives than regulations affecting trade in goods. Broadly, restrictions in services trade may account for one of the following four objectives: (a) prevent market abuse, (b) compensate for the lack of information and information asymmetries, (c) rationalize and internalize the cost of externalities,

(d) secure public policy (social, distributional, and so on) objectives.[63] The scope of the GATS is widened by the fact that it concerns measures "affecting" – not only those specifically "regulating" or "governing" – trade in services. Because of its wide scope, the breadth of the obligations imposed by the GATS is limited and varies from one state to another. Indeed, the GATS imposes two series of obligations.[64] First, it imposes limited unconditional obligations. These amount to the duty (a) not to discriminate between service providers from the various WTO members, by virtue of a general most favoured-nation (MFN) clause (Art. II), (b) to ensure transparency when adopting and implementing the various trade-related measures (Art. III), and (c) to put into place some procedural safeguards at the service of foreign service providers (Arts. VI, IX e.a.).[65] These "unconditional" obligations are themselves subject to exceptions. Second, GATS signatory states have undertaken conditional obligations, also known as "specific commitments" in respect of two legal obligations: market access (Art. XVI, covering essentially – but not exclusively – quantitative restrictions and measures having an equivalent effect) and national treatment (Art. XVII, non-discrimination between domestic and foreign service providers). Signatory states have filled in "schedules" annexed to the GATS agreement, whereby, for each of the two above legal obligations – and for each one of the four modes – they commit to a variable degree of liberalization, on a service by service basis.[66] For each one of the two disciplines (market access and national treatment) and for each mode of supply, states have (a) specified the restrictions thereto, (b) imposed no restrictions, or (c) declared themselves unbound (no liberalization at all). In areas where states have made commitments, some additional disciplines apply as of right, without any declaration being necessary (that is, Art. VI). States may also offer additional commitments (Art. XVIII). These schedules are extremely long (more than 30,000 pages for all signatory states) and complicated, with virtually no two states having made identical commitments.[67]

4.2. The GATS and migration: present and (tentative) future

Commitments in respect of mode 4 of the GATS are the least numerous and the most restricted of all. In the original negotiation of the GATS the intention was that there would be a rough reciprocity between liberalization under mode 3 (establishment of service outlets through FDI), which was mostly in the interest of developed countries, and mode 4 (temporary migration abroad), which was expected to be of more interest to developing countries. Such reciprocity never occurred despite (or because of) mode 4 negotiations being extended several months beyond the official end of the Uruguay round. More than two-thirds of the commitments offered concern executives, managers, and specialists and about one third of these are limited to intra-corporate transfers. The extent to which modes 3 and 4 are substitutes or complements one to the other is disputed among GATS specialists.[68] A further dispute, and a more relevant one for the purposes of the present contribution, is whether mode 4 GATS should be seen as entailing migration. According to trade negotiators, people providing services under mode 4 are not entering the local labour market because their stay is temporary, they do not form part of "labour", and they are not seeking residency or citizenship status. Immigration officials, on the other hand, argue that "temporary" often extends to periods as long as 3 years and, therefore, even if service providers do not seek to, they do in fact participate in the local labour market by providing a service a local person could probably do. "From this point of view, service providers have entered the local labor market and are implicated in local labor an[d] employment market conditions, including those arising from personal taxation, union representation and employer tax burdens in relation to employees. The service provider is therefore a 'laborer' with all the accompanying economic and social linkages" (Young, 2000, p. 186). This vision is further strengthened by the way in which statistical data is kept: in the "Statistical Yearbook" published by IMF, when service providers move across the borders for less than a year, their wages are registered as income for the sending state, while for longer periods service providers are considered to form part of the host economy and only their remittances towards the home state are taken into account.[69] Irrespective of the position adopted in the above dilemma, it is beyond any doubt that the GATS does not cover pure immigration control and police measures, typically in the form of entry conditions, visa requirements, extraditions, and so on, as this would seriously challenge state sovereignty. The GATS does, however, cover most other policies affecting migration. In the areas where signatory states have made commitments under mode 4, and unless they have made express reservations, they may neither restrict market access by imposing quantitative restrictions, either in absolute numbers or connected to an economic needs test, nor deviate from national treatment by imposing special requirements for access to or exercise of the service activity concerned. In the few areas where WTO states have made full commitments under mode 4 (if any), their obligations are very similar to the ones stemming under Article 56 TFEU for EC member states. Despite the fact that states have avoided making substantial commitments under mode 4, they are, nevertheless bound, by the unconditional obligations of the GATS. This may have several practical effects. For one, the MFN obligation prohibits any discrimination between different foreign service providers; therefore, any facility (if any) offered to the nationals of one signatory state should be opened up to all the others. Second, according to Article III, states are to inform one another of all existing and forthcoming measures affecting the application of the Agreement. This obligation, if properly implemented,[70] would account for a very high degree of transparency in respect of measures affecting service provision, such as opening hours, price levels (if regulated), territorial restrictions, conditions for access to the various service activities, national monopolies, and so on. Such transparency would, on its own, and without any further ado, affect migratory flows, both quality and quantity wise. Third, regarding professional qualifications and experience, Article VII GATS specifically provides the possibility for bilateral, plurilateral, or, indeed, multilateral agreements of mutual recognition. These, whenever adopted, will also exert pressure on migration flows. Last but not least, whenever states have not declared themselves to be "unbound" by the GATS, and irrespective of the amount of restrictions they have scheduled in respect of mode 4, the "additional obligations" become applicable as of right. In this respect, Article VI of the GATS, may be of paramount importance: it requires states to (a) administer measures in a reasonable, objective and impartial way; (b) to make sure that service providers obtain reasoned decisions in respect of the exercise of their activity subject to some kind of judicial control, and, most importantly (c) to make sure that the technical standards applicable to service provision are proportionate and objectively justified.[71] All the above obligations, stemming both from the specific commitments and from the unconditional obligations, are liable to receive special weight if combined with EC law: European migrant workers already enjoy a number of substantial rights and, questionably, such rights are not to be extended to TCNs under the MFN clause contained in Article II GATS. The main legal reason justifying preferential treatment of EU, compared to non-EU, nationals is Article V GATS allowing derogations for regional agreements of economic integration. However, the precise content of Article V is disputed in legal doctrine (Stephenson, 2000), and a restrictive interpretation thereof is favoured by many authors. Indeed, it is questionable whether Article V also covers new measures (that is, measures adopted by the regional organization after the entry into force of the GATS) and whether it is not restricted to measures which are strictly necessary to the fulfilment of the Regional organization's objectives – a test which makes measures subject to a test of necessity and proportionality.[72]

Finally, it should be kept in mind that the re-scheduling of GATS mode 4 is one of the major objectives underpinning the current (Doha) round of negotiations under the WTO. Therefore, if the effects of GATS mode 4 have gone unperceived up until now, this is very likely to change in the near future.

5. Conclusion

It is now well documented and widely accepted that democratic states have limited leeway in (not) accepting migrants for the purpose of family reunification, or when such immigrants seek asylum. In respect of economic migration, on the contrary, there is a widespread belief that states are not bound by any legal obligations. The preceding analysis shows that this perception is inaccurate and that there are various sources of legal obligations concerning economic migrants, whether they are self-employed or in a subordinate employment situation. These obligations are more or less compelling, depending on their source, and are more or less far reaching, depending on the degree of maturity of the relevant rules.

Being an early starter, the EU has a clear advance over the WTO, in relation to the free movement of workers. This advance explains that in the EU, the shortfalls of free movement – in particular in the form of social dumping – have already surfaced. In the framework of the WTO, the members of which are far more numerous and heterogeneous, a similar level of free movement of professionals is not to be expected any time soon, even if the Doha round concludes successfully. If in the field of trade in goods, the GATT was able to avoid social dumping by the imposition of anti-dumping duties, a comparable technique is hardly imaginable in the GATS framework, as it would run counter to the very principle underlying free trade, that is, comparative advantage. The rules described above, however, imperfect and problematic as they are, produce a secondary effect not directly perceptible at first reading. In the EU, this secondary effect, progressively developed by the Court's case law on free movement, has been termed "European citizenship" and has been written into the Treaty text itself, thus acquiring constitutional value. This consists of a series of procedural rights recognized to all European citizens when moving to another member state (and lately also even when they are not moving). Article VI GATS, which becomes applicable "automatically" as soon as a signatory state offers some commitments in its schedules under mode 4, also provides for a series of procedural rights in favour of service providers moving in other states. Could we then talk of the forthcoming emergence of a "global citizenship" for economic migrants?

Notes

1. Some authors even talk of "co-production" of services; see Rubalcaba, L. (2007) "Historical and Anthropological Origin of the Service Economy" in L. Rubalcaba (ed.) *The New Service Economy, Challenges and Policy Implications for Europe* (Cheltenham/Northampton: Edward Elgar) 14–42.
2. See Case 186/87 *Cowan* [1989] ECR 195 and, more recently, Case C-215/03 *Oulane* [2005] ECR I-1215.
3. In its 2007 communication on posted workers (COM (2007) 747) the Commission states that "[t]here are no precise figures or estimates of posted workers in the EU. However, the overall number of posted workers is estimated to be just under 1 million or about 0.4% of the EU working age population in 2005. They represent significant numbers in some Member States (Germany, France, Luxembourg, Belgium or Poland) but the phenomenon is increasingly widespread and affects now all Member States as sending and/or as receiving countries."
4. Case 205/84, *Commission v. Germany, Insurance* [1986] ECR 3755; subsequently broadened by Case C-55/94, *Gebhard* [1995] ECR I-4165, where the Court held that (para 27): "not only the duration of the provision of the service, but also its regularity, periodicity or continuity" should be taken into account.
5. See Hatzopoulos (2000) 45, where this restrictive approach of the Court was also criticized as being inappropriate in view of the current development and sophistication of services.
6. Case C-215/01, *Schnitzer* [2003] ECR I-14847.
7. See, for example, the *Tourist Guide cases*, see Cases C-154/89, C-180/89, and C-189/89, respectively *Commission v. France, Italy and Greece* [1991] ECR I-659.
8. *Schnitzer*, n. 6 above, para 30.
9. *Schnitzer*, n. 6, para 39; it is worth noting that the Services Directive (for which see below 3.1 and especially 3.1.1) follows broadly the same logic.
10. Some authors have observed the newness of the Court's approach but have hesitated to identify a fully new direction, see, for example, Prieto, C. (2004) "Liberté d'établissement et de prestation de services", *RTDE*, 543, which speaks of the temporal criterion as being *"dilaté"* in this case.
11. Case C-171/02, *Commission v. Portugal, Private Security Firms* [2004] I-5645.
12. For the concept of migration facilitators see, among several writers, Papademetriou, D. (2003) "Managing Rapid and Deep Change in the Newest Age of Migration", in Spencer, S. (ed.), *The Politics of Immigration, Managing Opportunity, Conflict and Change* (Massachusetts etc: Blackwell), 39–58.
13. Joined Cases 62/81 and 63/81, *Evi v. Seco* [1982] ECR I-223; Case C-113/89, *Rush Portuguesa* [1990] ECR I-1417; Case C-43/93, *Vander Elst* [1994] ECR I-3803.

14. For the importance of minimal pay agreements as a means to combat poverty see Funk, L. and Lesch, H. (2006) "Minimum Wage Regulations in Selected European Countries", *Intereconomics*, 89.
15. Directive 96/71/EC of the European Parliament and of the Council of 16 December 1996 concerning the posting of workers in the framework of the provision of services, OJ [1996] L 18/ 1; the word codified is oversimplifying in this context, as the exact content of the Directive and the extent to which it restricts or expands the scope of application of previous case law has been hotly disputed by legal scholars, see, for example, Davies, P. (1997) "Posted workers: Single market or protection of national labour law systems?" *CMLRev* 34: 571–602; Meyer, F. (1998) "Libre circulation des travailleurs et libre prestation de services, à propos de la directive 'détachement du travailleur' ", *RIDE*, 57–73.
16. Joined Cases C-369/96 and 376/96, *Arblade* [1999] ECR I-8453.
17. [1999] OJ C 67/12.
18. Case C-43/93 *Vander Elst* [1994] ECR I-3803.
19. Case C-445/03 *Commission v Luxembourg, posted workers I* [2004] ECR I-10191.
20. Case C-341/02 *Commission v. Germany, posted workers* [2005] ECR I-2733.
21. Case C-319/06 *Commission v Luxembourg, posted workers II* [2008] ECR I-4323, para 81.
22. Case C-165/98, *Mazzoleni* [2001] ECR I-2189.
23. Ibid., para 30, emphasis added.
24. Ibid., para 35.
25. Ibid., para 36.
26. Case C-164/99 *Portugaia Construções* [2002] ECR I-787.
27. Ibid., para 29.
28. This is a peculiar proportionality test: usually the restrictive measure is appraised as against a less restrictive one, while here the competing interests themselves are being compared.
29. Joined Cases C-49/98, C-50/98, C-52/98 to C-54/98 and C-68/98 to C-71/98, *Finalarte* [2001] ECR I-7831.
30. Case C-341/05 *Laval and Partneri* [2007] ECR I-11767; Case C-438/05 *Viking* [2007] ECR I-10779; and Case C-346/06 *Rüffert* [2008] ECR I-1989.
31. See, for example, *Viking*, para 72 and *Laval*, para 116.
32. *Laval*, para 116.
33. The Posted Workers Directive in fact creates an exception to the general private international law rules, as enshrined in the Rome Convention, now turned into Regulation (EC) 593/2008 on the law applicable to contractual obligations [2008] OJ L 177/6, according to which, unless otherwise agreed, workers in temporary postings remain subject to their home state rules; see for a full argument about the Regulation, the Posted Workers Directive and the judgments under consideration, Deakin, Simon, "Regulatory Competition after *Laval*" (2008) 10 CYEL 581–609, 590–595.
34. Case C-346/06 *Rüffert* [2008] ECR I-1989; Case C-319/06 *Commission v Luxembourg, posted workers II* [2008] ECR I-4323; the former case concerned the obligation imposed by a German Lander that all employees or subcontractors of undertakings executing works within its territory receive pay above the national minimum, while the latter concerned several aspects of

the Luxembourg legislation, including a system of automatic indexation of wages above the national minimum. Both were found incompatible with the Posted Workers Directive.

35. *Commission v Luxembourg*, para 26.
36. Ibid., paras 30–31.
37. *Laval*, para 80; *Rüffert*, para 33.
38. *Commission v Luxembourg*, paras 38–44.
39. The neoclassical theory of migration is just one – probably the most prominent – among several theories explaining modern migration; see Massey, D., Arango, J., Hugo, G., Kouaouci, A., Pellegrino, A., and Taylor, E. (1993) "Theories of International Migration: A Review and Appraisal" *Population and Development Review*, 19(3): 431–466.
40. *Vander Elst*, para 25.
41. It should be remembered that *Rush Portuguesa* as well as *Viking, Laval*, and *Rüffert*, all concerned EU citizens, but at a time when their individual right of free movement was suspended by virtue of a transitional period.
42. Council Directive 2009/50/EC of 25 May 2009 on the conditions of entry and residence of third-country nationals for the purposes of highly qualified employment [2009] OJ L 155/17. For this Directive see Section 3.3.
43. Case C-158/96 *Kohll* [1998] ECR I-1931; Case C-157/99 *Smits & Peerbooms* [2001] ECR I-5473; Case C-368/98 *Vanbraekel* [2001] ECR I-5363. For these cases and their progeny see, among many, Cabral, P. (2004) "The Internal Market and the Right to Cross-Border Medical Care" *ELRev* 673–685, Davies, G. (2002) "Welfare as a Service", *Legal Issues of European Integration* 27–40, and Hatzopoulos, V. (2002) "Killing National Health and Insurance Systems But Healing Patients? The European Market for Health Care Services after the Judgments of the ECJ in *Vanbraekel* and *Peerbooms*" *CMLRev* 683–729, and more recently (2005) "Health Law and Policy, the Impact of the EU", in De Burca (ed.) *EU Law and the Welfare State: In Search of Solidarity* (Oxford, OUP/EUI), 123–160.
44. Case C-456/02 *Trojani* [2004] ECR I-7573; Case C-138/02 *Collins* [2004] ECR I-2703; Case C-209/03 *Bidar* [2005] ECR I-2119; See in general on the "social sensibility" of the ECJ, Hatzopoulos, V. (2005) "A (more) Social Europe: A Political Crossroad or a Legal One-Way? Dialogues between Luxembourg and Lisbon", 42 *CMLRev.* 1599–1635; also, by the same author (2009) "Current Problems of Social Europe" in J. Baquero-Cruz and C. Closa (eds.) *European Integration from Rome to Berlin 1957–2007, History, Law and Politics* (Brussels, etc.: PIE Peter Lang), 147–180.
45. Case C-484/93 *Svensson & Gustavsson* [1995] ECR I-3955 annotated by the present author in (1996) *CMLRev* 569–588.
46. It should be recalled that nationality is a prohibited ground for discriminating between EC nationals, but as far as TCNs are concerned, the non-discrimination directives refer to various criteria for discrimination which may mirror nationality (ethnic origin, religion, colour) but do not explicitly mention nationality as a prohibited ground for discrimination; see Council Directive 2000/43/EC of 29 June 2000 implementing the principle of equal treatment between persons irrespective of racial or ethnic origin [2000] OJ L 180/22; Council Directive 2000/78/EC of 27 November 2000 establishing a general framework for equal treatment in employment and occupation

[2000] OJ L 303/16; and Council Directive 2004/113/EC of 13 December 2004 implementing the principle of equal treatment between men and women in the access to and supply of goods and services [2004] OJ L 373/37. The same is true for the proposed Directive on implementing the principle of equal treatment between persons irrespective of religion or belief, disability, age or sexual orientation, COM 2008 (426) *final*.

47. C-326/00 *IKA v Ioannidis* [2003] ECR I-1703, and for a thorough presentation of this case the comment by the present author in *CMLRev* (2003) 1251–1268; Case C-202/97, *Fitzwilliam* [2000] ECR I-883. See Moore (2002) "Freedom of Movement and Migrant Workers' Social Security: An Overview of the Case Law of the Court of Justice, 1997–2001", *CML Rev*, 807–839.

48. COM 2001 (702) *final*.

49. See the annual SOLVIT report at http://ec.europa.eu/solvit/site/docs/solvit2008_report_en.pdf.

50. SOLVIT's mandate covers the following areas: Recognition of Professional qualifications and diplomas; Access to education; Residence permits; Voting rights; Social security; Employment rights; Driving licences; Motor vehicle registration; Border controls; Market access for products; Market access for services; Establishment as self-employed; Public procurement; Taxation; Free movement of capital or payments.

51. Council Regulation (EC) 859/2003 [2003] OJ L 124/1.

52. Joined cases C-95/99 to 98/99 and 180/99 Khalil ea [2001] ECR I-7413.

53. Regulation (EC) 883/2004 [2004] OJ L 166/1.

54. Council Directive 2003/109/EC concerning the status of third-country nationals who are long-term residents [2003] OJ L 16/44.

55. On the issue of how to integrate immigrants and the role of the long-term immigrants directive see, among many, Gross, T. (2005) "Integration of Immigrants: The Perspective of EC Law", *EJML* 145–161; Halleskov, L. (2005) "The Long Term Residents Directive: A fulfilment of the Tampere Objective of Near-Equality?" *EJML* 181–201; Handoll, J. (2003) "The Status of Third-Country Nationals Residing on a Long-Term Basis", in De Bruycker, P (ed.) *The Emergence of a European Immigration Policy – L'émergence d'une politique européenne d'immigration* (Brussels: Bruylant), 269–362; Urth, H. (2005) "Building a Momentum for the Integration of TCNs in the EU", *EJML* 163–180.

56. Though not "equal" ... Art. 11 of the directive draws directly on the equivalent provisions of the "Citizenship directive" 2004/38/EC of the EP and the Council of 29 April 2004 [2004] OJ L 158/77, but does introduce various derogations.

57. It is true that Art. 14(5) of the Long Term Residence Directive excludes from its scope "the residence of long-term residents in the territory of the member states 'as providers of cross-border services' "; however, to the extent that this "exclusion" seems to be in stark contrast with the basic rule of free movement established in Art. 14 of the Dir, it should be seen as a vicious offspring of the requirement of unanimity in the Council and should be read restrictively, as meaning that the Dir does not specifically address any of the issues related to cross-border service provision; these are taken care by other texts, most importantly, by the Services Directive.

58. Council Directive 2009/50/EC of 25 May 2009 on the conditions of entry and residence of third-country nationals for the purposes of highly qualified employment [2009] OJ L 155/17; on this Directive see Zaletel, P. (2006) "Competing for the Highly Skilled Migrants: Implications for the EU Common Approach on Temporary Economic Migration", *ELJ* 613–635.
59. See Directive 64/222/EEC [1964] OJ L 56/857; Directive 64/427/EEC [1964] OJ L117/1863; Directive 68/364/EEC [1966] OJ L 260/6; and many other directives, repealed by Directive 2005/36/EC for the mutual recognition of professional qualifications [2005] OJ L 255/22.
60. Council Directive 89/48/EEC on a general system for the recognition of higher-education diplomas awarded on completion of professional education and training of at least 3 years' duration [1989] OJ L 19/16; Council Directive 92/51/EEC on a second general system for the recognition of professional education and training to supplement Directive 89/48/EEC [1992] OJ L 209/25, modified several times; both these Dirs have now been repealed and replaced by Directive 2005/36/EC of the European Parliament and of the Council on the recognition of professional qualifications [2005] OJ L 255/22.
61. Directive 2003/109, above n. 54, Art. 11(1).
62. Directive 2009/50, above n. 58, Art. 14(d).
63. This is just one classification among many, taken from Adlung, R. and Mattoo, A. (2008) "The GATS", in Mattoo, A., Stern, R., and Zanini, G. (eds.) *A Handbook of International Trade in services* (Oxford: OUP), 48–83, 68.
64. In reality there is also a third category, consisting of commitments which apply as of right (that is, they do not need to be specifically "scheduled") but only in the areas where states have made commitments, see, for example, Art. VI.
65. Ibid., 63.
66. Services are classified in 11 broadly defined categories, plus one residual category, which are further broken down into 160 sub-sectors; the main 12 categories are: business services, communication services, construction, distribution, education, environmental services, financial services, health and social security, tourism and travel, recreational and cultural services, transport, other.
67. Even the EU member states have made a body of common commitments and additional individual commitments.
68. Mode 4 could be seen as a first step, involving less permanent delocalization and less FDI, towards mode 3, while in practice it is clear that the movement of persons will very often occur in the framework of intra-corporate mobility; moreover both modes correspond to the same pattern of trans-border service provision, whereby the provider moves in the territory of the recipient. In general for the relationships between the two modes see Alan Winters (2008) "The Temporary Movement of Workers to Provide Services (GATS Mode 4)", in Adlung, R. Mattoo, A. "The GATS" in Mattoo, A., Stern, R. and Zanini, G. (eds.) *A Handbook of International Trade in Services* (Oxford: OUP), 480–541, 497; see also Allison Young (2000) "Where Next for Labor Mobility under GATS", in Sauvé, P. and Stern, R. (eds.) *GATS 2000, New Directions in Services Trade Liberalization* (Washington, D.C.: Harvard/Brookings Institution Press), 184–210, 189.
69. Ibid., 193.

70. Which is far from being the case at present.
71. This clause may be seen as reflecting the issue of prior notification of technical standards organized by Directive 98/34/EC laying down a procedure for the provision of information in the field of technical standards and regulations [1998] OJ L 204/37; this Directive repealed Directive 83/189; its scope was extended by Directive 98/48/EC [1998] OJ L 217/18 to cover information society services.
72. See, for example, Bartels, L. (2005) "The legality of the EC mutual recognition clause under WTO law", *Journal of International Economic Law* 8: 691–720; also Beviglia Zampetti, A. (2000) "Market access through mutual recognition: the promise and limits of GATS article VII", in Sauvé, P. and Stern, R. (eds.) *GATS 2000, New Directions in Services Trade Liberalization* (Washington, D.C.: Harvard/Brookings Institution Press), pp. 283–306; it is true that both authors reason by reference to the application of mutual recognition, but the reasoning is valid for any type of measure conferring preferential treatment to some but not all WTO states.

Bibliography

Adlung, R. and Aaditya, A. (2008) "The GATS", in A. Mattoo, R. Stern and G. Zanini (eds.) *A Handbook of International Trade in Services* (Oxford: Oxford University Press) 48–83.

Ashiagbor, D. (2009) "Collective Labor Rights and the European Social Model", *Law and Ethics of Human Rights*, 3(2): 222–266.

Barnard, C. (2008) "*Viking* and *Laval*: An Introduction", *Cambridge Yearbook of European Legal Studies*, 10, 463–492.

Bartels, L. (2005) "The Legality of the EC Mutual Recognition Clause under WTO Law", *Journal of International Economic Law*, 8(3): 691–720.

Blanpain, R. (ed.) (2009) "The Laval and Viking Cases. Freedom of Services and Establishment v. Industrial Conflict in the European Economic Area and Russia", *Bulletin of Comparative Labour Relations* (The Netherlands: Kluwer Law International), 69.

Cabral, P. (2004) "The Internal Market and the Right to Cross-Border Medical Care", *European Law Review*, 29(5): 673–685.

Cremers, J., Dolvik, J. E., and Bosch, G. (2007) "Posting of Workers in the Single Market: Attempts to Prevent Social Dumping and Regime Competition in the EU?" *Industrial Relations Journal*, 38(6): 524–541.

Dashwood, A. (2008) "*Viking* and *Laval*: Issues of Horizontal Direct Effect", *Cambridge Yearbook of European Legal Studies*, 10, 525–540.

Davies, P. (1997) "Posted Workers: Single Market or Protection of National Labour Law Systems?" *Common Market Law Review*, 34(3): 571–602.

Deakin, S. (2008) "Regulatory Competition after *Laval*", *Cambridge Yearbook of European Legal Studies*, 10, 581–609.

Funk, L. and Lesch, H. (2006) "Minimum Wage Regulations in Selected European Countries", *Intereconomics*, 41(2): 78–92.

Gross, T. (2005) "Integration of Immigrants: The Perspective of EC Law", *European Journal of Migration and Law*, 7(2): 145–161.

Halleskov, L. (2005) "The Long Term Residents Directive: A fulfilment of the Tampere Objective of Near-Equality?" *European Journal of Migration and Law*, 7(2): 181–201.

Handoll, J. (2003) "The Status of Third-Country Nationals Residing on a Long-Term Basis", in P. De Bruycker (ed.) *The Emergence of a European Immigration Policy – L'émergence d'une politique européenne d'immigration* (Brussels: Bruylant) 269–362.

Hatzopoulos, V. (2009) "Current Problems of Social Europe", in J. Baquero-Cruz and C. Closa (eds.) *European Integration from Rome to Berlin 1957–2007, History, Law and Politics* (Brussels: Peter Lang) 7–180.

Hatzopoulos, V. (2008a) "Que reste-t-il de la directive sur les services?" *Cahiers de droit européen CDE*, 43 (3/4) 299–358.

Hatzopoulos, Vassilis, (2008b) "Le principe de reconnaissance mutuelle dans la libre prestation de services" paper delivered in a conference on "Mutual Recognition" organised by the Université Robert Schuman de Strasbourg, on 5 December 2008, available at http://www.coleurope.eu/template.asp?pagename=lawpapers.

Hatzopoulos, V. (2005) "A (more) Social Europe: A Political Crossroad or a Legal One-Way? Dialogues between Luxembourg and Lisbon", *Common Market Law Review*, 42(6):1599–1635.

Hatzopoulos, V. (2005) "Health Law and Policy, the Impact of the EU", in G. De Burca (ed.) *EU Law and the Welfare State: In Search of Solidarity* (Oxford: Oxford University Press) 123–160.

Hatzopoulos, V. (2002) "Killing National Health and Insurance Systems But Healing Patients? The European Market for Health Care Services after the Judgments of the ECJ in *Vanbraekel* and *Peerbooms*", *Common Market Law Review*, 39(4): 683–729.

Hatzopoulos, V. (2000) "Recent developments of the case law of the ECJ in the field of free movement of services 1994–1999", *Common Market Law Review*, 37(1): 43–82.

Hatzopoulos, V. (1999) *Le principe communautaire d'équivalence et de reconnaissance mutuelle dans la libre prestation de services* (Athènes/Bruxelles: Sakkoulas/Bruylant).

Hatzopoulos, V. and Do, U. (2006) "The Case Law of the ECJ Concerning the Free Provision of Services: 2000–2005", *Common Market Law Review*, 43(4): 923–991.

Hös, N. (2009) "The Principle of Proportionality in the *Viking* and *Laval* Cases: An Appropriate Standard of Judicial Review?" EUI LAW Working paper 2009/06.

King, R. (2002) "Towards a New Map of European Migration", *International Journal of Population Geography*, 8(2): 89–106.

Malmberg, J. and Sigeman, T. (2008) "Industrial Actions and EU Economic Freedoms: The Autonomous Collective Bargaining Model Curtailed by the ECJ", *Common Market Law Review*, 45(4): 1115–1146.

Massey, D., Arango, J., Hugo, G., Kouaouci, A., Pellegrino, A., and Taylor, E. (1993) "Theories of International Migration: A Review and Appraisal", *Population and Development Review*, 19(3): 431–466.

Meyer, F. (1993) "Libre circulation des travailleurs et libre prestation de services, à propos de la directive 'détachement du travailleur' ", *Revue internationale de droit économique*, 57–73.

Meyer, F. (1998) "Libre circulation des travailleurs et libre prestation de services, à propos de la directive 'détachement du travailleur' ", *Revue internationale de droit économique*, 57–73.

Moore, M. (2002) "Freedom of Movement and Migrant Workers' Social Security: An Overview of the Case Law of the Court of Justice, 1997–2001", *Common Market Law Review*, 39(4): 807–839.

Papademetriou, D. (2003) "Managing Rapid and Deep Change in the Newest Age of Migration", in S. Spencer (ed.) *The Politics of Immigration, Managing Opportunity, Conflict and Change* (Malden, MA: Blackwell) 39–58.

Prieto, C. (2004) "Liberté d'établissement et de prestation de services", *Revue Trimestielle de Droit Européen*, 533–558.

Rubalcaba, L. (2007) "Historical and Anthropological Origin of the Service Economy", in L. Rubalcaba (ed.) *The New Service Economy: Challenges and Policy Implications for Europe* (Cheltenham/Northampton: Edward Elgar).

Scharpf, F. (2009) "The Only Solution is to Refuse to Comply with ECJ Rulings", *Social Europe Journal*, 4(1), available at http://www.social-europe.eu/2009/04/interview-the-only-solution-is-to-refuse-to-comply-with-ecj-rulings/ (accessed on 4 June 2009).

Shiubhne, N. N. (ed.) (2006) *Regulating the Internal Market* (Cheltenham/Northampton: Edward Elgar).

Stephenson, S. (2000) "Regional Agreements on Services in Multilateral Disciplines: Interpreting and Applying GATS Article V", in S. Stephenson, (ed.) *Services Trade in the Western Hemisphere, Liberalisation, Integration and Reform* (Washington, D.C.: Organization of American States/Bookings Institution Press) 86–104.

Triandafyllidou, A., Gropas, R., and Vogel, D. (2007) "Introduction", in A. Triandafyllidou and R. Gropas (eds.) *European Immigration. A Sourcebook* (Aldershot: Ashgate).

Triandafyllidou, Anna and Gropas, Ruby (2007) "Concluding Remarks", in Triandafyllidou, Anna and Gropas, Ruby (eds.) *European Immigration. A Sourcebook* (Aldershot: Ashgate) 361–376.

Triandafyllidou, A. (2009) "EU Migration and Asylum Policies", in O. Cramme (ed.) *Rescuing the European Project: EU Legitimacy, Governance and Security* (London: Policy Network) 123–135.

Urth, H. (2005) "Building a Momentum for the Integration of TCNs in the EU", *European Journal of Migration and Law*, 7(2): 163–180.

Winters, A. (2008) "The temporary movement of workers to provide services (GATS Mode 4)", in "The GATS" in A. Mattoo, R. Stern, and G. Zanini, Gianni (eds.) *A Handbook of International Trade in Services* (Oxford: Oxford University Press) 480–541.

Young, A. (2000) "Where Next for Labor Mobility under GATS", in P. Sauvé, and R. Stern, (eds.) *GATS 2000, New directions in services trade liberalization* (Washington, D.C.: Harvard/Brookings Institution Press) 184–210.

Zaletel, P. (2006) "Competing for the Highly Skilled Migrants: Implications for the EU Common Approach on Temporary Economic Migration", *European Law Journal*, 12(5): 613–635.

Zampetti, A. B. (2000) "Market Access through Mutual Recognition: The Promise and Limits of GATS article VII", in P. Sauvé, and R. Stern (eds.) *GATS 2000, New Directions in Services Trade Liberalization* (Washington, D.C.: Harvard/Brookings Institution Press) 283–306.

Section III

The Outsourcing of Migration Management

8
The Privatization and Outsourcing of Migration Management

Georg Menz

1. Introduction

One of the central themes in recent political science debates on European migration concerns the exercise of state sovereignty and the effective control over migration flows. The questions debated include why liberal democratic European states accept immigration at all (Joppke, 1998) and whether the state apparatus is still in a position to curb immigration, given the constraints imposed by activist courts (Guiraudon, 2001), the globalization of labour markets (Hollifield, 1992), transnational ethnic networks (Soysal, 1994), and the activities of special interest groups such as ethnic advocacy coalitions and employer associations (Freeman, 2001; Menz and Caviedes in this book). A gap is said to exist between restrictive rhetoric and often more permissive practice.

Existing political science scholarship on European migration is not only somewhat state-centric (Brochmann and Hammar, 1999; Cornelius et al., 2004; Geddes, 2003), its portrayal of the state as a monolithic entity is also somewhat flawed because the *nature* of the European state over the past two decades has undergone structural transformation with important implications for migration management. Consequently, migration scholars base their assumptions about state sovereignty on an outmoded concept of the state and risk losing sight of important outsourcing processes of migration control that arise from the internalization of neoliberal ideology. This neoliberalization does not only imply a change in policy output, but, more importantly perhaps, a change in institutional dynamics and the number and nature of actors involved in the formulation, design, and implementation of migration policy. However, it is also acknowledged that neoliberalization has not proceeded at the same pace across Europe. This chapter focuses on empirical developments regarding the privatization and outsourcing of migration management in the United Kingdom (UK), the Netherlands, and Germany, while including brief overviews of developments in the United States (US) and Australia. It argues that the involvement of private actors is most pronounced where neoliberalization is most advanced. This claim informs the case selection. Whilst not focusing on labour migration per se, the argument is put forward that migration management is increasingly influenced by broader macroeconomic considerations, including prominently the rise of new public management in public policy design, but also financial and political blame avoidance strategies. Privatization and outsourcing does not necessarily imply that migration control is carried out by private actors in lieu of actions otherwise taken by public authorities. Instead, the state involves private actors in migration enforcement in addition to maintaining – and often extending – a state migration management apparatus. The involvement of airlines, shipping companies, and private security companies thus provides an additional layer of migration management and does not automatically result in the retreat of the state. In fact, such private actors are commonly bound by contractual arrangements, though following the classic principal-agent dilemma, privatization, once pursued, may well create self-reinforcing dynamics with the growth of a prison industry complex that is difficult to control and curtail. In exploring the broader context of tectonic changes in political economy, it also becomes possible to account for changes in migration management that the seminal contribution by Guiraudon and Lahav (2000) charts, but ultimately struggles to make sense of. Migration control is indeed being extended "upwards, . . . downward . . . and outward" (Guiraudon and Lahav, 2000, p. 164), yet these are not mere empirical particularities, but rather significant subcomponents of a more general transformation of stateness, which is, however, advanced to varying degrees.

In terms of policy output, the internalization of the business-friendly economically liberal competition state (Cerny, 1997) agenda has pivotal implications. The neoliberalized state does not abandon migration control. Migrants are desirable in principle so long as they are perceived as useful human resources, while barriers are erected against the unsolicited entry of "undesirables". Migration policy thus becomes an additional mechanism for human resources procurement, especially if it complements existing production strategies (Menz, 2008). States have not lost their control capacity (*pace* Soysal, 1994; Sassen, 2001), but instead have sought new channels and mechanisms of control, including greater involvement of private sector actors. In fact, the competition state is not necessarily lean or residual. It simply has prioritized neoliberal preoccupations about establishing business-friendly investment conditions. By no means does this imply a retreat or reduction of the punitive and disciplinary state functions and related capacities. If anything, the repressive and controlling elements of state power are expanded, whilst economic "embedding" functions central to the Keynesian-dominated Fordist phase of mass production are shed. Gamble's (1988) depiction of Thatcherism as a "strong state and a free economy" succinctly summarizes this transformation, but earlier state theorists, including Poulantzas (2002) and Hirsch (1980), were aware of the dichotomy between a liberalized economy and an increasing control and surveillance regime towards those considered "deviant" regarding classic patterns of accumulation. "(I)t seems to be precisely this incapacity to make a clear distinction between 'threats' and 'resources', between the 'dangerous' and the 'labourious' classes or, to follow another sociologically successful dichotomy, between 'social junk' and 'social dynamite', which compels the institutions of social control to regroup whole sectors of the post-Fordist labour force as 'categories at risk', and to deploy consequent strategies of confinement, incapacitation and surveillance" (De Giorgi, 2006, p. 76).

In terms of policy design, new rules, incentive structures, and actors have emerged in the more neoliberalized polities. The state involves private sector actors in the detention, prevention, and control of migration flows. Transportation companies are incorporated into the design of migration flow management and, in some cases, private security companies manage detention facilities. This is migration management by "remote control" (Zolberg, 1999). By involving private actors in migration control, new policy dynamics are created in at least three different ways. Firstly, path-dependent lock-in effects are being created (Hansen, 2000) that shape – though note determine – subsequent developments. The privatization of detention facilities has proven in practice to be a self-perpetuating policy choice that seems difficult to limit or undo even after a change in government. Secondly, interest groups "by creating structures to control or adapt to uncertainty ... have contributed to the development of a more complex and rapidly changing policy environment" (Heinz et al., 1993, p. 371). New actors in migration policy present a potential for regulatory capture (Stigler, 1971) in the sense of agents successfully influencing the principal's position. Thirdly, involvement of private sector companies can also be seen as a way of outsourcing legal liability and the often unpleasant implementation of the most immediate and potentially aggressive forms of direct interaction with migrants. Responsibility can thus be shifted and a new venue in Baumgartner and Jones' (1993) sense is being created outside of the immediate remit of the state.

2. The changing nature of the European state and the domestic and international outsourcing of migration control

Existing accounts of state sovereignty in migration often portray it as a zero-sum game, overlooking the more complex dynamics of involving private actors into migration control. These developments are intrinsically linked to the bourgeois state's structural transformation. In the 1970s, scholars identified "overloaded states" (King, 1975) and serious legitimacy crises arising out of an excessive and internally contradictory remit of responsibilities (Habermas, 1976; Offe, 1972). In the 1980s, the embrace of neoliberalism first in the UK and subsequently to different degrees throughout Western Europe and elsewhere prompted the diagnosis of a "hollowed out" state (Peters, 1993, 1997; Rhodes, 1994). Concomitantly, new public management approaches introduced more market-oriented guidelines for procurement, internal management, and public resources policy of public administration so as to deliver similar results with greater cost efficiency.

The emergence of post-Fordist production patterns, the abandonment of Keynesianism and the embrace of neoliberalism as a dominant paradigm in macroeconomic policy design (Soederberg et al., 2005) have reshaped the nature of the contemporary state with important repercussions for migration management. This link between the neoliberal restructuring of the state and migration regulation remains underexplored and underappreciated (a cogent exception is Köppe, 2003). Cost shifting, blame avoidance, and ideological preference for private sector providers all play roles in the outsourcing of direct control functions to transportation companies, including airlines, trucking, and shipping companies. Migration control by remote control offers the advantage of shifting the financial burden – and also the blame in cases of non-compliance or accidents – on to third actors. States have also privatized detention of migrants, often concomitantly or even ahead of the privatization of prisons. Doing so can help shift blame and immediate legal responsibility to private sector actors.

Philip Cerny (1997) describes the neoliberal transformation of the state by sketching the contours of the new competition state. Central concerns embody providing a "relatively favorable investment climate tor transnational capital...[including a] circumscribed range of goods that retain a national-scale...public character...[such as] human capital,...infrastructure [and generally] maintenance of a public policy environment favorable to investment (and profit making)". But this comes at the expense of the much broader array of public service functions, which are simply often outsourced, privatized, or even abandoned altogether, inspired by neoliberal ideology. The competition state promotes flexibility and neoliberal response strategies to a changing economic global macroclimate, it endorses and enforces monetarist priorities on inflation control at the expense of other macroeconomic goals, notably employment, and its extent of welfare provision is extremely limited, proceeding through a reliance on second order effects of economic growth and private sector entrepreneurship. The competition state therefore merely promotes the "marketisation in order to make economic activities located within the national territory...more competitive in international and transnational terms" (Cerny, 1997, p. 258).

In this context, human resources matter greatly and migrants are welcome, as long as they promise to contribute to the prerogatives of a business-friendly national economic growth strategy. The flipside of newly liberalized economic migration policies are more restrictive practices towards unsolicited migration flows, characterized as constituting an economic drain and a potential political menace.

While neo-Marxist accounts have always emphasized the class bias of the bourgeois capitalist state, the neoliberalized competition state is even more inclined to a class-biased representation of interests because it considers its responsibilities towards lower socio-economic segments of society as consisting of control and surveillance (cf Poulantzas, 2002) and, where and if still possible, in re-commodifying "deviant" individuals that seek to escape the confines of wage labour. Such disciplining function can be outsourced to private sector actors, even if they touch upon the Weberian monopoly over the legitimate use of force. The competition state's core focus is an economistic obsession with securing and maintaining competitiveness.

But neoliberalization is not the only pertinent factor. Policy-making institutions and rules of the game shift drastically – and, it would appear, irreversibly – once private sector actors become involved in migration control. While the immediate rationale underpinning the involvement of private sectors was almost entirely due to a neoliberal obsession over alleged efficiency gains, the ideological faith in the superiority of private sector solutions per se, and possibly cost savings, once such transition has been made, it creates self-perpetuating and self-enhancing effects that are difficult to counter.

3. Appointing new gatekeepers: The outsourcing of control to transportation companies

Obvious problems affecting the accumulation process in the mid-1970s precipitated more restrictive migration policies and ended active recruitment of labour migration throughout Western Europe. However, in lieu of other sizable legal access channels, family reunion and increasingly political asylum emerged as principal migration categories. This rise in humanitarian categories of migration entailed individuals that could not as readily be integrated into national production strategies. Consequently, by the mid-1980s, West European governments were exploring new mechanisms of controlling and impeding migration flows that arrived spontaneously and outside of tightly constrained economic migration channels.[1] With the Iron Curtain still impeding land access, the key mode of transport was via air and to a less extent seaways. Classic emigration countries such as Australia and the US had long since implemented legal provisions permitting either the imposition of fines[2] or at least obliged transportation companies to remove non-admitted foreign nationals.[3] An early precedent can be seen in the 1793 UK Registration of Aliens Act, which obliged ship captains to report numbers, names, and occupations of foreign passengers to local ports authorities upon arrival and introduced a 10 pound fine, raised to 20 pounds in 1836, per passenger for which such information was not provided. One tool for closing this access channel was the delegation of control responsibilities to transportation companies, including airlines, shipping, and trucking companies. While airlines had always been required to check the documentation of passengers at point of embarkation under the terms of the 1944 Chicago Convention on International Civil Aviation (Annex 9),[4] this document does not prescribe carrier sanctions and in fact expressly forbids them: "[carriers] shall not be fined in the event that any control document in possession of a passenger are found by a Contracting State to be inadequate or if . . . the passenger is found to be inadmissible to the State" (Art. 3.36 Annex 9) *unless* "there is evidence to suggest that the carrier was negligent in taking precautions" (Art. 3.37.1).

The rationale behind the introduction of carrier sanctions was to impede unsolicited migration movements to Europe geographically. In practice, most of the burden fell on airlines, since few migrants chose to enter Europe as stowaways (interviews DE-TRANS-1, UK-TRANS-1) and trucking only played a minor role, and then primarily in the early 2000s as a means to cross the English channel and enter the UK in a clandestine fashion (interview DE-TRANS-2, UK-TRANS-2). Shipping today plays practically no role whatsoever anymore as a route of transportation for undocumented or "stowaway" migrants in Northern Europe, although people "trafficking" using naval vessels is, of course, commonplace in the Mediterranean.

The co-opting of airlines into co-management commenced in 1987, when four West European governments introduced carrier sanctions in rapid succession. In January, Art. 8(4) and (5) of the (West) German 1965 Aliens Law was modified, introducing a penalty (*Zwangsgeld*) of 2000 Deutschmarks, raised to 5000 Deutschmarks in 1990. But in addition, the transportation company is not only legally obliged to pay for repatriation (*Rückbeförderungspflicht*), a duty applicable for periods of up to 36 months after first attempted entry, but can also be held responsible for the cost of accommodation and living expenses of the migrant during this period (interview DE-TRANS-1; Cruz, 1991, pp. 67–68). An additional penalty (*Geldbuße*) of up to 20,000 Deutschmarks can be imposed in cases of negligence.

On 15 May 1987, the UK Immigration (Carriers' Liability) Act introduced a fine of 1000 pounds per non-admitted foreigner, doubled in August 1991 and extended to transit passengers without valid visa in 1993 (Asylum and Immigration Appeals Act 1993). Though a legal precedent to this regulation had existed in theory already and the obligation for transportation companies to return migrants at company expense to their country of origin had already been enshrined in the 1971 Immigration Act (Sched. 2, paragraph 8 + 19) (Nicholson, 1997, p. 588), the additional fine was a new instrument.

In a 14 July 1987 modification of the 15 December 1980 law governing entry, visit, and residence in the Kingdom of Belgium, carrier sanctions of approximately 80,000 Belgian francs were introduced in instances in which carriers carried five persons or more to the national territory (Cruz, 1991, p. 65ff.).

The Danish 8 June 1983 Aliens Act was modified on 17 December 1987, introducing a new Art. 59a. Effective as of 1 January 1989, fines of up to 10,000 Danish krone per passenger could be imposed. In practice, no consideration was even given to the question of whether any such undocumented migrant be an asylum-seeker.

Though these four countries came chronologically first, the rest of the EU member states were to follow suit. Since 1991, Austrian authorities can claim "compensation" (*Konstenersatz*) of up to 20,000 Austrian schillings per inadmissible passenger, unless a transportation company is willing to return the migrant immediately.

In France, law 92–190 of 26 February 1992 added Art. 20a to the 1945 Foreigner Law, introducing new responsibilities for carriers (Guiraudon, 2002, p. 3). However, the fine of up to 10,000 French francs cannot be imposed if the migrant's claim for asylum is accepted or at least not dismissed as manifestly unfounded or if the carrier can demonstrate that valid documents were presented at point of embarkation and not obviously fake or tampered with.

In the Netherlands, sanctions were first introduced in 1994, but were not applied in practice until December 1997. In the late 1990s, the Dutch government imposed fines on a number of airlines, including national flag carrier KLM, even involving the latter in a court case that was finally decided by the Supreme Court in 2000, entailing a 4.5 million euro fine (Supreme Court LJN AA6456, 112 986, 11 July 2000, cited in Scholten and Minderhoud, 2008, p. 141). In early 2000, the Dutch government signed a memorandum of understanding with the airline, entailing government-funded training for airline staff and obliging the airline in turn to apply due diligence, carry out detailed identification document controls at point of embankment and accept annually decreasing quotas for "non-admissibles". The Dutch border police dispatched immigration liaison officers to carry out pre-boarding checks, liaising with embassies abroad as well as the airlines. The first officers were seconded to immigration "hotspots" including Accra, Moscow, and Colombo as early as 1995 (Scholten and Minderhoud, 2008, p. 136). Elsewhere in Europe, Portuguese, Spanish, Italian, and Greek legislation was also modified to contain provisions for imposing carrier sanctions.

The 1990 Schengen Implementing Convention obliged EU member states to introduce carrier sanctions eventually, while the 27 June 2001 EU directive (EC 2001/51/EC, OJ L 187, p. 45), initiated by the French government, forces member states to do so with important ramifications both for the two member states without such provisions in national law – Ireland and Sweden – and, by implication, the 2004 and 2007 newcomers along with Norway, Iceland, and Switzerland.

This shedding of traditional responsibility to private sector actors met with little enthusiasm among the airlines. Though the authorities in some cases offered training and education measures (notably in Germany and the Netherlands) (interview DE-TRANS-1), they imposed significant financial burdens in terms of the obligation to repatriate and statutory fines. In Germany, there is the particularly punitive practice of forcing airlines to underwrite the accommodation expenditure of any such migrant throughout the entire sojourn on German territory. Even such training measures often involved a financial participation of the airlines. In practice, it often proved difficult to enforce payment of fines levied, especially on foreign airlines. Annual expenditure for major European airlines on this aspect of migration management is in the mid-double digit millions of euros (interview UK-TRANS-1). On top of preventive measures, constant training measures for employees, and even research on "hotspots" for emigration and passport fraud, the airlines face the unpleasant spectre of being obliged to carry deportees who commonly resist repatriation with the attendant negative implications for public relations, the hazardous impact on operational maintenance, and the undesired attention of anti-deportation political activists (interviews UK-TRANS-1, DE-TRANS-1, UK-SEC-1). For major European airlines who rely on revenues from transit passengers for the lucrative trans-Atlantic routes, the control obligations imposed by North American governments also have important financial ramifications as do transit passengers absconding themselves whilst in transit in the airlines' European hubs (interviews UK-TRANS-1, DE-TRANS-1, *The Independent*, 8 October 2007). However, airlines also profit from ticket sales; British Airways received 4.3 million pounds in 2006 alone for the transportation of returned migrants (Ginn, 2008, p. 14). In 2007, UK carrier XL Airways withdrew from a 1.5 million pound contract with the Home Office entailing the removal of failed asylum-seekers to the DR Congo. As the company could extract itself without legal repercussions, some doubt is cast on the allegedly legal obligation to partake in deportation.

Though in theory fines can also be imposed on other transportation companies, in practice this was mainly pursued with respect to British and continental European long-distance lorry companies, whose lorries were used – usually without knowledge or consent of the driver, but in a limited number of cases perhaps with tacit agreement – by immigrants who sought to cross from the northern French ferry ports, especially Calais, to Britain in the early 2000s. The UK Home Office reacted promptly and quite firmly by levying fines (interviews DE-TRANS-2, UK-TRANS-2), instigating protests among affected companies about being inadvertently blamed for border infractions outside of their immediate control and quite often even against their will (interviews UK-TRANS-3). The medium-term response was the introduction of more sophisticated technological means of spot-checking departing lorries in the French ports, which rendered the chances of success of such undocumented journeys much less likely.

4. Outsourcing migration detention

While the outsourcing of remote control was proceeding apace, the management of the detention of "undesirable" immigrants also commenced in the mid-1980s and coincided with an ideological infatuation with new public management principles. As the degree to which the privatization of migration detention seems to correlate directly with the neoliberalization of macroeconomic policy more generally, the empirical results from Europe are presented in the order of a continuum of neoliberalization. In addition, developments in the US and Australia are juxtaposed with European trends and will be presented briefly.

In Europe, the UK was the first country to embrace the management of migration detention by private companies. The legislative foundation for detention was created in the shape of the 1971 Immigration Act, however, detention was intended as a tool for brief periods immediately prior to deportation. The UK Border Agency's *Enforcement Instructions and Guidance* states, "Detention must be used sparingly, and for the shortest period necessary" (UKBA, 2009, chapter 55.1.3), though this appears to be frequently ignored in practice. As early as August 1970, the Conservative government contracted Securicor to manage a small detention facility in Harmondsworth near Heathrow airport and a second one near Manchester airport. However, the early 1970s also witnessed the practice to hold detained migrants in prison, a practice only rendered illegal after passage of the 1999 Immigration and Asylum Act. In the late 1980s, Securicor also used a converted car ferry to house detainees. In 2009, 11 detention centres in the UK focused exclusively on migration detention, seven of which are managed by private sector companies with a total capacity of 2935 places, representing a significant increase from its capacity of 250 in 1993 (Bacon, 2005, p. 2). In 2009, the Home Office announced plans to expand its detention capacity by building an 800-bed centre near Bullingdon prison in Oxfordshire, which would be the largest detention centre in Europe (*BBC News*, 2009). Strikingly, the contracts all involve only three multinational conglomerates, with recent consolidation and a bewildering array of trading names obfuscating the picture of an essentially oligopolistic market structure: Geo Group Limited, G4S, and Serco. The former two are active in the US and Australia as well. The contracts are lucrative, with total costs charged to the Home Office per detainee per week reaching 1230 pounds (Hansard, 2 October 2006). G4S is also responsible for providing transportation services to both the Home Office and HM Prison Services. Despite repeated attempts made over a two-year period, representatives refused to be interviewed for this study.

Jones and Newburn (2005) chronicle the privatization of select prisons in the UK in the late 1980s. Ideological zeal, advocacy by the hard-right think tank Adam Smith Institute, and persistent lobbying from a UK subsidiary of the American company CCA as well as a fairly ideologically biased composition of the 1988 House of Commons Home Affairs Select Committee, including *inter alia* John Wheeler MP who simultaneously served as Director General of the British Security Industry Association, were all contributory factors in the genesis of the 1991 White Paper *Custody, Care and Justice: The Way Ahead for the Prison Service in England and Wales* (Bacon, 2005, pp. 11–13). During 1991, two prisons were contracted out to private security companies, with Campsfield Detention Centre in Oxfordshire becoming Britain's first privately managed migration detention facility, run by Group 4 (later G4S). G4S also managed two offshore detention centres in Coquelles and Calais in northern France.

Despite promising that "at the expiry of their contracts a Labour government will bring these prisons into proper public control and run them directly as public services" in 1995 (*The Times*, 8 March 1995), the new Home Secretary Jack Straw broke his promise within 7 days of Labour wining the 1997 national elections. He agreed to two new privately financed prison deals immediately and was later to announce that all new prisons in England and Wales would be privately constructed and operated (Bacon, 2005, p. 19). Hopes for a fresh approach to migration detention or the promised end to the private sector involvement were quickly squashed. While the 1998 White Paper *Fairer, Faster and Firmer – A Modern Approach to Immigration and Asylum* promised a distinction between asylum-seekers and undocumented migrants in detention treatment, reserving it for the latter category, in practice detention continued and new facilities came on stream. In fact, all new detention construction was to be carried out by private companies under the Blair and Brown governments.

Negative publicity, direct action by political activists, and protests by inmates have arrested any additional market entrants. A fire and major unrest at Yarl's Wood in Bedfordshire in February 2002 that erupted over alleged mistreatment of inmates a mere 3 months after the opening of the site highlighted both the substandard quality of service and infrastructure provision and, in the detailed enquiry that followed the riots, the extremely tight schedule imposed on private contractors to construct the site. Yarl's Wood had been constructed in record time and an official enquiry into the causes of the disturbances found that the facilities were of questionable standard, staff was poorly trained and had been hastily recruited (Shaw, 2004). The report also quotes senior Home Office officials who suspect that this rapid pace of detention holdings expansion was at least partially a result of the public policy commitment to setting annual targets for deportations, itself an outcome of pandering to a vociferously xenophobic yellow press. Reports of abusive treatment of inmates were frequent (Ginn, 2008). One of the possible compounding factors was the poor state of working conditions in British detention centres, where unionization is generally discouraged, shifts can be up to 12 hours long and wages tend to lie barely above minimum wage level, as a Prison Inspectorate report on Campsfield House in 1998 uncovered (HMIP, 1998, para 2.01–2.02). Major disturbances have also been recorded at Campsfield, Lindholme, and Harmandsworth over the years. A number of these centres have been the subject of highly critical reports by the Chief Inspector of Prisons (2008).

In light of the high operating costs, perennially resurfacing problems with abusive treatment of inmates, and an uncertain deterrence effect on would-be migrants, it seems surprising that the privatization course was not seriously questioned. A number of scholars support the view that in the UK lock-in effects had been created. Harding (1998) argues that financing and contractual arrangements are designed to lock in governments with private contractor arrangements that are impossible to disentangle during the course of such contracts. In addition, continuous lobbying (UK-SEC-1) proceeded apace. The profitability of immigration detention induces companies to play an "originating role" (Newburn, 2002, p. 180) and act as policy entrepreneurs. Feeley (2002) concurs: "Historically, entrepreneurs may have been the single-most important source of innovation... Many – perhaps most – new forms of punishment in modern Anglo-American jurisdictions have their origins in the proposals of private entrepreneurs." The predominant role that private contractors play in British migration detention management also oddly places the government into a relatively weak bargaining position and perhaps partially contributes to the feeble degree of oversight and accountability exercised. While all immigration detention centres are subject to regular visits by HM Prison Inspectorate, it is not clear how consequential the sometimes highly critical reports are in practice. In any case, key operational and financial details of the contracts between the Home Office and private contractors are treated as confidential, which impedes oversight by parliament.

The privatization of detention facilities proved more politically contentious in most of other continental European countries. In the *Netherlands*, the Aliens Act 2000 created grounds for administrative detention in Sections 6 and 59. Section 6 on "border detention" reads: "An alien who has been refused entry into the Netherlands may be required to stay in a space or place designated by a border control officer", which "may be secured against unauthorised departure." According to Section 3, grounds for refusing entry include lack of valid travel document and/or visa, posing a threat to the public order or national security, and insufficient means to defray costs of staying in the country.

According to the government's accelerated asylum procedure a decision on whether to allow asylum-seekers to formally apply for asylum in the Netherlands should be determined within 48 working hours – or 5–8 days. During this initial period, asylum seekers are held at government-run "application centres" (interview NL-GOV-1). If the Immigration and Naturalization Service decides during the initial 48-hour period that further investigation is necessary, a "prolonged" procedure continues at a "temporary reception centre", which is run by an independent, government-funded agency called the Central Agency for the Reception of Asylum Seekers (COA) (interview NL-GOV-1).

There are six detention centres and three "application centres". In 2005, a total of 12,485 were detained; in 2006, 12,480; in 2007, 9595; and in 2008, 8585. G4S is involved in operating the Detentiecentrum Zeist with 540 inmates, which is located in Soesterberg near Schiphol airport. Public outcry over harsh conditions at detention sites, which was sparked in part by a 27 October 2005 fire at the Schiphol Airport detention facility that resulted in the deaths of 11 detainees due to poor fire safety procedures, has gradually led to some reforms, in particular with respect to safety regulations at detention facilities (interview NL-SEC-1). The minister of justice resigned over the ensuing protest and a subsequent study by this ministry confirmed poor health and safety practices (*The Dutch News*, 22 September 2006).

In the Dutch debate, the introduction of private sector companies has been relatively controversial and has consequently been undertaken only on a very limited scale. The main arguments used in favour were related to alleged efficiency and the potential for better value for money, yet the political backlash created by the incident at Schiphol has stalled any considerations of increased involvement of private sector companies. Lobbying activities are somewhat less pronounced than in the UK. However, despite the Schiphol scandal in 2005, with earlier fires on the site reported in 2004 and 2003, the contract with G4S was extended in 2007 for another 6 years, demonstrating a "lock-in" effect. G4S also provides approximately 50 per cent of all security personnel for detention centres elsewhere, including in Zaandam, Rotterdam, and the Rotterdam-based detention boats (Ministerie van Justitie, 2007, 2010, interview NL-SEC-1). Regular inspections are carried out by the Inspectorate for Sanction Implementation.

In *Germany*, the privatization of detention has proven highly politically contested and ultimately did not proceed fully. Detention and indeed prison management is the responsibility of the individual states. However, there are currently three prisons (in Burg, Offenburg, and Hünfeld) in which services are being provided by private sector companies. Hünfeld was a pilot project implemented by the Right-wing Hesse state government in December 2005 after political agreement in the coalition treaty of 1999, despite significant resistance and vociferous criticism from the unions, the political opposition, and a number of criminal justice experts. However, a legal panel within the Hessian state ministry of justice, briefed with examining the relevant legal framework, discovered that the criminal justice system is legally defined as being a component of the state legal remit (*Staatshoheit*) and this, in light of Art. 33.4 of the German Basic Law, could therefore not be privatized. Consequently, Serco is providing general services to the prison, yet the wardens are civil servants and direct employees of the state of Hesse (*Süddeutsche Zeitung*, 31 March 2008, interview DE-SEC-1). Both North Rhine-Westphalia and Brandenburg have tendered certain service provisions to private sector companies. European Homecare operates reception and detention facilities at Düsseldorf airport and at Büren. On a more modest scale, B.O.S.S. is providing auxiliary services in a migrant detention centre in Eisenhüttenstadt since 2000. However, due to both legal concerns and political resistance to involving private sector companies in such a sensitive policy domain, there is no interest in broadening the remit of private sector involvement.

Outside of Europe, the privatization of migration detention centre management was pioneered in Australia and the US. In both countries, the privatization of prisons and migration detention centres proceeded concurrently. Notably, the involvement of private actors has also been continued even after the election of centre-left governments. Both ideological neoliberal considerations and argument alleging costs savings have been used in justifying the outsourcing of detention management. In Australia, privatization commenced in 1997 under the conservative Howard government. The 1992 Migration Amendment Act modifying the original 1958 Migration Act has rendered mandatory the detention of "unlawful immigrants", which had previously been only permitted, but not prescribed, including all asylum-seekers. The new legislation also removed the previous maximum time limit to detentions of 273 days. The responsible Department of Immigration and Australian Citizenship (DIAC) first cooperated with Australasian Correctional Services (ACC), a subsidiary of the US Wackenhut Corrections Corporations, entering a ten-year general contract on 27 February 1998. Considerations of economizing, "value for money", the US as a role model, a new public management preference towards private sector solutions, and capacity concerns in the public sector were all factors in the initial decision (interview AUS-GOV-1). The Financial Management and Accountability Act 1997 obliges government procurement to be led by considerations of "value for money". By 2001, DIAC was no longer convinced that ACC was providing this, but rather than re-thinking privatization altogether, DIAC simply re-tendered the job in August 2001, eventually deciding to replace ACC with Group 4 Falck on 27 August 2003 (ANAO, 2006a). It is unclear to what extent intense criticism of this company's operations from NGOs and several incidents of inmate protests in the six centres managed by this company may have played a role in the re-tendering. In any event, Group 4 Falck (later to trade as G4S) had at this stage purchased the parent company of ACC and complaints about abusive treatment of inmates continued. Notably, a 2004 audit by ANAO had identified major shortcomings of accountability and a lack of documentation regarding project management, recordkeeping, roles and responsibilities of personnel and expert advisors (ANAO, 2006b) in the original tender. From a single detention centre in Maribyrnong near Melbourne, opened in 1966, the number of detention centres grew to include a centre in each province by 2009, including offshore facilities in the Christmas Islands.

After a change in government in 2007, there were expectations that the new Labour government of Rudd would modify immigration policy significantly (Evans, 2008), including an end to the controversial offshore processing of refugees in Nauru and the Christmas Islands, known as the so-called Pacific solution. Indeed, mandatory detention was modified somewhat and rendered no longer applicable to asylum-seekers not deemed to constitute a security threat. In addition, regular reviews of pending cases were introduced and a new Ombudsman was appointed to review decisions and avoid the somewhat opaque style that had prevailed, especially in the offshore centres. However, the facilities in the Christmas Islands were not closed down and, surprising to many, despite

Labour's promise in opposition, the tender underway in 2007 was continued. Accused of breaking an election promise, Minister of Immigration and Citizenship Chris Evans explained the rationale (Evans, 2008): "The absence of alternative public service providers would require the extension of the current contract arrangements for a minimum of two years. The cancellation of the tender process would expose the Commonwealth to potential compensation claims from the tenderers.... The broader policy issues of public versus private sector management of detention services will be addressed following an evaluation at the end of the term of the contracts concluded as part of the tender process." A parliamentary enquiry into migration detention in August 2009 highlighted the persistent concerns by NGOs over the lack of scrutiny and accountability of private service provision and reiterated earlier criticism regarding poor quality management, excessively high costs, and ineffective performance management systems (Parliament of Australia, 2009). The 2009 Migration Amendment (Abolishing Detention Debt) Bill independently ended the practice of charging detainees for the costs incurred during detention. Insisting that the standards of service provision had been raised in the new tender, in May 2009 GSL was selected as the provider of services at the more low-security immigration residential housing facilities and transit accommodation, while Serco was awarded the contract for the more high-security 11 detention centres and related transportation services. Despite the promise of better value for money and higher standards of service, the fundamental course of privatization had not been reversed.

In the *US*, immigration detention itself is a relative new phenomenon and the involvement of private companies spearheaded prison privatization. In 1983, the newly founded Corrections Corporations of America (CCA), established by the Corrections Commissioners of Tennessee and Virginia along with the Chairman of the Tennessee Republican Party in 1980, secured a contract with the then-Immigration and Naturalization Service (INS) to provide prison beds for detained immigrants. Shortly thereafter, the INS concluded a second contract with Wackenhut Services (since consolidated with GEO). Throughout the 1980s and 1990s, both companies rapidly expanded their share of prison place provision and – thanks in no small part to the Reagan administration's punitive Sentencing Reform Act of 1984 – the prison population rapidly swelled during these two decades. In immigration terms, the 1996 Illegal Immigration Reform and Immigration Responsibility Act proved a watershed, for it rendered even minor offences committed by legal residents grounds for mandatory detention and deportation and in such cases could also be applied retroactively. Consequently, the number of deportations doubled to nearly 60,000 between 1995 and 1997 (INS data in Ellermann, 2009, p. 114). The INS continued to own few facilities itself and cooperated with state and local authorities for the detention of immigrants. In 2010, 67 per cent of all detainees are kept in state and county jails, 13 per cent in facilities owned by the re-christened Immigration and Customs Enforcement (ICE), and 17 per cent in privately owned facilities (ICE, 2010; interview US-GOV-1). A recent study suggests that repeated cases of overcharging ICE for migrant detention by country government and the spectacular growth in local prison facilities are the result of wrong incentives created by the outsourcing of migrant detention to local government (Greene and Patel, 2007). Journalistic reports from California suggest that there and elsewhere such federal money had become a major source of revenue, amounting to 55.2 million dollars in 2008 alone (*San Diego Union-Tribune*, 4 May 2008, *Los Angeles Times*, 17 March 2009).

The revival in the economic fortunes of CCA and GEO, the two major private prison companies along with smaller companies such as Cornell Corrections and Management and Training Corporation, commenced during the Bush Jr. administration. In June 2003, the ICE set out a ten-year strategy to remove all "removable aliens" from US territory known as "Operation Endgame" (US Department of Homeland Security, 2003). Deportation levels rose to 349,000 by 2008 and average detention rates reached 31,345 (Detention Watch 2010). Supporting the expansion of privately managed detention facilities, CCA's total expenditure expanded from 410, 000 dollars in 2000 to 3 million dollars in 2004 (*San Diego Union-Tribune*, 4 May 2008). Consequently, 13 per cent of CCA's revenue, which reached 1.5 billion dollars in 2008, came directly from ICE that year, federal contracts in total for 40 per cent of revenue and the company provided 50 per cent of all private prison beds in the US. Geo, which reported 1.2 billion dollars in revenues for 2007, credits ICE for 11 and federal contracts for 27 per cent of its operating revenue.

The increased efforts to raise levels of deportation and mandatory detention have rapidly led to increases in capacity needs and the private providers have exploited this new demand.

5. Conclusion

Private actors have increased their role in the management of migration flows since the mid-1980s. Both control and enforcement functions have been outsourced to private companies. Debates over state sovereignty need to appreciate the embrace of a neoliberal competition state agenda, while future scholarly efforts need to consider in more detail the implications of a more diverse landscape of actors in immigration policy-making. While privatization and greater involvement of business facilitates the advancement of interest positions and agenda-setting for some, it also implies somewhat less voice for other civil society actors. The neoliberalized state does not lose sovereignty, nor does it endorse restrictive immigration policy. It outsources certain control functions to private sector actors. Immigration policy management of physical access is characterized by the co-opting of transportation companies, while private security companies are involved in the operation of detention facilities. Interestingly, this involvement of private actors is more advanced in the more noeliberalized Anglo-American cases of Australia and the US. Privatization of migration detention often accompanies prison privatization and creates powerful lock-in dynamics, which render policy reversals extremely difficult. Privatization of control and enforcement functions should, however, not be seen as a surrendering of control functions. Rather, the competition state is mean, though not necessarily lean, in its dealings with migration policy.

Interviews

DE-TRANS-1 interview with representative of German airline

DE-TRANS-2 interview with representative of German trucking sector interest association

DE-TRANS-3 interview with representative of German shipping sector interest association

DE-GOV-1 interview with senior official at German Ministry of Interior Affairs

DE-SEC-1 interview with representative of German sectoral employer association for security services

UK-GOV-1 interview with senior official at the UK Home Office

UK-BUS-1 interview with senior representative of British employer association

UK-BUS-2 interview with senior representative British sectoral employer association for gastronomy

UK-BUS-3 interview with senior representative British sectoral employer association for construction

UK-TRANS-1 interview with representative of British airline

UK-TRANS-2 interview with representative of British trucking sector interest association

UK-TRANS-3 interview with representative of British shipping sector interest association

UK-SEC-1 interview with representative of British security sector interest association

NL-GOV-1 interview with representative of Dutch Ministry for Interior Affairs

NL-SEC-1 interview with representative of Dutch security company

AUS-GOV-1 interview with Australian Ministry for Immigration and Citizenship

US-GOV-1 interview with US Immigration and Customs Enforcement

Acknowledgements

Field Research was facilitated by a grant from the Research Office at Goldsmiths College and the British Academy, for which the author would like to express his gratitude. The author would like to thank Alex Caviedes and Anke Ellermann for helpful comments on an earlier draft.

Notes

1. Commenting on the introduction of carrier sanctions in the UK, then Home Office Minister Douglas Hurd stated that: "The immediate spur to this proposal has been the arrival of over 800 people claiming asylum in the three months up to the end of February" (H.C Hansard, Vol. 122, col. 705).
2. The 1820 US Act Regulating Passenger Lists (section 4) required all captains of US-bound vessels to keep lists of their passengers. The duty of steamship owners to return non-admitted migrants at their own costs was enshrined in the 1902 Passengers Act.
3. The Australian 1958 Migration Act establishes in sects. 217 and 218 the obligation of owners of vessels to cooperate in the deportation of non-admitted foreigners. However, in most cases, the cost of this procedure is to be born by the deportee himself (sect. 210). An amendment, effective as of 1 November 1979 (sect. 229), introduces outright fines for carriers found guilty of having carried non-admitted foreigners, though extenuating circumstances shall be considered, especially if the owner or person in charge of the vessel can demonstrate that he or she acted in good faith and was presented with documents that appeared to be valid at point of embankment.
4. "[o]perators shall take precautions...that passengers are in possession of the documents prescribed by the states of transit and destination for control purposes....Contracting state and operators shall cooperate...in establishing the validity and authenticity of passports and visas that are presented by embarking passengers" (Arts. 3.39 and 3.40).

Bibliography

ANAO – Australian National Accounting Office (2006a) "Management of the Tender Process for the Detention Services Contract", Canberra: ANAO.

ANAO – Australian National Accounting Office (2006b) "Preparations of DIAC's Detention and Health Services Contracts", Canberra: ANAO.

Bacon, Christine (2005) RSC *Working Paper No. 27: The Evolution of Immigration Detention in the UK: The Involvement of Private Prison Companies.* Working Paper Series. Refugee Studies Centre, Department of International Development, Queen Elizabeth House, University of Oxford. September 2005.

Baumgartner, F. and Jones, B. (1991) "Agenda Dynamics and Policy Subsystems", *The Journal of Politics* 53 (4): 1044–1074.

Baumgartner, Frank R. and Jones, Bryan D. (1993) *Agendas and Instability in American Politics*, Chicago, IL: University of Chicago Press.

Brochmann, G. and Hammar, T. (eds.) (1999) *Mechanisms of Immigration Control: A Comparative Analysis of European Regulation Policies*, Oxford: Berg.

Castles, S. and Kosack, G. (1973) *Immigrant Workers and Class*, Oxford: Oxford University Press.

Cerny, P. (1997) "Paradoxes of the Competition State: The Dynamics of Political Globalization", *Government and Opposition* 32 (2): 251–274.

Chief Inspector of Prisons (2008) *Report on an Unannounced Full Follow-up Inspection of Harmondsworth Immigration Removal Centre,* London: HM Inspectorate of Prisons.

Cornelius, W., Tsuda, T., Martin, P. L., Hollifield, J. F. (eds.) (2004) *Controlling Immigration: A Global Perspective*, Stanford: Stanford University Press.

Cruz, A. (1991) "Carrier Sanctions in four European Community States: Incompatibilities Between International Civil Aviation and Human Rights Obligations", *Journal of Refugee Studies* 4 (1): 63–81.

Department of Justice, Equality and Law Reform (2005) *Strategy Statement 2005–2007*, Dublin: Department of Justice, Equality and Law Reform.

Ellermann, A. (2009) *States Against Migrants: Deportation in Germany and the United States*, New York: Cambridge University Press.

Evans, C. (2008) "New Directions in Detention: Restoring Integrity to Australia's Immigration System", Speech at Australian National University, Canberra, 29 July 2008.

Feeley, M. (2002) "Entrepreneurs of Punishment: The Legacy of Privatisation", *Punishment and Society* 4(3): 321–344.

Freeman, G. (2001) "Client Politics or Populism? Immigration reform in the United States" in V. Guiraudon and C. Joppke (eds.) *Controlling a New Migration World*, London: Routledge, 65–96.

Gamble, Andre (1988) *The Free Economy and the Strong State*, Basingstoke: Palgrave.

Geddes, A. (2003) *The Politics of Migration and Immigration in Europe*, London: SAGE.

de Giorgi, A. (2006): *Re-Thinking the Political Economy of Punishment*, Aldershot: Ashgate.

Ginn, E. (2008) "Outsourcing Abuse: The Use and Misuse of State-Sanctioned Force During the Detention and Removal of Asylum Seekers", London: Medical Justice Network.

Greene, J. and S. Patel (2007) "The Immigrant Gold Rush: The Profit Motive Behind Immigrant Detention", Geneva: UN Special Rapporteur on the Rights of Migrants.

Guiraudon, V. (2000) "European Integration and Migration Policy: Vertical Policy-making as Venue Shopping", *Journal of Common Market Studies* 38 (2): 249–269.

Guiraudon, V. (2001) "European Courts and Foreigners' Rights: A Comparative Study of Norms Diffusion", *International Migration Review* 34 (4): 1088–1125.

Guiraudon, V. (2002) "Logiques et pratiques de l'Etat délégateur: les compagnies de transport dans le contrôle migratoire à distance. Partie 1", *Cultures et conflits* 45, available at: http://www.conflits.org/index771.html

Guiraudon, V. and Lahav, G. (2000) "A Reappraisal of the State Sovereignty Debate: The Case of Migration Control", *Comparative Political Studies* 33 (2): 163–195.

Habermas, J. (1976) *Legitimation Crisis*, London: Heinemann.

Hansen, Randall (2000) *Citizenship and Immigration in Post-War Britain*, Oxford/New York: Oxford University Press.

Harding, R.W. (1998) "Private Prisons" in M. Tonry (ed.) *The Handbook on Crime and Punishment*, Oxford: Oxford University Press.

Heinz, J. P., Laumann, E. O., Nelson, R. L., and Salisbury, R. H. (1993) *The Hollow Core. Private Interests in National Policy Making*, Cambridge MA: Harvard University Press.

Hirsch, Joachim (1980) *Der Sicherheitsstaat: Das "Modell Deutschland", seine Krise und die neuen sozialen Bewegungen*, Hamburg: EVA.

Hirsch, Joachim (1998) *Vom Sicherheitsstaat zum nationalen Wettbewerbsstaat*, Berlin: ID-Archiv.

HMIP (1998) *Campsfield House Detention Centre: A Report by Her Majesty's Chief Inspector of Prisons Following an Unannounced Short Inspection*, London: HMIP.

Hollifield, J. (1992) *Immigrants, Markets and States: The Political Economy of Postwar Europe*, Cambridge, MA: Harvard University Press.

Home Office (2005) *Controlling our Borders: Making Migration Work for Britain – Five Year Strategy for Asylum and Immigration*, February, London: Home Office.

Huysmans, J. (2006) *The Politics of Insecurity: Fear, Migration and Asylum in the EU*, London: Routledge.

ICE (2010) "US Immigration and Customs Enforcement: Detention Management Program", available at: www.ice.gov/partners/dro/dmp.htm.

Jones, T. and T. Newburn (2005) "Comparative Criminal Justice Policy Making in the United States and the United Kingdom: The Case of Private Prisons", *British Journal of Criminology* 45: 58–80.

Joppke, C. (1998) "Why Liberal State Accept Unwanted Migration", *World Politics* 50 (2): 266–293.

King, A. (1975) "Overload: Problems of Governing in the 1970s", *Political Studies* 23 (1&2): 162–174.

Köppe, O. (2003) "The Leviathan of Competitiveness: How and why do liberal states (not) accept unwanted immigration?", *Journal of Ethnic and Migration Studies* 29 (3): 431–449.

Menz, Georg (2008) *The Political Economy of Managed Migration: Nonstate Actors, Europeanization, and the Politics of Designing Migration Policies*, Oxford: Oxford University Press.

Ministerie van Justitie (2007) "Detentibooten Zuid-Holland locatie Rotterdam Inspectiebericht Vervolgonderzoog", The Hague: Ministry of Justice.

Ministerie van Justitie (2010) "Detentiecentrum Noord-Holland locatie Zaandam Inspectierapport Doorlichting", The Hague: Ministry of Justice.

Los Angeles Times (17 March 2009) "Cities and counties rely on immigrant detention fees".

Newburn, T. (2002) "Atlantic Crossings: 'Policy Transfer' and Crime Control in the United States and Britain", *Punishment and Society* 4(2): 165–194.

Nicholson, F. (1997) "Implementation of the Immigration (Carriers' Liability) Act 1987: Privatisating Immigration Functions at the Expense of International Obligations", *The International and Comparative Law Quarterly* 46 (3): 586–634.

Noll, G. (2003) "Visions of the Exceptional: Legal and Theoretical Issues Raised by Transit Processing Centres and Protection Zones", *European Journal of Migration and Law* 5: 303–341.

Offe, C. (1972) *Strukturprobleme des kapitalistischen Staates*, Frankfurt: Suhrkamp.

Parliament of Australia (2009) "Immigration detention in Australia: Facilities, services and transparency", Canberra: House of Representatives Printing and Publishing Office.

Peters, B. G. (1993) "Managing the Hollow State" in K. Eliassen and J. Kooiman (eds.) *Managing Public Organisations: Lessons for Contemporary European Experience*, London: Sage.

Peters, B. G. (1997) "Shouldn't Row, Can't Steer: What's a Government to do?", *Public Policy and Administration* 12 (2): 51–61.

Piore, M. (1979) *Birds of Passage: Migrant Labor and Industrial Societies*, Cambridge: Cambridge University Press.

Poulantzas, N. (2002) *Staatstheorie*, VSA: Hamburg.

Rhodes, R. (1994) "The Hollowing Out of the State: The Changing Nature of the Public Service in Britain", *The Political Quarterly* 65: 138–151.

Rudolph, C. (2003) "Security and the Political Economy of International Migration", *American Political Science Review* 97 (4): 603–620.

Sassen, Saskia (2001) *The Global City*, Princeton: Princeton University Press.

San Diego Union-Tribune (4 May 2008) "Detention Dollars: Tougher immigration laws turn the ailing private prison sector into a revenue maker".

Scholten, S. and P. Minderhoud (2008) "Regulating Immigration Control: Carrier Sanctions in the Netherlands", *European Journal of Migration and Law* 10: 123–147.

Shaw, Stephen (2004) Investigation into Allegations of Racism, Abuse and Violence at Yarl's Wood Removal Centre: A Report by the Prisons and Probation Ombudsman for England and Wales March 2004, London: Prisons and Probation Ombudsman.

Soederberg, S., Menz, G. and Cerny, P. (eds.) (2005) *Internalizing Globalization: The Rise of Neoliberalism and the Decline of National Varieties of Capitalism*, Basingstoke: Palgrave.

Soysal, Y. (1994) *Limits of Citizenship: Migrants and Postnational Membership in Europe*, Chicago: University of Chicago Press.

Stigler, George (1971) "The Theory of Economic Regulation", *Bell Journal of Economics and Management Science* 3: 3–18.

UK Border Agency (UKBA) (2009) "Detention and Temporary Release", in *Enforcement Instructions and Guidance*. Last updated 23 April 2009. Available at: http://www.ukba.homeoffice.gov.uk/sitecontent/documents/policyandlaw/enforcement/detentionandremovals/.

U.S. Department of Homeland Security Bureau of Immigration and Customs Enforcement (2003) "Form M-592 (8/15/03) ENDGAME Office of Detention and Removal Strategic Plan, 2003 – 2012 Detention and Removal Strategy for a Secure Homeland", Washington: US Dept. of Homeland Security.

Watts, J. R. (2002) *Immigration Policy and the Challenge of Globalization: Unions and Employers in Unlikely Alliance*, Ithaca, N.Y.: Cornell University Press.

Zolberg, A. (1999) "The Handbook of International Migration: The American Experience", in C. Hirschan, P. Kasinitz, and J. DeWind (eds.), *Volume prepared for the Social Science Research Council*. New York: Russell Sag, pp. 71–93.

Section IV
Unauthorized Labour Migration

9
Strange Castle Walls and Courtyards: Explaining the Political Economy of Undocumented Immigration and Undeclared Employment

Michael Samers

1. Introduction

Anxiety among European states and publics about undocumented migration has been a feature of the political landscape of European countries since at least the early 1990s. That much is clear. What is perhaps less evident is the concern about "undeclared employment", which is ironically often conflated with undocumented (read "clandestine", "irregular", or "illegal") migration. There is little doubt that undocumented migration[1] and "undeclared employment"[2] are related, although as a number of scholars have stressed, undocumented migration does not produce undeclared employment (for example, Castells and Portes, 1989; Wilpert, 1998) and the bulk of undeclared employment is performed by citizens and not migrants, legal or otherwise (for example, Williams, 2009; Williams and Windebank, 1998).[3] Nonetheless, each *facilitates* the other (Castells and Portes, 1989; Quassoli, 1999; Reyneri, 1998; Sassen, 1996, 1998; Wilpert, 1998),[4] and it was widely surmised by European institutions, member states of the EU, and the popular press that undocumented migration increased during the 1990s and the early 2000s, although few if any time-series statistics have been available.[5] Likewise, undeclared employment is argued to be increasing since the 1970s (see, for example, the data presented by Schneider and Enste, 2000), and its alleged proliferation is now exercising European policy-makers (European Commission, 2006).[6] If the growth of both phenomena seems less dizzying now for *some* European governments, the vigilance of the latter has hardly waned. Witness the cavernous range of reports and studies, at the member state and European levels that have explored the implications of these phenomena. News-ready stories of migrants dying at sea or in the back of trucks, along with tales of unscrupulous employers paying extremely low wages, forcing migrants to work in terrible, and sometimes deadly, working conditions while undercutting citizen workers, have reinforced the image of a Europe besieged by illicit movements and criminal activity. If governments and a wide swathe of the European citizenry are so concerned, what explains the apparent growth of these phenomena? Are they simply beyond control in a world marked by more "intensive" and "extensive" flows of goods, people, capital, and ideas (Held et al., 1999), or are they purposely ignored while at the same time manufactured by states. The literature does not necessarily tell us much.

In fact, it is not an exaggeration to say that there is no political economic theory of *undocumented* migration, let alone a theory which solders it to the arguably twinned process of *undeclared* employment. Sure enough, there are a range of political economic accounts of *legal* migration, but a theory of *undocumented* migration and a theory of *undeclared* employment? This must be impossible since undocumented migration and undeclared employment might be both considered at least partially epiphenomenal – a product of the regulation of migration and of the labour market itself (Samers, 2003). As Walters (2008) argues "migration governance should be examined in terms of programs, discourses, experts, technologies and interventions which do not simply respond to something already there, but instead operate as an active and constitutive force that shapes the social world in particular ways with particular political consequences" (p. 43). The apparently epiphenomenal character of undocumented migration and undeclared employment raises significant questions about whether and how states respond to or indeed create these twinned processes. In fact, Walters (2008) locates a distinctly "anti-illegal immigration policy" in the European Union (EU). He insists that such a policy has developed alongside labour migration policy in order to make *legal* migration more palatable to a broadly sceptical public. Similarly, states such as France have taken aggressive steps to deter undeclared employment through a familiar but uniquely effective set of punitive actions such as fines and worksite raids.

My purpose in this chapter is certainly not to propose a *singular* theory of undocumented migration and undeclared employment, but rather to develop a more plausible, synthetic, and combinatory set of arguments that explain how and why states both respond to *and* produce undocumented immigration and undeclared employment. This is accomplished through an analysis of France and Italy in the period after September 2001 but before the emergence of the global recession in 2008. While I discuss some of the different processes and state policies in these two countries, my aim is to tease out the commonalities in state actions. I begin first by briefly citing some existing theories of migration or at least arguments that might explain the political economy of undocumented immigration and undeclared employment. I conclude this section with my own synthetic argument and in Section 2 I provide some empirical evidence for such a political economy from the two countries indicated above.

2. On the political economy of migration – some theoretical considerations

Over the last 35 years or so, a number of contrasting and competing theories have attempted to explain the relationship between states and immigration. Let me review very briefly these approaches for the purposes of framing the empirical analysis that follows. Thus, in the 1970s, Marxist arguments remained popular, demonstrating the role of the state (the "executive committee of the bourgeoisie") in securing an exploited "reserve army of labour" for capital accumulation while lowering the costs of social reproduction (for example, Castells, 1975; Castles and Kosack, 1973; Granotier, 1970; Miles, 1982). Arguments concerning "post-Fordism" or "neoliberalism" in the late 1980s and 1990s continued this tradition but in a different guise. Many scholars continued to stress the function of immigrants as low-wage workers in growing service industries in Europe. Migrants provided "flexibility" and "docility" for employers in order to respond to rapidly changing economic demands (for example, Burgers and Engbersen, 1996; Pugliese, 1993; Quassoli, 1999). With the apparent rise of neoliberalism and the tightening of welfare states, including the extension of social and economic rights (however limited they be) to long-settled immigrants, undocumented migrants in particular are argued to become more rather than less attractive to both employers and the state (Samers, 2003). Alongside these critical political economy-inspired arguments, a vigorous debate grew out of Freeman's (1995) agenda-setting "client politics thesis". Though influential, Freeman's thesis attracted substantial criticisms. First, in the context of so-called "unwanted family reunification" in Europe, Joppke (1998) argues that Freeman neglects *legal* process as a force in liberalizing immigration, since judges are often shielded from the political clamoring of Freeman's clients, and more beholden to constitutional rights and statutes. That is, legal constraints and moral obligations prevent courts from either inhibiting entry or quickly ordering deportations, whatever the rhetoric of "zero immigration" (Favell and Hansen, 2002). Geddes (2008), echoing Soysal (1994) reminds us of the additional significance of European legislation in this regard. Wielding the concept of "venue-shopping", others have developed an argument that migration actors seek new decision-making jurisdictions through which they can more easily carry out their intended objectives, for example, by moving decision-making from national states to the European level (Guiraudon, 2000; Guiraudon and Lahav, 2000; Lahav, 1998; Menz, 2008), or by moving the location of repressive migration practices outwards beyond Europe to the "source" areas of undocumented migration (Samers, 2004; Zolberg, 2002).

A barrage of studies began to focus on the discourse and practice of "migration management", in which states develop sophisticated migration systems to filter out "unwanted" migrants such as asylum-seekers and refugees, while facilitating the immigration of the highly skilled, the entrepreneurial, or the very rich. Such a framework sits uneasily with the alleged market orthodoxy of neoliberalism, since migration management often involves quite sophisticated statist measures. What can be said is that migration management is both at odds with, but also complementary to neoliberalism. Alongside the umbrella of migration management, a vast range of studies have emerged which align the politics of undocumented migration with "securitization" *as a discourse* (the so-called "Copenhagen School"), or a discourse associated specifically with terrorism (Boswell, 2007). Many have argued that EU migration policy is increasingly securitized in both discursive and practical terms (for example, CASE collective, 2006; Cholewinski, 2000; Huysmans, 2000; Samers, 2004) as are individual states through deportations, detentions, and dispersals (for example, Schuster, 2005). From a considerably different angle, others develop Foucauldian and other cognate critiques of state or partisan-based exclusionary discourses that mark and code "unwanted" (racialized, gendered, sexualized) bodies (for example, Papastergiadis, 2006; Tesfahuny, 1998; Walters, 2008). Somewhat in contrast, I have argued in a neo-Marxist vein that the political economy of migration and undeclared employment involves a "malign neglect" whereby states ensure adequate numbers of undocumented migrant workers for undeclared employment (Samers, 2003, 2005). This may reflect, as Jahn and Straubhaar (1999) note, the relative benefits and costs of policing undocumented migration. These two epiphenomena are too economically costly to control; too politically costly to ignore completely.

This bewildering range of approaches suggests that teasing out a distinct political economy of undocumented migration, let alone one that includes the study of undeclared employment, is nothing short of an enormous challenge. Indeed, none of these approaches have sought to understand why undocumented immigration *and* undeclared employment persist. What makes the task so difficult is the plausible character of most of these arguments for understanding the relationship between states and at least undocumented migration, and the difficulty of developing a comparative analysis. In order to undertake this Herculean task, I privilege an inductive approach by drawing out the commonalities and divergences from a study of France and Italy. In doing so, I hold that six – often contradictory – processes constitute the political economy of undocumented migration and undeclared employment, namely:

1) **the desire among elected representatives to maintain restrictive and oppressive policies** towards migrants on behalf of publics *broadly* sceptical towards at least certain *kinds* of migrants and migration. This may be as much a *perception* among elected officials of electoral opposition to more liberal migration and residence policies as it is *explicitly stated* opposition by the same electorate. In any case, state policies towards undocumented migration may also reflect the particular classed, racialized, and gendered perspectives of policy-makers themselves, irrespective of public attitudes. This may include state representatives' and policy-makers' undue conflation of at least undocumented migration (if not undeclared employment) with terrorists and acts of terrorism, or other security-related issues. While anxiety about undocumented migration appears to be far more palpable amongst the public than undeclared employment, the latter is of special, technical concern to governments concerned about social and employment issues (see further below). Thus, the two phenomena are related but are asymmetrical in their degree of political debate. In any case, many of the policies and measures against both phenomena are symbolic and/or designed to meet limited objectives in order to demonstrate state capacity in the sphere of migration, immigration, and employment policy;

2) **the difficulty of deporting** the majority of undocumented migrants because of legal intervention on the part of national constitutional or other high courts – what Joppke calls "self-limited sovereignty", though

European courts may also become involved in a very limited number of cases;

3) **the relative financial costs and benefits of policing undocumented migration** (Jahn and Straubhaar, 1999) or undeclared employment (Samers, 2003). This results in "malign neglect", that is the recognition or a resignation that completely eliminating undocumented migration is either undesirable (quite simply migrant workers may be paid less and thus increase profitability for businesses relying on them)[7] or unachievable (the difficulty and cost of eliminating undeclared employment or controlling clandestine cross-border movements and locating and deporting even a fraction of the undocumented residents);

4) **humanitarian protest** emanating from Left-leaning political parties, pro-migrant groups, and undocumented migrants themselves, which is partly manifested in regularization policies;

5) with respect to "malign neglect" (see point 2 above), it is also **practically and politically difficult to punish employers** for hiring workers in an undeclared fashion, even if states are concerned with the "imbalances" that undeclared employment might pose to social welfare systems and employee rights, as well as "fair competition";

6) **political confusion** amongst both parties and "social partners" with respect to a response to (the undeclared employment) of undocumented migrants.

These six arguments suggest why these phenomena are both challenged as well as tolerated at the same time. In short, it explains the strange castle walls and inner courtyards of at least France and Italy. Let us begin with the French case.

3. The exterior walls and inner courtyards of European countries: A study of France and Italy

3.1. France

To fathom the political economy of undocumented migration and undeclared employment in France, one might begin by questioning the novelty of the former. To be more specific, what is remarkable but perhaps little known about undocumented migration to France is that large numbers of migrants were undocumented during the 1960s, but were later regularized by the French government, in part because of the enormous demand for manual labour in "Fordist" industries (for example, Tripier, 1990; Weil, 1991). During the post-World War II period, local prefects had "discretionary power" in granting legal residence status to undocumented migrants, and some 20,000 migrants were granted such status during the 1990s. A 1945 Ordinance laid the groundwork for their discretionary power, which prevented authorities from deporting the spouses of French citizens, children who migrated to France before they were 10 years old or parents who have children with French citizenship. In this sense, the idea of "regularization" could be located in the constitutional notion that the family should be protected (Laubenthal, 2007). Thus, undocumented migration is not by any means a new phenomenon in France. Perhaps it is equally surprising that the practice of undeclared employment by employers only became a "crime" in 1985, after being a legal "infraction" since the 1940s (Marie, 2000). As such, it is not possible to date an expansion of undeclared employment to, let us say, the late 1980s and the apparent growth of undocumented migration, though its "criminalization" may be related to stricter controls on migration. By the late 1980s, these two phenomena and particularly undocumented migration became more prominent issues in political debates in France.

By the early, 1990s, repressive discourses and policies with regard to these two phenomena proved to be pervasive, not least through the 1993 Pasqua Law which sought "zero immigration" (at least in rhetoric; later modified to zero illegal immigration) and to tighten the reins on undocumented migration. At the same time, undeclared employment became the target of increasing scrutiny through the creation of a battery of laws, institutions and measures aimed at tackling undeclared employment during the 1990s (in particular the creation in 1997 of the DILTI and later the COLTI (*Comité Opérationnel de Lutte contre le Travail Illégal*), which has proven to single out the French administrations of the 1990s and 2000s as among the few administrations in Europe to actually achieve the institutional goals of reducing the undeclared employment of citizens, if not of undocumented migrant workers (Eurofound, 2008; Marie, 2000; Samers, 2003).

Nonetheless, while scrutiny and repression have been features of migration and residence control since the early 1990s, there is another very different story to be told, and that concerns regularization. As Laubenthal (2007) points out, in the mid-1990s, pro-migrant groups increasingly appeared on the scene, such as *Droits Devant!* (Rights first!). They gained credence from the support of celebrities and other notable groups. In order to legitimize regularization, Laubenthal points out that such groups stressed colonialism and the contribution of former colonized populations in fighting on the side of France, in order to "evoke a sense of national moral obligation that could justify claims for regularization" (p. 108). Such protest, if not moral persuasion, would eventually have an effect on the governments' decisions to deport migrants. For example, in response to a number of protests by undocumented migrants in the Fall of 2002, Sarkozy, then Interior Minister, announced that he was re-launching the possibility of regularization and claimed that the cases of thousands of undocumented migrants would be dealt with "realistically, and with compassion", and promised to regularize some 80,000–400,000 undocumented migrants. This, however, may have been little more than a move to thwart an issue around which the opposition Socialist party might mobilize. In fact, his advisors would later state that only those "able to prove that they are in a special situation" will benefit from a regularization, and he was careful to distinguish the French government's more hesitant position *vis-à-vis* regularization from that of Italy and Spain. This "special situation" included parents with children born in France and attending French schools, and undocumented migrants able to prove that they had been living in France for at least 10 years. The result is that very few of the estimated 80,000–400,000 migrants were actually regularized (Zappi, 2002).

Any ideological and practical gestures towards regularization aside, successive French governments have – generally speaking – become less rather than more willing to regularize undocumented migrants. One might trace this political shift to at least 2002, and the Right-wing election gains of Le Pen, who managed 16.9 per cent of first round presidential voting (Marthaler, 2006). In its wake, a November 2003 law (the MISEFEN law or so-called Sarkozy Law) restricted family unification and stepped up efforts to more rapidly deport failed asylum-seekers and prevent "false marriages". In February 2005, France's Interior Minister Dominique de Villepin published a report arguing that the French government "needed" to intensify its "fight" against undocumented migration, while opening legal channels for further migration. He sought to create a new 600-person immigration police to coordinate the migration-related activities of the various law and order agencies, as well as local and national government organizations. This gained momentum when the French public voted "no" against the European constitution at the end of May 2005, providing the French government with more flexibility in devising a more restrictive migration policy for low-skilled/low-income migrants (*Migration News*, July 2005). By June 2005, the French government announced that it was adopting a stricter immigration policy. The policy was designed to accelerate the deportation of undocumented migrants, while introducing an annual quota/point system for "highly-skilled" migrants. The French government believed that these new measures would bring down the rate of unemployment (then hovering at around 10 per cent) by creating new jobs. Sarkozy, claimed that the new policy would move France from "immigration by submission to immigration by choice". The government hoped to increase the expulsion rate by 50 per cent from 15,000 a year to 22,500, and sure enough deportations increased from 11,000 in 2003, to 16,000 in 2004, and to about 23,000 in 2005. The government wished to see the new special police force (see above) given the capacity to enter into areas that undocumented migrants were believed to reside in. At the same time, human rights organizations were vocal in their opposition to the government's handling of undocumented migration under the guise of anti-terrorism (*Migration News*, October 2005).

The 2005 riots seemed to harden the opinion of large swathes of the French public against low-income migration from poorer, especially Muslim-dominated, countries, even though Islam had apparently nothing whatsoever to do with the riots (for example, Dikec, 2007). In early 2006, Sarkozy (at that point both Interior Minister and conservative presidential candidate) sought to once more increase the number of deportations to 25,000 in 2006, while remaining staunchly against any blanket regularizations (*Migration News*, October 2006; Tanaka, 2007). Some of the undocumented migrants that were subject to deportation were chosen precisely because they had children in French schools. Not surprisingly this led to protests from pro-migrant groups at airports, as they watched families escorted into planes. Paradoxically, the government also considered regularizing the residence applications of 30,000 undocumented migrants who had children in French schools for at least 2 years. While an April 2006 poll revealed that the majority (53 per cent) of French citizens seemed to support Sarkozy's more hard-line approach to undocumented migrants, agreeing with a statement that France had "too many immigrants", Ségolène Royal, the Socialist contender to Sarkozy in the 2007 presidential elections, remained heavily critical of Sarkozy's efforts to deport undocumented migrants (*Migration News*, October 2006; Tanaka, 2007). She favoured a "case-by-case" approach to regularization, which would be based on the length of residence, whether the migrant had children in school, and whether they held a work permit (Tanaka, 2007). Ultimately, the July 2006 *Loi Sarkozy* (or the so-called second Sarkozy law) overturned the 1998 Chevènement law, and eliminated the automatic regularization of, and legal residence for, undocumented migrants after 10 years of residence in France (against the proposals of Ségolène Royal who wished to re-instate the 1998 law); it limited family reunification and sought to crack down on "false marriages". In any case, the French government further stipulated that an adult undocumented migrant would be paid 2400 dollars and their children 600 dollars if they "voluntarily agreed" to return to their country of origin, and again, some undocumented families were singled out and identified because they had children in school. Lastly, Sarkozy created the ELOI index (an abbreviation of *l'eloignement* – a euphemism for deportation) which would provide data on undocumented migrants as well as anyone housing them or visiting them in detention centres. This was quickly struck down by the *Conseil d'Etat* (the highest administrative court) on administrative grounds (Tanaka, 2007).

The route to the French presidential elections of May 2007 opened up yet another round of contentious migration and immigration politics in the wake of the 2005 riots that spread across France. In general, immigrants would have to *demonstrate* their reasons for remaining in France. This would be challenged in 2007 by Ségolène Royal's Socialist bid for Presidency, and her calls to reintroduce regularization for undocumented migrants but on a case-by-case basis (see above). While she insisted that the "*sans papiers'* were not being treated humanely" (Marthaler, 2006, p. 392), she wished to remain "firm" on undocumented migration, proclaiming that "we cannot, any more than our neighbours, simply open up our borders without creating intolerable economic and social imbalances, in particular a strong downward pressure on pay" (cited in Marthaler, 2006, p. 391). Marthaler explains this as a dilemma between the need for the Socialists to appeal to both their progressive middle-class voters and to the working classes with respect to immigration and employment and wages. Sarkozy proposed a Ministry of Immigration, Integration, National Identity and Co-Development (*Migration News*, April 2007). The head of the new Ministry (the French Immigration Minister Brice Hortefeux) instructed local governments in September 2007 to once again increase the number of deportations of undocumented migrants, and Sarkozy, now the newly elected President, established a target of 25,000 deportations in 2007 (*Migration News*, July, October 2007). Such moves to increase the number of deportations should be partly read as symbolic, since the number of deportations appears to be only a small fraction of the apparent number of undocumented residents in France.

As undocumented migrants became the victim of ever increasing deportation targets, it also became abundantly clear that the French government wished to further step up its "fight" against undeclared employment by the early 2000s, including devoting more funds and personnel to this aim. Indeed, the first *"Plan national de lutte contre le travail illegal"* (National Plan to fight against illegal work) was introduced and implemented in 2004. It has to be said that the DILTI and later the COLTI and CNLTI (see bibliography) have remained relatively high-profile organizations in French political debate, at least compared to many European countries, and there is substantial cross-Ministerial cooperation (Eurofound, 2009). The COLTI has specifically targeted the building and public works sector, the hotel and restaurant sector, and agriculture, to name just a few sectors in which "raids" have been carried out.[8] Notably in agriculture, the Plan calls for a more "efficient control over the return of seasonal migrant workers to their country of origin" (DILTI, 2004, p. 4), thus contributing to the soldering of migration and labour market control.

3.2. Italy

Does the political economy of undocumented migration and undeclared employment in Italy differ substantially from France, a supposedly "Northern European" country? To begin to answer this question, let us explore the type and volume of undeclared employment in Italy. Although it is difficult to quantify, a significant proportion of employment in Italy is undeclared. Most of it is to be found in agriculture, construction, domestic, and other care work, low end services such as street selling, and other small businesses (for example, Ambrosini, 2001; Finotelli and Sciortino, 2009; Reyneri, 2001). None of this is surprising and more or less mirrors the sectors in which undeclared employment is pervasive in most European countries. Thus, it is perhaps not the type, but the *extent* of undeclared employment which *may* set it apart from Northern European countries (but see Finotelli, 2009).

Beginning in the early 1990s, *undocumented* migrants increasingly filled the ranks of the jobs in the sectors mentioned above. The reasons for and the relationship between both are, however, needless to say complicated. While migrants were subject to strict visa regulations, the cancelling of readmission agreements, and frequent rounds of deportations, there were also two regularization schemes in the 1990s, and internal controls and employer sanctions have proved infrequent. Finotelli and Sciortino (2009) also speak of a "civic culture" which does not view undeclared employment in a criminal light, and any clamp-downs on such employment are likely to spark vociferous debate. It would, however, be remiss to not mention the creation of the largely ineffective *Comitato nazionale per l'emersione del lavoro non regolare* (National Committee for the Regularization of Informal Work) in 1998, whose *de facto* role seems to be mostly limited to monitoring undeclared employment (Eurofound, 2008). In this respect, regularization programmes seem to be the preferred solution, especially when and where internal controls are difficult or undesirable.[9] As Finotelli and Sciortino (2009) point out, the Italian government's migration policies "try to repress irregular migration through the control of spatial movements, rather than acting on the internal factors – such as the size of the Italian shadow economy – that motivate and reward these movements" (p. 127). In fact, as these same authors argue: "The fight against illegal work is the real missing piece of Italian immigration legislation" (ibid.).

At the same time, it was not until the 1990s that channels opened up for the recruitment of *legal* labour through quotas, though the legal migration of domestic workers remained under the aegis of the employer–worker contract-based *chiamata nominativa* (nominative call system) until the mid-1990s (Finotelli, 2009; Nare, forthcoming). The Catholic Church figured centrally in mediating these contracts for domestic workers between Italian employers and migrant workers overseas (Nare, forthcoming). Nonetheless, channels for legal labour migration remained limited and cumbersome until 2006, after which time, legal labour migration accelerated (Finotelli and Sciortino, 2009). Partly as a consequence of the problems that employers faced in recruiting *legal* migrant workers, employers turned to illegally recruiting undocumented migrants and most of the migrants to Italy have been undocumented from the mid-1980s to the mid-2000s, finding work in undeclared employment. This undocumented migration has consisted of either over-staying or clandestine entry, and despite salacious stories of migrant-filled boats destined for the Italian coast, most undocumented migration has been composed of over-stayers (Finotelli and Sciortino, 2009; Geddes, 2008; Zincone, 2006). In fact, sea landings in Italy fell from a high of nearly 50,000 in 1999 to 20,165 in 2007, while the number of undocumented migrants was estimated at some 500,000 by 2008 (Finotelli and Sciortino, 2009).

How has Italian immigration policy shaped the relationship between undocumented migration and undeclared employment? I have already mentioned inadequate and cumbersome legal recruitment channels as well as weak internal controls. We could add to this severe visa policies in Italy and a formerly liberal German asylum system which allows migrants to enter "Schengen space" legally and then move from

Germany to settle illegally in Italy – what Finotelli and Sciortino call Fortress Europe's "soft underbelly" (2009, p. 131). Political scientists have also focused on the Italian political system as an *explanans*. In this respect, it is difficult to simply align restrictive immigration policies along partisan lines, as Zincone (2006) shows in her detailed analysis of the passing of the 1998 Turco-Napolitano Act (T-N act) and the 2002 Bossi-Fini immigration law (B-F law). Zincone argues that the two main coalitions (centre-left and centre-right) have implemented remarkably similar immigration policies despite divergent attitudes and rhetoric (see also Geddes, 2008). While this chasm between immigration rhetoric and reality is hardly surprising (Geddes, 2008) (see, for example, Cornelius et al. "gap hypothesis" (1994)), it deserves exploration. For Zincone (2006) and Geddes (2008), then, part of the explanation of this gap lies in the character of the Italian political system, which has mediated the relationship between partisan politics and actual policies.

Our focus here will be on the formation of, contestation against, and actual policy contours of the B-F law in 2001–2002, although I will also examine certain policy developments since this law. Concerning the former, the second Berlusconi government (2001–2006) and the ruling Centre-Right coalition more broadly (especially the racist, ethnicist, regionalist, xenophobic, anti-Islamic *Lega Nord* and the somewhat more centrist *Alleanza Nazionale*), aimed to tackle clandestine entry and overstaying, while at the same time promoting "integration" through legal labour channels and other means. By the same token, the *Lega Nord* (LN) opposed regularization for the most part, threatening to break from the Centre-Right coalition if regularization were to remain an option (Hepburn, 2009). The LN were also worried about the "black economy", especially its effect on Italian businesses and workers, and they sought to eliminate the "job-seeker's residence permit" whereby a migrant could enter Italy and then search for work. The LN envisioned the replacement of a residence permit by a "unified contract of employment and residence" in which employers were required to sign an employment contract with a potential worker outside Italy. The employer would have to guarantee accommodation and pay the cost of repatriating the migrant workers, if and when the employment came to an end. In turn, the migrant worker would then have to leave the country after the cessation of the employment contract. Other individuals in the *Lega Nord* actually favoured the regularization of care and other domestic workers because they served to support families,[10] yet *in general* (partly as an effect of the *Lega Nord's* staunch opposition to regularization) the ruling coalition continued to argue against a wider regularization (Finotelli and Sciortino, 2009; Geddes, 2008; Zincone, 2006).

The proposals quickly drew fire from within the coalition and what might be considered more right-leaning political circles, including business voices. For example, the Director of *Confindustria* (the Italian employers' confederation) opposed the immediate expulsion of migrants after the cessation of their employment contract, and a year before the B-F law came into being, businesses in the north of Italy formed the scarcely believable "Pro Illegal Labour Committee" in response to migrant workers they had lost through deportations. Likewise, the CCD-CDU within the ruling Centre-Right coalition cited the impacts it would have on care and other domestic workers specifically, who might easily slip into illegality with the proposed legislation (Zincone, 2006).

At the same time, the proposals were immediately opposed by the Centre-Left and the Catholic Church as too ideological, impractical, unconstitutional, and ripe with xenophobia. This led to immediate revisions on the part of the Centre-Right coalition; clandestine migration would no longer be criminalized; other repressive measures would also be eliminated such as the use of Italian naval forces against boats carrying migrants, the use of weapons in general, and the collection of biometric data with long-term residence cards and their renewal. The required number of years for permanent residence would be reduced from the proposed 8 to 6 years. However, the implementation of the "unified contract of employment and residence" would remain. The CCD-CDU, the advocacy coalition and immigrant families pushed for a wider regularization beyond domestic/care workers, with support from business owners and the Church. The ruling coalition had to concede to Catholic and business organizations, and the initial proposals for deportation without trial were modified so that they complied with existing Italian legal frameworks as well as those of international, and specifically European legislation (Geddes, 2008). Judges remained concerned about the Constitutional legality of the proposed B-F law and sided with the advocacy coalition's defence of migrants. Moreover, the Constitutional courts were cushioned from lobbyists while hearing controversial referrals from lower courts figured centrally in attenuating the repressive measures of the B-F law.

The two Constitutional court judgments ruled firstly that mandatory imprisonment of a person who fails to comply with an order to leave the country of origin after being found without a residence permit or with an expired permit is unconstitutional, as a person cannot be deprived of his freedom for committing a mere administrative offence; and secondly that arrest and immediate escorting to the border (also measures affecting freedom) by means of simple endorsement by a judge, without any hearing or possibility of defence, is likewise unconstitutional.

(Zincone, 2006, p. 367)

In the end, many of the initially repressive measures of the B-F law (which was mainly drafted by the centre-right coalition without the opposition's formal input) were eliminated because of the sheer costs of enforcing them. A trial and deportation for every undocumented migrant were considered too expensive (Zincone, 2006). Nonetheless, the B-F law contained a number of features: first, undocumented migrants would be arrested only if they were found to be in an egregiously illegal status for the second time, with a prison sentence of 6 months, and for a third offence – a one to three year prison sentence. (This would later be changed to one of four, and four to five years respectively for *clandestine* migrants – not over-stayers – under a harsher 2004 decree.) The practice of deportation without a trial, especially for "persistent offenders", continued from the T-N law. Resident permits were renewable for precisely the period for which they were granted, as opposed to the previous period of double the initial residence period, and were not renewable for more than 2 years (later three for seasonal workers) (ibid.). The period of unemployment could not exceed 6 months before the government would request departure or deport the individual. The relatively liberal framework of family and social entitlements for both legal *and* undocumented migrants remained unchanged (Finotelli and Sciortino, 2009; Zincone, 2006), although as Kofman (2004) admonishes, the definition of the family changed (see Nare, forthcoming). Care and domestic workers could be regularized, and some 634,000 individuals were then regularized in 2002 under this provision (Zincone, 2006). And as Zincone points out, this regularization represented the largest regularization ever in the history of Europe, and it was approved by a Centre-Right administration.[11] At the same time, immigration quotas for seasonal and other workers increased to the highest number in Italian history (some 79,500 and 159,000 workers, respectively) even while unemployment remained relatively high (Finotelli and Sciortino, 2009; Zincone, 2006).

4. Conclusion

This chapter has sought to understand the political *economy* of two phenomena that have only been rarely connected to each other theoretically. My aim in this sense has not been to locate a unified theory, but to establish a set of plausible arguments (six to be precise) that explain the state oppression *and* "toleration" of these two phenomena. To what extent does the actual political economy in France and Italy during the period under study (roughly 2002–2007) correspond to my six arguments, and what commonalities and divergences with respect to these phenomena do we find in the two countries?

My first argument related to internal and external restriction and oppression in order to appease *largely* anxious and reluctant publics. In this sense, evidence of xenophobia and racism were clearly visible in Right-wing partisan politics and public opinion. At the same time, the now commonplace policy of "migration management" prevailed in both countries, whereby those deemed "highly skilled" were favoured over those deemed not to be, with carefully guarded visa controls in both countries. Whether this is evidence of ever increasing *external* restriction would have to be evaluated carefully from a historical perspective, not least because Italy doubled the number of seasonal visa permits for migrant workers in the mid-2000s. Nevertheless, there seems to be evidence of numerically increasing *internal* controls during the study period, measured by the number of deportations in at least France, if not Italy. A blatant exception to the nature and extent of internal controls during the early part of the study period is evidenced in the largest regularization programme in European history which the Italian government carried out in 2002. My second argument concerned the difficulty of deporting the majority of undocumented migrants. In this respect, more restrictive migration or immigration legislation proposed by Right-leaning political parties had to be modified, either to meet European legislation (in the case of the B-F law in Italy) or administrative and constitutional courts (for example, the ELOI law in France and again certain elements within the B-F law). This lends some credence to Joppke's (1998) self-limited sovereignty thesis, but also to the Europeanization or communautarization of migration policies (Geddes, 2000).

The third argument revolved around the relative financial costs and benefits of policing undocumented migration or undeclared employment. In terms of the former, deportations were considered too expensive to use as strategy *en masse* by both state representatives and legislators alike. Although the French government dramatically increased the amount of public funds to police undocumented migration, this may be as much a symbolic gesture of state capacity to regulate such migration in order to appease anxious (Right-leaning) publics, as it is a desire to completely eliminate the presence of undocumented migrants. I maintain that this represents a "malign neglect", and this is precisely why I used the term "political *economy*". That is, I wished to underscore the economic "benefits" that states derive from only partially controlling undocumented migration, but also undeclared employment. In short, the French and Italian economies "benefit" from the presence of an ethnicized and racialized class of individuals that serve as extremely low-wage, undeclared workers in a range of economic sectors (for a similar argument, see Balibar and Wallerstein, 1991). To eliminate this "supply" of workers completely would prove immediately de-stabilizing (both economically and politically) to states such as France and Italy. This is, no doubt, hardly news to anyone who has considered the economic function of undocumented migrants, and it is presumably not news to the migrants themselves? Nevertheless, since it is either the *absence* or the *limited degree* of state responses that are significant, it is more difficult to reveal such a structuralist-functionalist argument through empirical research (a few exceptions notwithstanding as I mention below) as most state representatives are unlikely to admit to ignoring the control of undocumented migration because of the economic benefits of undocumented migrants.

In terms of undeclared employment, there seems to have been much more concern about undeclared employment *in general* in France than in Italy, perhaps because of the long-standing centrality of undeclared employment to the structure of Italian labour markets. So what are we to make of periodic regularizations then? That they are periodic is tell-tale, since they hardly eliminate the undocumented migrant population that employers can draw upon. Indeed, regularizations in France and Italy (even the largest ones) are only partial both in terms of the permanence of the migrants' legality, and the number of those regularized. An historical review of the estimated number of undocumented migrants in both countries suggests that there has been an unlimited "reserve army" of undocumented migrant workers in France and Italy despite numerous regularizations in the 1990s and 2000s.

My fourth argument concerned humanitarian protest and here there is much similarity between the two countries. The governments of both countries were dominated by Right-leaning political parties during the study period, but were subject to considerable contestation from

Left-leaning political parties and pro-migrant groups. In France, political contestation from the Socialist Party, along with a number of high profile protests from undocumented migrants and a surrounding coterie of celebrities mediated the contours of the two *Sarkozy* laws. In the case of Italy, the ruling coalition's repressive policy proposals on migration and immigration met with protest from the Centre-Left coalition, and especially the Catholic Church and NGOs such as Caritas. My fifth argument centred on the limitations and challenges that states face in sanctioning employers. While the French government has proven itself to be uniquely efficacious in reducing the degree of undeclared employment through a battery of institutions and measures (though always with "targets" that do not significantly reduce its presence), it has remained difficult to prosecute the bulk of employers. In Italy, the organization that has dealt with undeclared employment is either unable or unwilling to uphold a similar level of scrutiny and prosecution.

My final argument concerned the political confusion of partisan politics: The rhetoric and policies of both Left and Right-wing political parties remained somewhat ambiguous and reflect, I would maintain, their political confusion. In Right-leaning political parties, nationalist tendencies conflict with the desire of employers to secure a low-paid workforce. Recall the explicit mobilization by employer representatives such as the Italian Employers' Association and the remarkable northern Italian "Pro-illegal Labour Committee" which rallied against the expulsions, and which provides some intellectual weight to Freeman's client politics thesis. Even a fraction of the *Lega Nord* party stood in favour of regularization. In contrast, such mobilization on the part of French employer groups would seem unimaginable in light of the French government's response to undeclared employment, and its continual flirtation with piece-meal regularizations in a political climate of restrictionism towards both low-income/low-skilled migration and undeclared employment. Left-leaning parties are equally ambivalent, especially in France. In particular, the Socialist party leaders wished to appeal to two constituencies: the middle classes and poorer income groups. This in turn had to be balanced with the concern for the safety and well-being of undocumented migrants, while at the same time seeking to maintain the social protections and ostensibly higher pay that more "formal" employment offers.

As a closing point, the six arguments that I have elucidated in this chapter *might* be generalizable to other so-called liberal democratic states, and perhaps they may even be tenable in different times and at different sub-national scales. Whether they are is a matter of further theoretical and empirical work. In the meantime, this chapter has served as a modest attempt to sketch out an explanatory framework, in lieu of an encompassing theory, which may be impossible to construct.

Notes

1. While governments draw a sharp distinction between legal and undocumented (or illegal or irregular) migration, Walters (2008) rightly asks whether such a definition of "illegal migration" is ever provided by states and if it is, questions the way in which it is defined. Clearly, undocumented migrants should not be lumped into a single category, either for explanatory or normative purposes. Depending on their mode of entry and their length of residence, so-called undocumented migrants will have varying statuses and varying potentialities for escaping from their undocumented status. For example, Anderson et al. (2006) speak of "semi-compliance" – the condition whereby migrants may satisfy their legal residence requirements, but violate their visas' employment terms by working either in an undeclared manner or working longer than the number of hours stipulated by their visas. To muddy the waters further, the term "undocumented" has a different meaning in the EU than it does in, for example, the US. In the EU, this literally refers to someone who has lost, destroyed, or had their citizenship or travel documents stolen. While such diversity poses a problem for an analysis of the political economy of undocumented migration, it should not rule it out, since for migrant and civil society groups, states and public alike often strategically envision "undocumented migrants" as a particular *group* of people. It is therefore meaningful in political terms.
2. There are a variety of names for such work including "informal", "underground", "unauthorized", "hidden", "black", "irregular", "*travail dissimulé*" (in France), and so forth. The term "undeclared" seems to be the latest, and perhaps one of the most apposite names for such economic activity in the Anglophone literature, as it suggests a direct relation to tax and labour laws. Yet, like undocumented migration, undeclared employment also involves heterogeneous situations that involve a continuum of "informality" and "formality" (see, for example, Sassen, 1998; Samers, 2005; Williams, 1998, 2009).
3. Consider as a proxy, for example, that "only" 10 per cent of the infractions recorded in 2002 in France involved the undeclared employment of undocumented migrants (DILTI, 2004).
4. I critically review some of the evidence for European countries in Samers (2005).
5. Some exceptions include Finotelli and Sciortino (2009).
6. See the nascent European platform for tackling undeclared work at http://www.emits.group.shef.ac.uk/blog/?p=75.
7. As we will see in the French case, an exception is the Socialist candidate Ségolène Royal's claim that migration would undermine wages, an argument also firmly stated by the primary institutions involved in regulating undeclared employment in France.

8. For example, in 2005, the number of firms that were subject to raids increased from 148 in 2003 to 562 to in 2005, an increase of 73% (see http://www.tripalium.com/gazette/Gazette2006/Apge21/dard02.asp, accessed March 31, 2010).

9. Finotelli and Sciortino (2009) claim that regularization policies (which might regularize the migrant on the basis of residence or their connection to at least undeclared employment) "have little political and monetary costs for the Italian governments" (p. 131), and turn " 'wanted but not welcome' migrants into welcome workers" (p. 132). Yet it is clear from the various analyses of the politics of migration and immigration during the 2000s that not all political parties favour system-wide regularization policies (see my discussion further below).

10. Einaudi (2007) argues, for example, that domestic workers compensate for insufficient welfare services in Italy (cited in Geddes, 2008).

11. Nonetheless, as Geddes (2008) observes, it became easier for immigrants to regularize their status, but more difficult to renew their residence permits, and thus the greater inflexibility of the residence permit renewal made falling into an "illegal status" more likely from temporary unemployment.

References

Ambrosini, M. (2001) "The role of immigrants in the Italian labour market", *International Migration*, 39, 3, 61–77.

Anderson, B., Ruhs, M., Rogaly, B., and Spencer, S. (2006) "Fair enough? Central and East European migrants in low-wage employment in the UK", Report Prepared for the Joseph Rowntree Foundation, available at http://www.jrf.org.uk/sites/files/jrf/1617-migrants-low-wage-employment.pdf.

Balibar, E. and Wallerstein, I. (1991) *Race, Nation, Class: ambiguous identities* (London: Verso).

Boswell, C. (2007) "Migration control in Europe after 9/11: explaining the absence of securitization", *Journal of Common Market Studies*, 45, 3, 589–610.

Burgers, J. and Engbersen, G. (1996) "Globalisation, migration, and undocumented immigrants", *New Community*, 22, 4, 619–635.

CASE collective (2006) "Critical approaches to security in Europe: A networked manifesto", *Security Dialogue*, 37, 4, 443–487.

Castells, M. (1975) "Immigrant workers and class struggles in advanced capitalism", *Politics and Society*, 5, 1, 33–66.

Castles, S. and Kosack, G. (1973) *Immigrant Workers and Class Structure in Western Europe* (Oxford: Oxford University Press).

Castells, M. and Portes, A. (1989) "World underneath: The origins, dynamics, and effects of the informal economy", in A. Portes, M. Castells, and L.A. Benton (eds.) *The Informal Economy: Studies in Advanced and Less Developed Economies* (Baltimore: Johns Hopkins University Press).

Cholewinski, R. (2000) "The EU *acquis* on irregular migration: reinforcing security at the expense of rights", *European Journal of Migration and Law*, 2, 361–405.

CNLTI (*Commission Nationale de lutte contre le Travail Illegal*). Dossier de presse, 21 March 2007.

CNLTI (*Commission Nationale de lutte contre le Travail Illegal*). Dossier de presse, 26 November 2009.

Cornelius, W, Martin, P.L. and Hollifield, J. (1994) "Introduction: the ambivalent quest for immigration control", in Cornelius, W, Martin, P.L, and Hollifield, J. (eds.) *Controlling Immigration: A Global Perspective* (Stanford: Stanford University Press).

Dikec, M. (2007) *Badlands of the Republic* (London: Royal Geographical Society).

DILTI (2004) *Commission national de lutte contre le travail illegal.* 18 June.

Droits Devant!! (1999) *Liberté, égalité, sans papiers,* Paris: L'esprit frappeur.

Einaudi, L. (2007) *Le Politiche dell'Immigrazione in Italia dall'Unita' a Oggi* (Rome: Laterza).

Eurofound (2008) National committee for the formalisation of irregular work, Italy. Document available at http://www.eurofound.europa.eu/areas/labourmarket/tackling/cases/it007.htm (accessed on 26 March 2010).

Eurofound (29 October 2009) Coordinated strategy again undeclared work, France, document available at "L'année 1997 correspond par ailleurs à un changement dans la politique de lutte contre le travail illégal, avec la création des COLTI" (Comité Opérationnel de Lutte contre le Travail Illégal), www.colti.fr (accessed 26 March 2010).

European Commission (2006) "Communication from the Commission on Policy Priorities in the Fight against Illegal Immigration of Third-Country Nationals". COM/2006/0402.

Favell, A., and Hansen, R. (2002) "Markets against politics: migration, EU enlargement and the idea of Europe", *Journal of Ethnic and Migration Studies,* 28, 4, 581–601.

Freeman, G. (1995) "Modes of immigration politics in liberal democratic states", *International Migration Review,* 29, 881–902.

Finotelli, C. (2009) "The North-South myth revised: A comparison of the Italian and German migration regimes", *West European Politics,* 32, 5, 886–903.

Finotelli, C., and Sciortino, G. (2009) "The importance of being southern: The making of policies in immigration control in Italy", *European Journal of Migration and Law,* 11, 119–138.

Geddes, A. (2000) *Immigration and European integration.* (Manchester: Manchester University Press).

Geddes, A. (2008) "*Il rombo dei cannoni?* Immigration and the centre-right in Italy", *Journal of European Public Policy,* 15, 3, 349–366.

Granotier, B. (1970) *Les travailleurs immigres en France.* (Paris: Francois Maspero).

Guiraudon, V. (2000) "European integration and migration policy: vertical policy-making as venue shopping", *Journal of Common Market Studies,* 38, 2, 251–271.

Guiraudon, V., and Lahav, G. (2000) "A reappraisal of the state sovereignty debate: the case of migration control", *Comparative Political Studies,* 33, 2, 163–195.

Held, D. McGrew, A. Goldblatt, D. and Perraton, J. (eds.) (1999) *Global Transformations* (Cambridge: Polity Press).

Hepburn, E. (2009) "Regionalist party mobilisation on immigration", *West European Politics,* 32, 3, 514–535.

Huysmans, J. (2000) "The European Union and the securitization of migration", *Journal of Common Market Studies,* 38, 5, 751–777.

Jahn, A., and Straubhaar, T. (1999) "A survey of the economics of illegal migration", in Baldwin-Edwards, M., and Arango, J. (eds.) *Immigrants and the Informal Economy in Southern Europe,* (London: Frank Cass).

Joppke, C. (1998) "Why liberal states accept unwanted immigration", *World Politics,* 50, 266–293.

Kofman, E. (2004) "Family-related migration: a critical review of European studies", *Journal of Ethnic and Migration Studies*, 30, 2, 243–262.

Kofman, E. (2008) "Managing migration and citizenship in Europe: towards an overarching framework", in Gabriel, C. and Pellerin, H. (eds.) *Governing International Labour Migration: Current Issues, Challenges and Dilemmas* (London and New York: Routledge).

Lahav, G. (1998) "Immigration and the State: the devolution and privatisation of immigration control in the EU", *Journal of Ethnic and Migration Studies*, 24, 4, 675–694.

Laubenthal, B. (2007) "The emergence of pro-regularization movements in Western Europe", *International Migration,* 45, 3, 101–133.

Le Monde (7 January 2010) "29,000 sans-papiers expulses en 2009 par la France".

Le Monde (25 January 2010) "Clandestins de Bonifacio: une affaire traitee 'avec precipitation' ".

Le Monde (7 February 2010) "A Calais, le hangar ou s'etaient refugies une centaine de clandestins evacuee par la police".

Le Monde (26 January 2010) "Tous les clandestins de Bonifacio sont libres".

Marie, C-V. (2000) "Measures taken to combat the employment of undocumented foreign workers in France: their place in the campaign against illegal employment and their results", in OECD (ed.) *Combating the Illegal Employment of Foreign Workers* (Paris: OECD).

Marthaler, S. (2006) "Nicolas Sarkozy and the politics of French immigration policy", *Journal of European Public Policy*, 15, 3, 382–397.

Menz, G. (2008) *The Political Economy of Managed Migration* (Oxford: Oxford University Press).

Miles, R. (1982) *Racism and Migrant Labour* (London: Routledge).

Nare, L. (2008) "The informal economy of paid domestic work – The Case of Ukrainian and Polish migrants in Naples", in M. Bommes and G. Sciortino (eds.) *Foggy Social Structures: Irregular Migration and the Eastern Enlargement* (Amsterdam: IMISCOE).

Papastergiadis, N. (2006) "The invasion complex: the abject other and spaces of violence", *Geografiskar Annaler*, 88 B, 4, 429–442.

Pugliese, E. (1993) "Restructuring of the labour market and the role of third world migrations in Europe", *Environment and Planning D: Society and Space*, 11, 5, 513–522.

Quassoli, F. (1999) "Migrants in the Italian underground economy", *International Journal of Urban and Regional Research*, 23, 2, 212–231.

Reyneri, E. (1998) "The role of the underground economy in irregular migration to Italy: cause or effect?", *Journal of Ethnic and Migration Studies*, 24, 2, 313–331.

Reyneri, E. (2001) *Migrants in Irregular Employment in the Mediterranean Countries of the European Union*, International Migration Papers, no. 41 (Geneva: ILO).

Samers, M. (2003) "Invisible capitalism: political economy and the regulation of undocumented immigration in France", *Economy and Society*, 32, 4, 555–583.

Samers, M. (2004) "An emerging geopolitics of 'illegal' immigration in the European Union", *European Journal of Migration and Law*, 6, 27–45.

Samers, M. (2005) "The underground economy, immigration and economic development in the European Union: an agnostic-skeptic perspective", *International Journal of Economic Development*, 6, 3, 199–272.

Sassen, S. (1996) "New Employment Regimes in Cities: the impact on immigrant workers", *New Community*, 22, 4, 579–594.

Sassen, S. (1998) *Globalization and its Discontents* (New York: New Press).

Schneider, F. and Enste, D. (2000) "Shadow Economies: Size, Causes, and Consequences", *Journal of Economic Literature*, 38, 77–114.

Schuster, L. (2005) "A sledgehammer to crack a nut: Deportation, detention and dispersal in Europe", *Social Policy and Administration*, 39, 6, 606–621.

Soysal, Y. (1994). *Limits of Citizenship* (Chicago: University of Chicago Press).

Tanaka, H. (2007) "Immigration and the 2007 French Presidential Elections", Migration Policy Institute, May, No. 3.

Tesfahuny, M. (1998) "Mobility, Racism, and Geopolitics", *Political Geography*, 17, 5, 499–515.

Tripier, M. (1990) *La classe ouvriere en France* (Paris: L'Harmattan).

Walters, W. (2008) "Anti-illegal immigration policy", in C. Gabriel and H. Pellerin (eds.) *Governing International Labour Migration: Current Issues, Challenges and Dilemmas* (London and New York: Routledge).

Weil, P. (1991) *La France et ses étrangers* (Paris: Calmann-Levy).

Williams, C.C. (2009) "The Hidden Economy in East Central Europe", *Problems of Post-Communism*, 56, 4, 15–28.

Williams, C.C. and Windebank, J. (1998) *Informal Employment in Advanced Economies* (London: Routledge).

Wilpert, C. (1998) "Migration and informal work in the new Berlin: new forms of work or new sources of labour?", *Journal of Ethnic and Migration Studies*, 24, 2, 269–294.

Zappi, S. (2002) "After protests, France's undocumented community hopes for permits", *Migration Information Source*, available at http://www.migration information.org/Feature/display.cfm?ID=67 (accessed 3 April 2010).

Zincone, G. (2006) "The making of policies: immigration and immigrants in Italy", *Journal of Ethnic and Migration Studies*. 32, 3, 347–375.

Zolberg, A.R. (2002) "Guarding the gates", on-line paper available at http://www. newschool.edu/icmec/guardingthegates.html.

10
Unauthorized Migration and the Politics of Regularization, Legalization, and Amnesty

Willem Maas

1. Introduction

Unauthorized migration is a major component of labour migration and a function of the opportunities for regular migration.[1] Facing the choice between ignoring the underground economy or attempting to control it, states constantly adjust their policies regarding residence and employment rights. As industrialized state's reduced legal avenues of labour migration in the 1970s, the international response generally focused on humanitarian concerns and the rights of workers, portraying unauthorized migrants as victims rather than law-breakers or criminals. Nevertheless, northern European states began sharpening their administrative controls. The introduction and expansion of the Schengen system in 1985, which removed border controls between various European states, resulted in enhanced cooperation regarding control of the common external border as well as changes in the administration of third country nationals, including unauthorized migrants. Driven by a combination of humanitarian concerns, labour market needs, and a relative lack of administrative capacity compared with northern European states (which had earlier pursued similar policies), southern European states such as Spain, Italy, Greece, and Portugal enacted a series of large-scale immigration amnesties and regularization campaigns. These programmes prompted arguments that legalization should not be regarded as a way of managing migration flows but should be confined to exceptional situations. This chapter explores the political response to unauthorized migration, focusing on the shifting legality of migration over time and paying particular attention to the case of Spain within the context of southern European states attempting to balance the demands of European integration with domestic labour market needs, humanitarian concerns and a relative lack of state capacity for managing migration.

Regulating migration has emerged as a key government task, and states must weigh economic forces encouraging increased migration against security and political forces favouring greater closure (Hollifield, 2004). Maintaining this balance is particularly difficult in states experiencing sharp increases in immigration. But political opposition to immigration does not everywhere grow linearly with increasing immigration: public opinion in some states remains more tolerant while harsher attitudes prevail elsewhere.

Unauthorized migration continues to grow in political salience, yet the delineation between legal and illegal migration remains in constant flux. Despite widespread agreement that some kinds of migration are always illegal – migrant trafficking for exploitation, for example – other kinds of migration often switch from legal to illegal status or the reverse as governments continually adjust their nationality and migration laws and policies, changing the administrative application of those laws and policies even more frequently (Maas, 2008, 2009). Compounding the uncertainty, different states have significantly different migration policies. Despite the elimination of border checks for travel among their countries, and despite years of efforts to construct a common approach, European states continue to pursue strikingly different policies concerning both legal and illegal migration.

2. The Shifting Legality of Migration

The regulation of immigration to southern European states did not become a major concern until the Schengen treaty resulted in the elimination of border controls between member states. Other European states also had a long history of tolerating if not actively encouraging irregular migration, particularly the seasonal migration of workers in the agriculture or construction sectors. During the 1950s and 1960s, French governments regarded large-scale irregular migration to France as a benign or even positive phenomenon (cf. Samers and Menz in this book) – an attitude that changed in the late 1960s when violent political opposition to so-called *immigration sauvage* prompted restrictive measures (Tomasi, 1984, p. 406). By the 1970s, the number of people crossing borders without permission or engaging in activities other than that for which they had been admitted – such as staying beyond the length of time authorized, working without authorization, or working in an unauthorized way – was increasing, most notably in France and the United States (US) (Houdaille and Sauvy, 1974). As labour migration grew in importance, the numbers of unauthorized or irregular migrants grew correspondingly. This was particularly true after European and other states reduced the legal means of labour migration in the 1970s.

The response of the international community to new restrictions on migration generally focused on the rights of workers. In late 1972, for example, the United Nations General Assembly expressed its deep concern at "the *de facto* discrimination of which foreign workers are the victims in certain countries of Europe and of other continents", urging states to combat "illicit trafficking in foreign labour, which is a form of exploitation" and to strengthen the protections for migrant workers.[2] Similarly, in 1974 the General Assembly urged all states to "promote and facilitate by all means in their power the adoption of bilateral agreements which would help reduce the illicit traffic in alien workers", and to "adopt the appropriate measures to ensure that the human rights of workers who enter their territory surreptitiously are fully respected."[3]

In 1976, the European Commission proposed a Directive intended to benefit and protect workers' rights (European Commission, 1976). The logic behind the proposed Directive was that, by raising the costs of irregular labour to the same level as the cost of legal workers, employers would lose any incentive to hire irregular workers. Once it had been discussed, however, the proposed Directive languished. In subsequent years, the European Council declined to pursue the proposed Directive, for reasons that "are not entirely clear" (Cholewinski, 2004: p. 166) – presumably a lack of political will in the member states, which the Community institutions lacked the legal competence to override.

Unauthorized migration into Western European countries continued to grow during the 1970s and into the 1980s, despite the adoption of a Council of Europe resolution on combating clandestine immigration and the illegal employment of foreign workers.[4] Strikingly, however, the focus of international agreements did not shift to penalizing unauthorized migrants but remained on safeguarding the rights of migrant workers. In 1984, for example, the Parliamentary Assembly of the Council of Europe invited member governments to "contemplate, as a first step, regularisation of the situation of migrant workers who have already settled, but only as an exceptional and non-renewable arrangement."[5] It also advocated "laying down severe administrative and penal sanctions for employers of clandestine workers, intermediaries and traffickers, so as to impose the same charges on all firms and to prevent illicit migration by providing equal treatment and working conditions for migrant workers."[6] The resolution targeted employers, intermediaries, and traffickers for sanctions, but spared the migrants themselves. This because, in the opinion of the parliamentarians, "clandestine migrant workers are the victims of a process created by many combined factors, *inter alia* the needs of certain employers in the host countries, the role played by those engaged in trafficking in labour, and the need for all migrant workers to escape from poverty in their country of origin and earn a living".[7]

Portraying migrant workers as victims rather than purposeful agents served to legitimize their continued presence in countries of destination, while blaming traffickers and employers for creating or exacerbating the problem. Moreover, many international observers castigated states for creating a problem out of migration phenomena which had hitherto not been seen as problematic. Thus, the Council of Europe lamented the fact that, "under the pressure of xenophobic movements, the authorities in certain host countries have been induced to take administrative measures, the effect of which was that situations not previously irregular actually became irregular, and newcomers were subjected to procedures taking no account of fundamental human rights."[8]

An example of this latter trend is the case of the United Kingdom (UK). At the time, immigration to the UK was regulated through a 1971 law. Yet observers found that, though the 1971 law remained unchanged, the UK government responded to perceived negative public opinion by tightening the administrative application of the law, broadening the definition of illegal immigration (Couper and Santamaria, 1984). The UK case illustrates well the reality that unauthorized migration is a function of authorized migration; they are two sides of the same coin.

Because irregular migration is a function of the opportunities for regular migration, the distinction between authorized and unauthorized immigration is murky and constantly being transformed as states change their immigration policies. Some states provide few opportunities for legal immigration, while others are more open. Some states provide easier access to residence rights than to employment rights, or the reverse. This allows many different typologies concerning whether a person is an illegal resident, an illegal worker, both, or neither. Because modern states have long-imposed restrictions on migration, irregular migration is a long-standing phenomenon. New is the scope and scale of irregular migrations, which appear to be constantly increasing (Jandl, 2004). This should not be surprising. In a world where goods, capital, services, and information move ever more freely, increased mobility of people should be expected. Despite significant efforts on the part of states to secure their borders, all borders remain porous. This allows individual migrants – and, increasingly, migrant smugglers – to exploit weaknesses in borders. Amnesties may temporarily succeed at "wiping the slate clean", but they rarely address the root causes of migration. Analysis of the world's largest amnesty, the US' 1986 Immigration Reform and Control Act, which granted amnesty to nearly 2.7 million irregular immigrants, suggests that the amnesty programme did not change long-term patterns of irregular immigration (Donato et al., 1992; Orrenius and Zavodny, 2003). Similarly, stricter border enforcement generally does not reduce the number of migrants, although migrants may find it more difficult to cross the border. Enforcement increases the cost of crossing the border illegally, thereby encouraging irregular immigrants to stay longer to recoup the cost of entry. The result is that irregular immigrants are *less* likely to return to their home countries, causing an increase in the resident stock of irregular immigrants (Massey, 2005). The budget devoted to US border control rose 20-fold over a period of two decades but the estimated number of unauthorized foreigners rose from 3 million to 9 million despite several regularization programmes (Martin, 2003, p. 7). Since states cannot control their borders, they all face the choice between ignoring the underground economy or attempting to control it. The next section examines this tension by focusing on the case of Spain.

3. The Case of Spain

Starting in the mid-1990s, Spain rapidly emerged as Europe's key immigrant destination: the number of non-Spanish citizens resident in Spain mushroomed from just over 100,000 in 1990 to 500,000 in 1995 to over 3.5 million by 2005 and an estimated 5.5 million by 2010, representing a 50-fold increase over two decades. This development transformed Spanish immigration politics, as Latin America and Eastern Europe became more important sources of immigrants than Africa. Since Spain lacked the administrative or legal infrastructure to allow regular immigration, most migrants arrived without proper authorization to obtain residence or employment. Given large-scale irregular immigration, successive Spanish governments opted to register workers in an attempt to incorporate them into the formal economy rather than ignoring them by letting them remain in the underground economy. The economic demand for new workers, coupled with the irregularity of the migrants responding to that demand, resulted in labour market rationales for amnesty similar to the rationales operating in other Southern European states such as Italy, Portugal, and Greece, which also held large-scale amnesties. Granting amnesty provided immediate economic benefits to state coffers, but did nothing to dissuade new migrants from entering Spain.

As Spain rapidly became Europe's most important immigrant destination, there was relatively little political pressure to reduce immigration, despite the explosive growth in migration, mostly unauthorized. The repeated granting of immigrant amnesties is doubly puzzling given the rise of xenophobic or anti-immigrant parties in other European states, coupled with an increased emphasis on security throughout the region. Rather than moving to restrict migration, successive Spanish governments responded to the growing influx of irregular migrants by granting one amnesty after another. In 2005, Spain carried out the largest amnesty program to date. Over 1 million people – almost 700,000 workers from Ecuador, Romania, Morocco, and elsewhere, along with 400,000 of their family members – applied in the 3 months between February and May 2005 to regularize their immigration status in Spain. To qualify, they needed proof of residency in Spain since at least August 2004, a work contract of at least 6 months' duration, and no criminal record. The new socialist administration of Prime Minister Zapatero justified the amnesty in terms of managing migration and bringing above ground the underground economy, which in turn would ensure that workers would pay taxes and benefit from legal protections. The government pursued the amnesty despite heightened security concerns following the terrorist bombings in Madrid (Chari, 2004). The amnesty also demonstrated how membership in the European Union (EU) continues to have only marginal effects on national immigration policies. Since the abolition of border controls within Europe, scholars had long anticipated that EU member states would move to harmonize their immigration policies (Philip, 1994). But the new Spanish government ignored appeals from other EU member states in its decision to grant amnesty. This raised the ire of other EU member states, which claimed that Spain was harming efforts to develop a more robust common European policy concerning irregular immigration. Similarly, the European Commission grumbled that Spain's move contravened the common EU return policy for irregular residents.

Amnesties by their nature reward individuals who have engaged in an illegal action or activity. They thus represent an admission of defeat for governments, whose other attempts to control the activity failed. It may be easier for a new government to propose an amnesty – blaming the failure to manage the situation on the previous government's blunders. Amnesty can then be justified as a means of "wiping the slate clean" so that, henceforth, immigration and the underground economy will be better managed and controlled. The Spanish example demonstrates the systematic failure of such hopes. States may expect migrants who are regularized to continue to work in the formal rather than underground economy, and to leave when their permission to work or stay expires. In reality, however, many migrants sink back into irregularity upon the expiration of their permits. The Spanish case also provides an example of a state choosing amnesty because it does not possess the administrative infrastructure and bureaucratic capacity to maintain a more active or stringent immigration policy – helping to explain why there are so many irregular migrants in Spain in the first place (Cornelius, 2004). Spain's struggles with irregular migration are also evidence of success: although it now faces difficulties adapting to large-scale immigration, this immigration arose as a result of stunning economic growth and a reversal of long-term historical trends of emigration rather than immigration.

4. Spain's Emergence as Immigration Destination

Spain was traditionally a country of emigration rather than one of immigration. Between 1846 and 1932 some 5 million Spaniards emigrated, primarily to Latin America (Arango and Martin, 2005). In the aftermath of the civil war, hundreds of thousands of Spaniards fled the Franco dictatorship. Many left to work in the more vibrant economies of Northwestern Europe. When Spain – together with Portugal – joined the European Community in 1986, the existing member states restricted the free movement of Spanish workers with provisions similar to the transition arrangements instituted with the 2004 enlargement for workers from central and Eastern European countries. The phase-in was sparked by fears in the existing member states that free movement of workers would cause massive emigration from Spain as Spanish workers sought employment elsewhere in Europe. In fact, Spain's accession marked a demographic turning point: immigration started to outpace emigration. At first, workers returning to Spain from Northwestern Europe accounted for much of the immigration. But Spain's entry into the Community also solidified its place as a popular retirement destination for Northern Europeans. Between 1990 and 2005, the number of citizens of other EU15 states officially resident in Spain increased over eight-fold, from 60,000 to almost half a million, or 1.1 per cent of the total Spanish population.[9] Even more striking, however, is the jump in the number of Spanish residents who are not citizens of EU15 states: from just over 50,000 in 1990 to almost 3 million in 2005 and an estimated 5 million by 2010. Non-EU15 foreigners comprised almost 7 per cent of the total Spanish population in 2005, meaning that approximately one out of every 12 Spanish residents in 2005 was a non-Spanish citizen, compared with only one out of every 350 residents 15 years earlier. These numbers include neither dual citizens or others who naturalized to become Spanish citizens nor irregular migrants or others who failed to officially register their residence. Northern Africa was supplanted as the chief source of immigrants: most of the recent newcomers were Spanish-speaking immigrants from Latin America. Ecuador displaced Morocco in 2003 as the single most important country of origin. Other immigrants arrived from Eastern Europe: by 2004, Romania was the fourth most important country of origin after Ecuador, Morocco, and Colombia. Argentina, Bulgaria, Peru, and Ukraine were other important sources.

Abundant employment opportunities fuelled both the demand for and the supply of immigrants. Between 1995 and 2005, the Spanish workforce grew to 21 million people from just over 16 million – a staggering 30 per cent increase. Spain's total population grew less than 12 per cent during this time, and over two-thirds of the increase (3.23 million out of 4.51 million) was attributable to foreigners (primarily non-EU15 citizens) moving to Spain (Table 10.1).

Labour market participation increased for Spanish citizens, EU15 citizens, and especially the new non-EU15 citizens. Between 1995 and 2005, the proportion of Spanish citizens in the workforce increased from 41.7 per cent to 46.7 per cent. In other words, while in 1995 fully 58.3 per cent of Spanish citizens were neither employed nor seeking employment, a decade later that proportion had shrunk five points to 53.3 per cent. But the labour market participation of non-Spanish citizens was even more striking. By 2005, over seven out of every ten non-EU15

Table 10.1 Spain: Population (000s) by citizenship and work status, 1995

	Spanish		Other EU15		Non-EU15		Total	
Employed	12,391	32.2%	39	37.9%	64	42.4%	12,495	32.3%
Unemployed	3,632	9.4%	10	9.7%	22	14.6%	3,664	9.5%
Inactive	22,445	58.3%	55	53.4%	65	43.0%	22,564	58.3%
Total	38,468	100%	103	100%	151	100%	38,723	100%

Source: Compiled from Eurostat Labour Force Survey, second quarter 1995. Due to rounding, not all percentages add to 100.

Table 10.2   Spain: Population (000s) by citizenship and work status, 2000

	Spanish		Other EU15		Non-EU15		Total	
Employed	15,200	38.9%	135	44.6%	347	56.3%	15,682	39.2%
Unemployed	2,377	6.1%	15	5.0%	76	12.3%	2,468	6.2%
Inactive	21,495	55.0%	153	50.5%	193	31.3%	21,842	54.6%
Total	39,072	100%	303	100%	616	100%	39,992	100%

Source: Compiled from Eurostat Labour Force Survey, third quarter 2000. Due to rounding, not all percentages add to 100.

residents were employed or seeking employment, as were just over half of EU15 residents (Table 10.2).

Even as the number of economically active individuals rose significantly, unemployment fell dramatically: in 1995, almost 2.5 million residents, fully 9.5 per cent of all Spanish residents (and 22.7 per cent of the economically active) were unemployed. By 2005, the proportion had dropped to 4.1 per cent of Spanish residents (and only 8.4 per cent of the economically active), with Spanish citizens continuing to do better than either EU15 residents or non-EU15 foreigners (Table 10.3).

Some immigrants came legally, but most did not. The strait of Gibraltar became one of the deadliest crossings in the world, as each year hundreds of would-be migrants drowned attempting to reach the Spanish shore from Morocco. Similarly, the Canary Islands became a destination for would-be migrants departing from Morocco or, since Morocco increased surveillance, Mauritania. In 2005, after the end of the largest amnesty programme to date (discussed below), hundreds of would-be immigrants from sub-Saharan Africa attempted to storm the fences separating Morocco and the Spanish enclaves of Ceuta and Melilla. After similar mass attempts to storm the border, Spain built a second razor

Table 10.3   Spain: Population (000s) by citizenship and work status, 2005

	Spanish		Other EU15		Non-EU15		Total	
Employed	17,046	42.9%	230	46.6%	1915	64.0%	19,191	44.4%
Unemployed	1,523	3.8%	21	4.3%	221	7.4%	1,765	4.1%
Inactive	21,172	53.3%	243	49.2%	858	28.7%	22,273	51.5%
Total	39,741	100%	494	100%	2994	100%	43,229	100%

Source: Compiled from Eurostat Labour Force Survey, third quarter 2005. Due to rounding, not all percentages add to 100.

wire fence around Ceuta in 2001, reducing the number of migrants getting through from around 10,000 per year to about 1500.[10] For those who arrived safely on the mainland, it was usually not difficult to find work. Indeed, Spain experienced significant economic growth in a number of sectors in which migrants can readily work, such as construction. The housing boom, particularly along the coast, was of course itself fuelled by immigration. Given plentiful work, it is perhaps not surprising that Spain became the top destination for immigration into Europe. But the Spanish government's immigration policy was slow to adapt to the rapid changes in migration. One measure of this is that immigration and emigration continued to be handled within the Ministry of Labour. In a way perhaps analogous to Germany's longstanding fiction of guestworkers – that immigrants would arrive, work for awhile, and then leave – Spain's immigration policy also remained geared to the fiction that migrants are workers who will return home. Furthermore, given the limited legal means of immigrating to Spain, migrants often choose to enter or stay in violation of the law. Because of its periodic amnesties for irregular migrants, Spain became, in the words of the Secretary of the Spanish Police union, "a paradise for illegal migrants".[11]

5. Managing Irregular Migration

Spain – like Italy, Portugal, and Greece – stepped up its migration control efforts largely as a result of the desire to meet European norms and fulfil requirements for joining the Schengen system, which removed border controls on travel between Schengen states.[12] In the words of the European Council, free movement within the territory of the Schengen members is "a freedom which as a counterpart requires not only the strengthening of the common external borders and the administration of third country nationals, but also enhanced co-operation between law enforcement authorities of Schengen states" (European Council, 2003: p. 32). Spain was characterized by poor administration of its third-country nationals, and thus needed to change its administration of immigrants – as well as the legislative framework for immigration – in order to meet the requirements. Other Southern European states also held amnesties: Italy had five between 1987 and 2002; Portugal held three major amnesties, in 1992–1993, 1996, and 2001–2003; and Greece held two major amnesties, in 1998 and 2000–2001. This spate of large-scale regularization campaigns prompted the European Commission to argue that "regularisations should not be regarded as a way of managing migration flows.... [They should] be avoided or confined to very exceptional situations" (European Commission 2004). In Spain, however, regularizations became the norm rather than the exception. Immigrant amnesties also arose in the context of partisan differences, which explains why amnesties often occur following a change in government.

Spain's first regularization programme dates from the Foreigners' Law of 1985, which provided amnesty for foreigners without proper authorization if they or their employers requested regularization and provided necessary documents.[13] Applicants were required to have an employment contract and to have been present in Spain before 24 July 1985, when the regularization period started. Although the regularization period lasted until 31 March 1986 (it was initially scheduled to run only 3 months, but was extended due to poor response), only 43,815 foreigners applied – less than half and perhaps as few as one quarter of all irregular migrants in Spain at the time – of whom 38,191 were regularized. Most numerous were citizens of Morocco (18.1 per cent of all applications), Portugal (8.8 per cent), Senegal (8.2 per cent), Argentina (6.6 per cent), the UK (5.7 per cent), and the Philippines (4 per cent) (Gortázar, 2000). The regularization was slow and badly managed, and the Spanish authorities lacked the infrastructure to properly handle the applications they did receive. Furthermore, it was difficult for those who regularized to renew their visas, so that many of those who had been regularized reverted to unauthorized status when their permits expired (Gortázar, 2000).

In 1991, the government held another regularization, for workers who had resided in Spain since before 15 May 1991 and asylum-seekers whose applications had been rejected or were under review. It ran from 10 June to 10 December. Out of the 135,393 requests for regularization, only 128,068 cases were considered – partially as a result of applicants' incomplete documentation and partially as a result of bureaucratic bungling – and 109,135 were accepted (Gortázar, 2000; Levinson 2005, p. 48). Although the 1991 regularization improved somewhat on the mismanagement of the 1985–1986 programme, it did not succeed in registering all irregular migrants in Spain. Indeed, more and more workers kept arriving to take jobs in a range of temporary sectors. Starting in 1993, the government introduced annual labour quotas to attempt to manage this migration. In the first year of the quota system, only 5220 workers were approved to fill the 20,600 available positions, but this was due to the limited application time and poor publicity. In 1994, when the government again made available 20,600 slots, it ended by approving 25,604 applications – more than the allotment but far less than the number of applications. In 1995, the government provided 25,000 slots, including 17,000 reserved for the overflow from 1994. In that year, the authorities approved 19,953 out of 37,206 applicants (Gortázar, 2000). Many of the rejected applications nevertheless moved to or remained in Spain. At the same time, just as during the 1985–1986 regularization programme, many of those who had been regularized in the 1991 programme reverted to unauthorized status when their visas expired.

In the legislative elections of 3 March 1996, the conservative Partido Popular narrowly defeated the Socialists, who had governed for the previous 14 years: the Partido Popular won 38.8 per cent of the votes and 156 seats in the 350-seat parliament, compared to 37.6 per cent of the votes and 141 seats for the Socialists. Faced with the growing number of irregular migrants, the new government introduced yet another amnesty between 23 April and 23 August 1996, targeted at immigrants who had fallen into irregular status by not renewing their documents from the previous regularization. To be eligible, applicants needed to prove that they had been employed (without a permit) since 1 January 1996, have a working or residence permit issued after May 1986 (regardless of current employment status), or be a family member of an applicant. The amnesty regularized 21,300 foreigners (13,800 workers or former workers and 7500 family members) out of approximately 25,000 applicants (Levinson, 2005, 48).

In 2000, there was yet another amnesty. The new Foreigners' Law provided for the regularization of foreigners who had been in Spain before 1 June 1999 and who applied for a residence or work permit, as well as anyone who actually received such a permit.[14] The new law was passed in January, against the wishes of the Partido Popular government of President José María Aznar, which did not have a parliamentary majority. Aznar was particularly concerned with Article 29.3, which allowed permanent regularization to anyone able to prove 2 years' uninterrupted residence in Spain. On 30 January 2000, some 10,000 Spaniards in the agricultural city of El Ejido, in Andalucia, demonstrated against Moroccan workers following the killing of a 26-year-old local woman by a mentally disturbed Moroccan. Anti-immigrant violence injured 80 people in El Ejido between 5–8 February 2000 and led to the arrests of 55 Spaniards (Zapata-Barrero, 2004).

The Partido Popular again emerged victorious in the parliamentary elections of 12 March 2000, winning 44.5 per cent of the votes and 183 out of the 350 seats in the Cortes. The Socialists won 34.1 per cent of the votes and 125 seats, while the pro-immigrant United Left halved its share of the vote (to 5.5 per cent, from 10.5 per cent in 1996) and dropped to eight seats, compared to the 21 it had won in 1996. The strengthened Partido Popular administration adopted a somewhat harsher policy, and only 153,463 out of 247,598 applications for the 2000 regularization were approved, mostly citizens of Morocco, Ecuador, Colombia, and China (Levinson, 2005, p. 48). In December, the government changed the Foreigners' Law, against the wishes of all the other parties.[15] It removed the article that would have allowed automatic regularization after 2 years' residence and generally "toughened up" the immigration system (Silveira, 2002).

Despite these legal reforms, explicitly aimed at discouraging immigration, immigrants kept arriving in record numbers. The new laws not only failed to prevent the entry of immigrants but were also "one of the main factors in the generation of 'undocumented' labour supply", since immigrants needed an employment contract to enter Spain legally for work (Zapata-Barrero, 2003, p. 30). To attempt to register those who had entered the country without a work contract and were hence working illegally, the government held another amnesty during June and July 2001, targeting those who had been in Spain since 23 January 2001 and were employed or were family members of a foreign worker or Spanish citizen. Approximately 350,000 applications were filed, and 221,083 permits issued to citizens from Ecuador, Colombia, Morocco, Romania, and elsewhere. There was also a special amnesty in 2001 for citizens of Ecuador (Geronimi, 2004; Geronimi et al., 2004). Immigration continued to vex the rest of the Partido Popular's term, as the number of irregular migrants rose unabated.

The Seville European Council of June 2002, which marked the end of Spain's six-month presidency of the EU, focused largely on controlling terrorism and irregular migration. European governments congratulated themselves with developing a "comprehensive plan to combat illegal immigration [that represents] an effective means of bringing about proper management of migration flows and combating illegal immigration" (Presidency conclusions, point 30). Observers characterized the Spanish proposals for combating irregular immigration as "poorly prepared" (Barbé, 2002). This lack of preparation reflected the fact that, while Spain had long looked to the EU for multilateral support for its objectives, it found that bilateral relationships remained fundamental on major issues such as northward migration (Gillespie, 2002).

6. The 2005 Amnesty

Spain's parliamentary elections of 14 March 2004 – a mere 3 days after the bombing of several train stations in Madrid, which killed 191 and wounded 1500 others – resulted in a somewhat unexpected return to power for the Socialists (Chari, 2004). Under the leadership of José Luis Rodríguez Zapatero, the Socialists won 164 seats to the Partido Popular's 148. Although the elections occurred in the shadow of the bombing, the result reflected not a swing from the Partido Popular to the Socialists but rather strategic voting by Left-wing and other minority party supporters who voted Socialist in order to remove the Partido Popular from power (Torcal and Rico, 2004). The new Socialist government quickly moved to defuse tensions between indigenous Spaniards and immigrants from Northern Africa and elsewhere. A major part of this effort was the largest amnesty programme in Spanish history. The amnesty was criticized by many other EU states, but Spain emphasized that border control was also a problem for other states, with Minister of Labour Jesús Caldera affirming that Spain was spending considerable resources on monitoring its southern borders. Highlighting the many Romanian immigrants living without authorization in Spain, who had entered the Schengen zone by way of Germany, Austria, and Italy, Caldera criticized these states for improperly guarding their borders.[16]

At the end of the amnesty period in May 2005, Minister Caldera announced that the programme would legalize over four-fifths of the estimated 800,000 irregular migrants.[17] The opposition Partido Popular claimed that only about 20,000 of these 800,000 people were actually employed and called on the government to construct "a real immigration policy like all European countries have".[18] The Minister responsible for immigration in the previous Partido Popular government described the amnesty as a "massive" and "chaotic" display of the new government's "open door policy".[19] Emphasizing that it had been agreed in consultation with businesses, labour unions, immigrants' associations, and all political parties except the Partido Popular, Minister Caldera heralded the amnesty as "one of the greatest processes of exposing the hidden economy in Europe in the last forty or fifty years."[20] He boasted that no other OECD (Organisation for Economic Co-operation and Development) country had ever exposed so many workers in the underground economy in such a short period: "they said it would be impossible to get more than 400,000."[21] United Left unsuccessfully petitioned the government to extend the amnesty for a further 90 days.[22] Minister Caldera explained that those who had chosen not to legalize themselves would be repatriated, and claimed that the government had already repatriated 120,000 illegal migrants during the Socialists' first year in office.[23]

After the amnesty, Minister Caldera congratulated Spanish businesses for being honest and registering their employees. At the same time, the Secretary of State for Immigration warned businesses to no longer employ unauthorized immigrants because the government would conduct 500,000 workplace inspections before the end of 2005 to ensure that no one employed irregular migrants.[24] The president of the Labour Inspectors' Union promptly claimed that this was "materially impossible", since there were not nearly enough inspectors to carry out so many inspections.[25] The government reacted by promising to hire new inspectors, so that 1700 would be available to check for irregular migrants.[26] Inspectors complained that, even with the new hires, they would have to double their workload to meet the new productivity targets.[27] In response, the government increased the inspectors' salaries by 8.7 million euros, spent 18 million euros on a new computer system, and doubled the budget devoted to inspections to 3.3 million euros.[28]

According to Minister Caldera, the amnesty provided "an 'x-ray' of the economic map of Spain. Knowing the number of regularization requests and the numbers of employed foreign citizens in each province, we know in which provinces and in which economics sectors businesses [comply]. And that will provide an excellent guide to fighting fraud."[29] This "x-ray" works because irregular migrants have a strong incentive to register with local authorities: if they are registered, they benefit from free medical care. Caldera estimated that bringing the migrants into social security would add 1.5 billion euros in social security contributions in the first year.[30] In contrast to the earlier regularizations conducted under the Partido Popular government, he claimed that his government's programme would oblige migrants to enter the social security system as part of their regularization. This would "save" the system by guaranteeing there would be enough money for pensions.[31] The conservative daily *El Mundo* responded that while the amnesty may have solved one problem (increasing social security contributions and aiding economic growth), it created a much larger one: "new migratory avalanches that could bring problems of integration and delinquency."[32] Despite one regularization after another, immigration to Spain ceaselessly increased, making Spain the paradigmatic example of the perverse effects of amnesty (Recaño and Domingo, 2005, p. 21).

At the end of December 2005, the government announced that 572,961 out of the 691,655 applications for regularization had been approved, while a further 115,178 had been rejected and 3516 were still under consideration. Of those approved, 548,720 workers had already been registered with Social Security. Employers were given 1 month from the date their employees received the approval notice to register them with Social Security, explaining part of the 24,241 difference. The majority (almost 56 per cent) of those approved and registered were men, and most were young: 18 per cent were between 16 and 24 years old, 61 per cent were between 25 and 39 years old, and the remaining 21 per cent were between 40 and 65 years old. Ecuador, Romania, Morocco, Colombia, and Bolivia accounted for the bulk of those approved and registered (Spanish Ministry of Employment and Social Affairs, 2005). One estimate placed the Social Security contributions of the newly registered workers at approximately 120 million euros per month, validating the government's earlier estimate of 1.5 billion euros annually in new contributions.[33] The 2005 amnesty illustrates well the political calculations underlying decisions concerning regularizing unauthorized migration.

7. Conclusion

Unauthorized migration is a major component of labour migration and a function of the opportunities for regular migration. Facing the choice between ignoring the underground economy or attempting to control it, states constantly adjust their policies regarding residence and employment rights. The introduction and expansion of the Schengen system, which removed border controls between European states, resulted in enhanced cooperation regarding control of the common external border as well as changes in the administration of third country nationals (Maas, 2005a). Free movement had always been a prime aim of European integration, and the development of European Union citizenship – giving citizens of the member states rights in all the other member states, including the right to live and work without a residence or work permit – significantly increased the salience of individual member state immigration policies (Maas, 2005b, 2007). Driven by a combination of humanitarian concerns, labour market needs, and a relative lack of administrative capacity compared with Northern European states (which had earlier pursued similar policies), Southern European states such as Italy, Greece, Portugal, and Spain enacted a series of large-scale immigration amnesties and regularization campaigns. These programmes prompted arguments that legalization should not be regarded as a way of managing migration flows but should be confined to exceptional situations. The Spanish case demonstrates the difficulty of balancing the demands of European integration with domestic labour market needs and humanitarian concerns, as well as the tension between efforts to control migration and insufficient state capacity, a tension that exists wherever there are unauthorized migrants.

Notes

1. Earlier versions of this chapter were presented at meetings of the International Studies Association and Western Political Science Association and I thank conference participants as well as the editors of this book, Georg Menz and Alexander Caviedes, for their helpful comments. All shortcomings are mine.
2. G.A. Resolution 2920 (XXVII) of 15 November 1972.
3. G.A. Resolution 3224 (XXIX) of 6 November 1974. Compare COM (1974) 2250 of 18 December 1974. Action Programme in Favour of Migrant Workers and Their Families.
4. Committee of Ministers Resolution 78 (44) of 26 October 1978 on clandestine immigration and the illegal employment of foreign workers.
5. Council of Europe. Recommendation 990 (1984) on clandestine migration in Europe.
6. Ibid.
7. Ibid.
8. Ibid.
9. "EU15" refers to the 15 EU member states before the 2004 enlargement: besides Spain, these are Austria, Belgium, Denmark, Finland, France, Germany, Greece, Ireland, Italy, Luxembourg, the Netherlands, Portugal, Sweden, and the UK. Two out of every five EU15 citizens officially resident in Spain are British citizens, another one in four are German, with Italians and French citizens representing the next largest contingents.
10. *BBC News*, 29 September 2005.
11. *El Mundo*, 7 May 2005, p. 16.
12. Because of its efforts, Spain became one of the states in which Schengen was first fully implemented in 1995, alongside Belgium, France, Germany, Luxembourg, the Netherlands, and Portugal. It took longer for Italy and Austria (implementation in 1998) and Greece (implementation in 2001) to convince the other member states that they met the border control requirements.
13. Ley Orgánica 7/1985, de 1 de julio, sobre derechos y libertades de los extranjeros en España (Law on the rights and freedoms of foreigners in Spain), commonly known as the Ley de Extranjería.
14. Ley Orgánica 4/2000, de 11 de enero sobre derechos y deberes de los extranjeros en España y su integración social.
15. Ley Orgánica 8/2000, de 22 de diciembre, de reforma de la Ley Orgánica 4/2000. United Left's condemnation of these changes is available at www. extranjeria.info/publico/area_recursos/loex/opinion/izquierda_unida.PDF.
16. *Financial Times*, 4 February 2005, p. 18; El Mundo, 9 May 2005, p. 20.
17. *Cinco días*, 10 May 2005, p. 47.
18. *El País*, 7 May 2005, p. 21.
19. *El Mundo*, 10 May 2005, p. 17.
20. *Agence France Presse*, 7 May 2005.
21. *El Mundo*, 10 May 2005, p. 17.
22. *El País*, 7 May 2005, p. 21.
23. *El País*, 7 May 2005, p. 21.
24. *Agence France Presse*, 7 May 2005; El Mundo, 8 May 2005, p. 1.

25. *El Mundo,* 8 May 2005, p. 1.
26. *El Mundo,* 9 May 2005, p. 20.
27. *El Mundo,* 10 May 2005, p. 17.
28. *El País,* 13 May 2005, p. 28.
29. *El País,* 11 May 2005, p. 260.
30. *El Mundo,* 9 May 2005, p. 20.
31. *El Mundo,* 10 May 2005, p. 17.
32. *El Mundo,* 8 May 2005, p. 5.
33. *El País,* 26 December 2005, p. 21.

Bibliography

Arango, J. and P. Martin. 2005. "Best Practices to Manage Migration: Morocco-Spain". *International Migration Review* 39 (1): 258–269.

Barbé, E. 2002. "The Spanish Presidency of the European Union 2002". *South European Society & Politics* 7 (1): 90–102.

Chari, R. S. 2004. "The 2004 Spanish Election: Terrorism as a Catalyst for Change?" *West European Politics* 27 (5): 954–963.

Cholewinski, R. 2004. "European Union Policy on Irregular Migration: Human Rights Lost?" In *Irregular Migration and Human Rights: Theoretical, European and International Perspectives,* ed. B. Bogusz, R. Cholewinski, A. Cygan and E. Szyszczak. Leiden: Martinus Nijhoff.

Cornelius, W. A. 2004. "Spain: The Uneasy Transition from Labor Exporter to Labor Importer". In *Controlling Immigration: A Global Perspective,* ed. W. A. Cornelius, T. Tsuda, P. L. Martin and J. F. Hollifield. Stanford CA: Stanford University Press.

Couper, K. and U. Santamaria. 1984. "An Elusive Concept: The Changing Definition of Illegal Immigrant in the Practice of Immigration Control in the United Kingdom". *International Migration Review* 18 (3): 437–452.

Donato, Katharine M., J. Durand, and Douglas S. Massey. 1992. "Stemming The Tide? Assessing the Deterrent Effects of the Immigration Reform and Control Act". *Demography* 29 (2): 139–157.

European Commission. 1976. "Proposal for a Council Directive on the Harmonization of Laws in the Member States to Combat Illegal Migration and Illegal Employment". In *COM(76) 331.*

European Commission. 2004. "Communication from the Commission to the Council, the European Parliament, the European Economic and Social Committee and the Committee of the Regions – Study on the links between legal and illegal migration". In *COM(2004) 412.*

European Council. 2003. *EU Schengen Catalogue, Vol. 4 (June).*

Geronimi, E. 2004. "Admisión, contratación y protección de trabajadores migrantes: Panorama de la legislación y la práctica nacionales de Argentina, Bolivia, Brasil, Chile, Colombia, Ecuador, España, Perú, Portugal y Uruguay". Geneva: International Labour Organization.

Geronimi, E., L. Cachón, and E. Texidó. 2004. "Acuerdos bilaterales de migración de mano de obra: Estudio de casos". Geneva: International Labour Organization.

Gillespie, R. 2002. "Spain's Pursuit of Security in the Western Mediterranean". *European Security* 11 (2): 48–74.

Gortázar, C. J. 2000. "The Regularisation of Illegal Immigrants in Spain". In *Les régularisations des étrangers illégaux dans l'Union européenne*, ed. P. d. Bruycker and J. Apap. Brussels: Bruylant.

Hollifield, J. F. 2004. "The Emerging Migration State". *International Migration Review* 38 (3): 885–912.

Houdaille, J. and A. Sauvy. 1974. "L'immigration clandestine dans le monde". *Population* 29 (4/5): 725–742.

Jandl, M. 2004. "The Estimation of Illegal Migration in Europe". *Studi Emigrazione/Migration Studies* XLI (153): 141–155.

Levinson, A. 2005. "The Regularisation of Unauthorized Migrants: Literature Survey and Country Case Studies". Oxford: Centre on Migration, Policy and Society.

Maas, W. 2005a. "Freedom of Movement Inside 'Fortress Europe'". In *Global Surveillance and Policing: Borders, Security, Identity*, ed. E. Zureik and M. B. Salter. Portland: Willan.

Maas, W. 2005b. "The Genesis of European Rights". *Journal of Common Market Studies* 43 (5): 1009–1025.

Maas, W. 2007. *Creating European Citizens*. Lanham: Rowman & Littlefield.

Maas, W. 2008. "Migrants, States, and EU Citizenship's Unfulfilled Promise". *Citizenship Studies* 12 (6): 583–595.

Maas, W. 2009. "Unrespected, Unequal, Hollow?: Contingent Citizenship and Reversible Rights in the European Union". *Columbia Journal of European Law* 15 (2): 265–280.

Martin, P. L. 2003. *Bordering on Control: Combating Irregular Migration in North America and Europe*. Geneva: IOM International Organization for Migration.

Massey, D. S. 2005. "Backfire at the Border: Why Enforcement without Legalization Cannot Stop Illegal Immigration". In *Trade Policy Analysis, no. 29*.

Orrenius, P. M. and M. Zavodny. 2003. "Do Amnesty Programs Reduce Undocumented Immigration? Evidence from IRCA". *Demography* 40 (3): 437–450.

Philip, A. B. 1994. "European Union Immigration Policy: Phantom, Fantasy or Fact?" *West European Politics* 17 (2): 169–191.

Recaño, J. and A. Domingo. 2005. Factores sociodemográficos y territoriales de la inmigración irregular en España. Paper read at XXV International Population Conference, 18–23 July, at Tours, France.

Silveira, H. C. 2002. "La Ley de Extranjería y la formación de un sistema dual de ciudadanía". *El vuelo de Ícaro* (2–3): 517–540.

Spanish Ministry of Employment and Social Affairs. 2005. "Proceso de Normalización de Trabajadores Extranjeros".

Tomasi, S. M. 1984. "Introduction to Special Issue: Irregular Migration: An International Perspective". *International Migration Review* 18 (3): 406–408.

Torcal, M. and G. Rico. 2004. "The 2004 Spanish General Election: In the Shadow of al-Qaeda?" *South European Society & Politics* 9 (3): 107–121.

Zapata-Barrero, R. 2003. "Spain". In *EU and US Approaches to the Management of Immigration*, ed. J. Niessen, Y. Schibel and R. Magoni.

Zapata-Barrero, R. 2004. "The 'Discovery' of Immigration in Spain: The Politicization of Immigration in the Case of El Ejido". *Journal of International Migration and Integration* 4 (4): 523–39.

Index